THE SIBLING EFFECT

THE SIBLING EFFECT

BROTHERS, SISTERS, *and the* BONDS

THAT DEFINE US

Jeffrey Kluger

RIVERHEAD BOOKS
a member of Penguin Group (USA) Inc.
New York
2011

RIVERHEAD BOOKS
Published by the Penguin Group
Penguin Group (USA) Inc., 375 Hudson Street, New York, New York 10014, USA •
Penguin Group (Canada), 90 Eglinton Avenue East, Suite 700, Toronto, Ontario M4P 2Y3, Canada
(a division of Pearson Penguin Canada Inc.) • Penguin Books Ltd, 80 Strand, London WC2R 0RL, England •
Penguin Ireland, 25 St Stephen's Green, Dublin 2, Ireland (a division of Penguin Books Ltd) •
Penguin Group (Australia), 250 Camberwell Road, Camberwell, Victoria 3124, Australia
(a division of Pearson Australia Group Pty Ltd) • Penguin Books India Pvt Ltd,
11 Community Centre, Panchsheel Park, New Delhi–110 017, India • Penguin Group (NZ),
67 Apollo Drive, Rosedale, North Shore 0632, New Zealand (a division of Pearson New Zealand Ltd) •
Penguin Books (South Africa) (Pty) Ltd, 24 Sturdee Avenue, Rosebank, Johannesburg 2196, South Africa

Penguin Books Ltd, Registered Offices: 80 Strand, London WC2R 0RL, England

Library of Congress Cataloging-in-Publication Data

Kluger, Jeffrey.
The sibling effect : brothers, sisters, and the bonds that define us / Jeffrey Kluger.
p.   cm.
ISBN 978-1-59448-831-3
1. Brothers and sisters.   2. Interpersonal relations.   3. Parent and child.   I. Title.
BF723.S43K58   2011   2011013623
155.9'2—dc22

Printed in the United States of America
1   3   5   7   9   10   8   6   4   2

Book design by Michelle McMillian

With love to

Steve, Garry, Bruce, Adam, and Allison,

with whom I'm sharing the ride

CONTENTS

THE SIBLING EFFECT

ONE

Band of Brothers—and Sisters

At the time, it seemed like a good idea to put my baby brother Bruce in the fuse box. Technically speaking, it wasn't a fuse box—it was more of a fuse cabinet, something larger than a medicine chest and much deeper, made of the same 1950s knotty pine that covered the rest of our playroom. Technically speaking again, my brother wasn't a baby. He was four years old—but to me, two years older than he was, that seemed pretty close to babyhood.

In any event, Bruce was small enough to fit inside the fuse cabinet, and if he scrunched up tight, there was just enough clearance for the door to be closed and latched behind him. Whether locking a four-year-old in a cabinet next to a panel of high-voltage, old-style, unscrewable fuses really was wise was something I honestly had not thought much about. The way I saw it then, he was probably safer inside than out.

I wasn't the only one who believed that putting Bruce inside the fuse cabinet was a smart plan. So did my other two other brothers; in fact, the oldest, Steve, was the one who came up with the idea. Steve was good at thinking on his feet.

Steve was just over eight years old at the time; I was six and Garry was five. The spacing between children got shorter as my parents went along, until, at the end, there was only a thirteen-month gap between Garry and Bruce. That thirteen months made a difference, though. Garry was an unusually pretty child, with extravagantly long eyelashes and almost absurdly perfect features. But he found a way to compensate for his elegant appearance with a sort of alley-cat toughness that belied his looks—a toughness that I was sure he would not hesitate to call on when he needed it. Bruce was another matter. By the time he was three he was already nearsighted enough to have begun wearing glasses; they had tortoiseshell frames, which went nicely with his fair skin and red hair, giving him an incongruously academic look. He had not lost his baby belly entirely and thus often wore his pants hiked well above his waistline, in the manner of a retiree whose belt can no longer accommodate his shape. Like the rest of us, he wore his hair in a velvety semi–crew cut, but his was offset by a small tuft of red curls at the front. I might have been just a child myself, but I recognized adorable and I recognized vulnerable, and I reckoned he was both. That was the reason that he, more than any of us, needed the protection of the fuse cabinet.

Our mother wasn't aware of what we were up to when we decided where to stash Bruce. Our father didn't know, either—and the fact is, our father's not knowing was precisely the point. My brothers and I were by no means battered children. We never suffered the hard and regular beatings that can wreck minds and scar bodies and lay waste to whole childhoods. But we did get hit—often enough and hard enough that, even during periods of peace, we were always aware of a distant, angry danger. It was a danger posed mostly by our father.

A smart, funny, hotheaded man, our father was just twenty-two years old when he got married and twenty-four when he had his first son. I thought of him as tall, though at five feet seven, he was nothing of the kind. He wore black-framed glasses, had what seemed to be a permanent shadow of whiskers, and smoked L&Ms—a great, great many L&Ms, enough that they would kill him when he was only sixty-seven, though, as a child, I had no way of suspecting that. Long before his cigarettes claimed his health, they claimed the clarity of his voice, and even as a young man he spoke in a rasp. When he found something funny, which he did quite often, the rasp gave his laugh a particularly happy, full-throated sound. When he was angry and shouting—something that happened quite often, too—that rasp became a roar.

I didn't know the source of my father's temper, and I still don't. Some of it, I suspect, was born of frustration. The son of a wealthy Manhattan businessman who'd made his bankroll during World War II, my father had gone to the University of Pennsylvania with the understanding that when he was finished, he would help run his father's various business interests. Shortly before graduation, however, my grandfather liquidated his assets, parked them in his own portfolios, and announced that he would spend the rest of his life investing and reinvesting them.

My father's plan B was decidedly less glamorous: he got married; moved to Baltimore, my mother's hometown; and opened a wholesale toy business. My brothers and I—who were often the happy beneficiaries of the surplus swag he brought home from his stockroom—could imagine no better profession for a man, and we naturally assumed our father delighted in his work. But I suspect he stewed in it, too.

A week's worth of such slow-cooked anger had to blow at some point, and it generally blew on weekends. Whatever my father might have imagined his Saturday and Sunday mornings would be like after the fourth of his rambunctious sons was born, he could not have realistically assumed they'd be quiet. My brothers and I played boisterously, fought frequently, and broke things constantly. We'd jump on beds until the frames collapsed. We'd split into pairs and climb onto dressers to play a game we called "wrapping up and falling," which, as its name suggests, involved nothing more than wrapping up in a shared blanket and falling—loudly—to the floor. The appeal is elusive now; it wasn't then.

Most weekend mornings, we'd confine ourselves to the downstairs playroom, a perfectly appropriate choice, except for the fact that it was directly below my parents' bedroom. My mother was a heavy sleeper—thanks, perhaps, to the early stages of a prescription-drug habit, which we knew nothing about at the time, but would come to know very well later—and did not seem disturbed by the din that always came from below. My father was another matter. He could be awakened easily—and stirred to anger quickly. And when he was, he became a frightening man.

The first indication we'd have that trouble was coming was the sound of pounding footsteps from above. Though the thumping started directly over our heads, the only way our father could reach us was by walking along a hallway outside the bedrooms, then down a short flight of stairs to the living room, turning through the kitchen and descending a half flight to the playroom level. That would take about a minute for an adult walking at a normal pace—less for an angrily striding one. To us, it seemed to take a whole lot longer.

When my father would finally reach the playroom, where we'd all be frozen in more or less the same spots in which we'd been standing when we first heard the footsteps, there was nothing disciplined or systematic about his hitting. He would lash out at whoever was there, landing opportunistic blows rather than planned ones. He did not aim for our faces as far as I knew, but I don't recall him taking pains to avoid them, either. I do recall him picking me up once by the front of my pajama top, his fisted hand holding a wad of fabric just under my chin, and being vaguely aware that I'd seen that move many times in cartoons, and that it always looked effortless on the screen. In real life, it was awkward and extremely scary. I also remember raising my hand once to protect myself, causing my father's incoming blow to land squarely on a new wristwatch he had given me not long before. It seemed ironic to me that he would be the one to break a gift he himself had bought, but the watch was a Timex, and it took the punishment.

The hitting never lasted long and we would reliably quiet down afterward. But the memory of the episode and the fear of the next one would leave us shaken, so much so that we—Steve, really—decided we needed a plan. From now on, in the forty-five or so seconds it took our father to reach us in the morning, we would all conceal ourselves in different corners of the playroom. Garry would dive into a window-seat toy chest and close the lid. Steve would slide under the couch. I would duck into the playroom closet and climb to a shelf about midway up the wall. Bruce would get the fuse box. He balked at first when we suggested the plan, but we encouraged him.

"It's a space capsule!" we said. "Just like Alan Shepard's!" We had all watched Shepard's Mercury flight on TV not long before and had been thrilled by it. Bruce went in willingly when we drew the comparison.

We practiced our scatter drill now and then to improve our stealth and timing. When we first put it into practice during a real Sunday emergency, I don't recall how well it worked, but I suspect any memo-

5

ries I have now are conflated with how we wanted it to work. In my recollections—and certainly in my brothers' and my retellings—our father would appear at the playroom door, look around confusedly, and begin calling our names, getting angrier and more frustrated at the silence that would greet him. We, of course, would preserve that silence perfectly, and he, mystified, would eventually turn and leave, mumbling and scratching his head. In our tellings, too, this worked weekend after weekend.

I doubt things ever played out this sit-comically. I suspect our father quickly caught on to what we were doing or we quickly gave ourselves away, and the hitting probably followed. We may not have even tried the stunt more than a few times—and, mercifully, we always collected Bruce safely from the fuse box afterward. It was only in later years that I would go a little cold, thinking about the deadly danger we courted on those mornings, squeezing a small child and high voltage so close to each other.

But if my memories of those episodes are murky, my brothers and I did take from them something clear and hard and fine: a deep and primal appreciation of the life-giving—and lifesaving—bond that we shared. The four of us, we came to know at a very deep level, were a unit—a loud, messy, brawling, loyal, loving, lasting unit. We felt much, much stronger that way than we did as individuals. And whenever the need arose, we knew we'd be able to call on that strength. Even now, several decades on, we still can.

The universe of human relationships is an impossibly varied one. Wives have their husbands; children have their parents; lovers have their partners; friends have one another. There are cousins and aunts and uncles and grandparents, schoolmates and colleagues and rivals and peers. Every one of those relationships plays out under its own set of rules and rituals, each unique, each elaborate. For all that richness and complexity, however, there may be no relationships that can run quite as deep or survive quite as long as those among siblings. You know it if you grew up with one. You know it if you're raising some. You know it if you've merely watched a group of them interact.

From the time we're born, our brothers and sisters are our collaborators and co-conspirators, our role models and our cautionary tales. They are our scolds, protectors, goads, tormentors, playmates, counselors, sources of envy, objects of pride. They help us learn how to resolve conflicts and how not to; how to conduct friendships and when to walk away from them. Sisters teach brothers about the mysteries of girls; brothers teach sisters about the puzzle of boys. Bigger sibs learn to nurture by mentoring little ones; little sibs learn about wisdom by heeding the older ones. Our spouses and children arrive comparatively late in our lives; our parents leave us too early. "Our brothers and sisters," says family sociologist Katherine Conger of the University of California, Davis, "are with us for the whole journey."

In a sense, the sibling bond should not run as deep as it does, if only because brothers and sisters are among the more commonplace of kin. You have just one mother; you have just one father; if you do marriage right, you have just one spouse for life. But siblings can claim none of that uniqueness. They are fungible, replaceable—a kind of genetic commodity. Parents set up shop and then begin laying in inventory, producing as many children as they choose until they decide their shelves are full. The exact size of the brood is limited only by sperm, eggs, and economics. As long as Mom and Dad are able to breed and support more young, they may as well keep having them. Even when families are exceedingly—sometimes regally—special, there's a product-line quality to the children they produce. It's not for nothing that Britain's princes William and Harry are referred as "an heir and a spare." It's not for nothing that each time a Kennedy boy died, his parents—and later the nation as a whole—began turning to the next one to fill the breach, as if he were a mere familial replacement part that could simply be snapped into place.

For scientists studying childhood and human development, this mass-produced quality always relegated siblings to a vaguely secondary station. A noisy group of comparative peers who wield little or no authority over you could not possibly have the same power to shape what you become as your parents or your teachers or—even more fundamentally—your genes. And even if there were useful data to be uncovered by studying siblings, trying to unearth it would be a bloody nuisance.

"There are so many variables to juggle," says Laurie Kramer, professor of applied family study at the University of Illinois at Urbana-Champaign. "There's age difference, gender difference, the number of kids; there's income, geography, culture, education. The complexity just turned people off."

But if scientists never showed much interest in studying sibling relationships, the rest of human society seems always to have understood that those bonds involved something special—at least judging by the high place sibling imagery holds in our language and our art. There's a reason Dostoyevsky did not write a novel about the comrades Karamazov. There's a reason the signature song of the Great Depression was not called "*Mister*, Can You Spare a Dime?" Twentieth-century women found strength not through solidarity or unity but through sisterhood. Soldiers march into battle not just as squad members or platoon mates

but as bands of brothers. America's good are crowned with brother-
hood; its Civil War is cursed as an act of national fratricide.

Even now, with the much-lamented fragmentation of so many families, brothers and sisters transfix us. There can be dignity in the sibling
bond: Think of Cooper Manning, his own football dreams smothered in
the cradle by a congenital narrowing of the spine, standing on the side-
lines and cheering with seemingly genuine joy as little brothers Peyton
and Eli go on to win Super Bowls. There can be petulance, too: Think
of Neil Bush, sibling of a president and a governor, and veteran of both
a savings-and-loan scandal and a messy public divorce, famously grip-
ing, "I've lost patience for being compared to my brothers." There can
also be greatness: The whole of the Wright brothers was more inven-
tive than the sum of its parts. The whole of the Marx Brothers was fun-
nier than the sum. Would the Gershwins, with the perfect key-in-lock
fit of their music and lyrics, have been what they were if one of them
had been named Jones? Would the Williams sisters have become the
athletes they are if there had been no Venus to push Serena, nor Serena
to push Venus?

Most of us will experience our relationships with our siblings much
more privately and much less spectacularly, but we'll feel them no less
acutely. A household with multiple siblings is a parliament of personalities that are forever in motion—and often in conflict. There are
alliances and feuds, loyalties and betrayals. Slights are remembered and
favors are banked. Daily wars erupt in the playroom, requiring compro-
mises to be negotiated and peace deals to be struck—deals that last only
until the next outbreak of hostilities, which can easily happen within the
hour. "Getting along with a brother or sister," says Kramer understat-
edly, "can be a complicated experience."

But it can be an educational one, too: Adulthood, after all, is practically defined by peer relationships—the workplace, the marriage, the community group. As siblings, we may fight and sulk and fume, but by nighttime we still return to the same twin beds in the same shared room. Peace is made when one sib offers a toy or ventures a thought or throws a pillow in mock provocation that releases the lingering tension in a burst of roughhousing or laughter. Somewhere in there is the early training for the e-mail joke that breaks an office silence or the husband who signals that a fight is over by asking his wife where she thinks they should go on that fast-approaching vacation anyway.

And all of that complexity comes just from the civil wars among the sibs themselves. There's also the constant jostling for the precious resource of parental love and attention, with each child struggling practically from birth to establish an identity that will best catch Mom and Dad's eye: *I'm the smart one! I'm the funny one! I'm the athlete! I'm the pretty one!* If one niche is filled, a child switches to another. Parents inevitably wind up playing favorites, and kids, cleverly, learn to game their parents—sending the adored oldest son to ask Mom a favor, sending the adorable youngest daughter to wheedle a treat from Dad. Mom and Dad themselves are entangled in all of this but also somehow above it, too busy with bills and meals and playdates to remember fully from their own childhoods what these kinds of quotidian dramas mean to the kids. The kids, on the other hand, are defined by it.

"In most households," says psychologist Daniel Shaw of the University of Pittsburgh, "parents serve the same big-picture role as doctors on grand rounds. Siblings are like the nurses on the ward; they're there every day."

The exact nature of life on those wards can be determined by countless other X factors, and affect siblings in countless other ways. There is birth order, with its common notions of the smart and studious older sib, the lost-in-the-thickets middle sib, and the wild-child younger sib. Are who you are and what you become really governed by something as capricious as the order in which you pop from the womb? There is divorce—when the home is suddenly blown to pieces and the family becomes a bipolar thing, with Mom in one house and Dad in the other, and the kids pulled like iron filings between two emotional magnets. There is the blended home, in which elements of two broken families and two sets of sibs try to combine themselves into a coherent whole under a single roof. Does the biology of your birth brood trump the proximity of the new, unrelated brood, or can children raised together become de facto brothers and sisters without a scrap of shared DNA?

Even if you can figure out all those variables, there are always others waiting. What about risk-taking behavior—the way smoking, drug use, drinking, teen pregnancy, and even criminality can be passed from older siblings to younger ones as easily as last year's sweater? What about the unique bond shared by twins and triplets and other multiple womb-mates, or the powerful influence of culture—the way Asian sibs differ from American ones, and Americans in turn differ from Africans and Europeans? Most enigmatically, there's the puzzle of the singleton—the only child who feasts on the concentrated love of two parents but is forever starved of the company of a sib. Is the one-child playroom really the lonely place it can seem, or are there quiet rewards that no one but the singletons themselves truly know?

Still, family studies sidestepped many of these questions for decades, focusing heavily on the husband-wife and parent-child bonds. But once the scientists had strip-mined all the findings from that work, they still came away with as many questions as answers. Somewhere, there was a sort of temperamental dark matter exerting an invisible gravitational pull all its own. And that force, the investigators finally began to accept, could only be our brothers and sisters.

With that realization, the dam finally broke. Over the past fifteen years or so, psychologists, sociologists, anthropologists, even biologists and zoologists, have begun studying brothers and sisters as never before—teasing apart the genetic, sociological, and psychological threads of the sibling relationship. They are videotaping brothers and sisters as they interact and breaking down the tapes like football coaches studying plays. They are tracking sibling genes and seeing how the shared biological software that makes them what they are either pulls them together or drives them apart. They are venturing into the field to study sibs in their natural family habitats—intact families, single-parent families, families with young parents, families with old parents, families with grandparents or other relatives doing the parents' job. In 2005, the *Journal of Family Psychology*, one of the psychology field's most prestigious publications, devoted an issue exclusively to siblings, and the clamor to publish in its pages was overwhelming.

"[Sibling research] has been one of the more neglected areas until recently," says Kimberly Updegraff, a professor of family and human development at Arizona State University. "But over time it snowballed and more people have become involved and reached consistent findings about the important ways siblings influence one another."

"Siblings," adds Katherine Conger simply, "are the last-explored territory of family relationships."

This book grew out of a pair of cover stories I wrote for *Time* magazine in 2006 and 2007, exploring the burgeoning field. The first of the stories covered sibling relationships in general, the second focused on the power of birth order. But my interest grew from something far more primal. My own life has in some ways been a decades-long tour of the sibling experience. I have full sibs, I have half sibs, and for a time I had stepsibs. My family went through divorces and remarriages and the later, blended home—and then watched that home explode, too. My brothers and I have fought the birth-order wars and struggled with ongoing rivalries for parental attention that define so many sibs. We lived in the total-immersion testosterone environment of an all-boy household, and then watched how things effervesced when sisters were suddenly dropped into the mix. We came together when drug addiction ravaged the family; we learned to accept—and then celebrate—what decades ago could be a traumatic announcement: that one of the members of our all-boy band had a hankering for other boys, outside the home. Most important, I, like my sibs, am now raising children of my own—two grade-school daughters, in my case—and find myself observing and refereeing the same sibling chess matches I spent my whole life playing.

If self-interest is partly behind my fascination with the sibling bond, I am hardly alone. The near universality of the sibling experience makes it something that powerfully affects all families. What's more, that effect continues later and later in life. With Americans living longer than ever, increasing numbers of us will be launched into an old age in which we've outlived our friends, our parents, and even our spouses, while our children and grandchildren have scattered to distant cities. For plenty of us, the only ones left at the end of the dance will be the ones what brung us—the brothers and sisters who have been with us the longest, loved us the hardest, and, by a wide margin, know us the best.

TWO

Stocking the Team

Siblings in a Growing Family

Think it was hard growing up in your house? It could have been worse; you could have been an egret. Egrets are not the most intelligent of nature's creatures. Even grading on the generous curve of the bird world, they finish near the back of the classroom. Just how far back? "Assume the IQ of sewage," says Douglas Mock, professor of zoology at the University of Oklahoma. "That's pretty much what you're working with when it comes to egrets."

But that's not to say that the species is entirely lacking in guile— particularly when it comes to the mother of an egret brood. Like all animals of breeding age, egret moms spend much of their time and most of their energy involved in a sort of reproductive marketing game. They've got a biological product to sell and distribute, and that product is their genes. Mating dances and courtship rituals are all about finding the fittest male to buy what's being offered. Once the female succeeds— once the nest is built and the mating is done and the eggs are laid—she still has to protect her investment, and that requires a lot of strategizing.

There is no fixed number of eggs in an egret clutch, but four is a pretty common count. Even the mother can't tell much about the chick inside each egg simply by looking at the shell. If one contains a frail baby that's not likely to survive the season and another contains a bruiser that will grow fast and well and leave plenty of the family's genes to later generations, she has no way of telling them apart. But she doesn't have to intuit which chick will be the biggest and fittest; she can actually control it.

When a nest is full of eggs, a mother egret staggers the way she incubates them. All of the eggs get enough warmth and enough turning to keep them alive, but the mom will favor one slightly, giving it a little more brooding and care. This ensures that it hatches a day before the rest. She then lavishes similar attention on the next egg, and the next and the next, causing all of the birds to pop out sequentially—each about twenty-four hours after the one before it. That may be a sensible strategy for an overworked mother, sparing her the chore of having to keep four chicks fed on her very first day of parenthood, but it can make things awfully nasty in the nest.

Hatching before the other chicks means that the first one out—Mock calls it the A Chick—gets a head start on drying off, opening its eyes, and finding its footing, not to mention a full day of uncontested food. The moment the weaker B Chick hatches, the A Chick exploits its advantage and begins pecking at the newcomer—not enough to kill it, but enough to establish who's in charge. When the C Chick comes along the following day, the B Chick administers a similarly harsh hello.

"As soon as the C Chick arrives," Mock says, "the A Chick stops fighting altogether. It retires undefeated and most of the pecking is directed by B against C. The pattern then repeats itself between C and D."

The mom knows this will happen—to the extent that an egret knows anything at all—and she's pleased by it, too. In the wild, no year is just like the year before it in terms of food supply, weather, and the abundance of predators. A mother thus can't handicap in advance if she's producing too many chicks for what will turn out to be a lean and dangerous season, or too few for what will turn out to be a fat and secure one. A modern human mother in the same situation would probably play it safe and keep her output relatively low no matter what, since it is far better to have only three children when you would have liked four or five than to have four or five and watch one or more of them languish and die. To egrets, however, chicks are interchangeable—one healthy hatchling is as good as another. So the mother errs on the side of excess, laying more eggs than she can be sure will survive, and letting the peck-happy babies sort things out themselves.

"She overproduces a little bit," says Mock. "That way there is a natural mechanism in place for the weakest bird to be dropped by the wayside if it turns out that it's a typical year with a typical budget." Mock, who wrote his seminal egret paper in 1991, and later authored the book *More Than Kin and Less Than Kind: The Evolution of Family Conflict* in 2004, dedicated his book to his three older brothers. He likes to say that one day he is going to print up a T-shirt that reads "D Chick Survivor."

The animal kingdom is stuffed with similar examples of siblings ensuring their own survival at the expense of their litter mates, nest mates, and brood mates—perhaps none more savagely than the shark. In keeping with its rep for bloodlust, one shark species—the sand tiger shark—begins its murderous ways even before it's born. After mating, a mother shark releases a clutch of fertilized eggs into her womb, where they hatch and produce a cluster of fetal young. No sooner have those incubating babies begun to develop mouths and teeth than they start to use them, thrashing and biting and systematically killing one another off, with the victors eating the remains of the vanquished. Only one baby survives this orgy of siblicide, and when that winner is at last determined, it settles back to continue its gestation in peace. The mother keeps her sole offspring fed throughout its remaining time in the womb by releasing ten thousand or so more eggs—ten thousand or so potential brothers and sisters—which the baby devours, surviving entirely on this cannibalistic diet of roe until at last it is born and can turn its carnivorous attentions to the outside world.

Domestic pigs, a decidedly more peaceable species, also can be rough on their same-age litter mates. Piglets are born with a set of eight irregular teeth that grow in a suspiciously lateral direction, jutting outside of the jawline. The babies' first job—and pretty much their only job throughout infancy—is to secure a steady milk supply from Mom. All of the siblings quickly learn that the best nursing spots are generally in the middle of the mother's abdomen, with the ones closer to her front and hind end producing a comparative trickle of milk. In the scrum that forms for the choicest places at the maternal table, the bristle of lateral teeth can start and settle a whole lot of fights. Indeed, within days of birth, it's evident which piglets have the strongest teeth, since those are also the ones that fatten up quickest. When farmers intervene and remove the milk teeth immediately after birth, all of the piglets grow to more or less the same size. The piglets themselves are happy not to use these natural weapons if they don't have to, and when the mother gives birth to a small litter and there's plenty of milk to go around, the babies do a lot less fencing and jabbing.

The first scientist to study this phenomenon, David Fraser of the Animal Research Center in Ottawa, Canada, was so struck by what he observed that in his published paper—a sober work that appeared in the sober journal *Behavioral Ecology and Sociobiology* in 1990—he took the unheard-of liberty of writing the opening summary in verse. The journal took the equally unheard-of step of publishing it:

> *A piglet's most precious possession*
> *Is the teat that he fattens his flesh on.*
> *We studied pig sisters and brothers,*
> *When some had their teeth, but not others.*
> *We found that when siblings aren't many,*
> *The weapons help little if any.*
> *But when there are many per litter,*
> *The teeth help their owners grow fitter.*

If pigs usually strike us as harmless animals, penguins can seem downright comical, and yet they, too, may take a pitiless approach to selecting the fittest babies for survival. Biologist Colleen St. Clair of the University of Alberta, one of Mock's former grad students, studied crested penguins in Tasmania and observed a surprising maternal pattern. The penguin mother generally lays just two eggs, spaced a few days apart, and in almost all cases, the chick inside one will outweigh the chick in the other by as much as 80 percent—though it's never certain whether the first or second egg will contain the bigger sib. Whichever one it is, the larger chick typically outcompetes the smaller one, limiting the food it gets so severely that the smaller one eventually dies. On occasion, the mother is able to expedite things, stopping the competition before it even begins.

"Before the second egg is laid," Mock says, "the mother appears to pay attention to internal signals that tell her if it will hold the bigger chick. If those signals are strong enough, she may simply drop-kick the small egg out of the nest."

Black eagles have a similar one-baby policy, with the A Chick always outweighing the B Chick, but they settle the matter more messily than the penguins do: When the little sib is born, the big chick rips it to bits. "The mother," Mock says, "just stands around yawning. The function of the second egg is insurance. If the first chick is healthy, the policy is canceled."

Humans, we like to think, approach things differently. We love our babies. We dote on them. We produce a lot of them because we find rapture in raising them, and far from abiding or encouraging warfare among our children, we spend most of our time settling fights and brokering peace. No egret or shark or nursing sow could say the same. All of that is undeniably true. But it's also true that, like the beasts, we commoditize our kids. And like the beasts, we've found a lot of ways—including stockpiling offspring—to ensure that our genes make it to the next generation and beyond.

As recently as the beginning of the twentieth century, a child born in the United States had no more than a 50 percent chance of making it to adulthood. Parents who bred and then lost a child would face the same break-even odds of keeping or losing the next one and the next. The only way to get ahead of the reaper was to produce so many babies that the probabilities would eventually tip your way. If you owned a farm or a business that required a lot of unpaid hands to run, you'd need more offspring still. If, in the course of producing your brood, you had too many girls—who are fine for certain kinds of work, but not others— you'd need to keep going till you manufactured more boys.

The sensible answer for a species like ours would be to breed in

litters—cranking out an entire mixed-sex workforce in a single go—
and if an economist had had a hand in designing human beings, that's
surely how things would work. But *Homo sapiens* has a big brain, and
big brains mean big heads, and those take up a lot of space in the womb.
One baby at a time thus became our general reproductive rule. What's
more, in order for the sole offspring—and that big head—to make it
through the birth canal, gestation must be relatively short, meaning
that we give birth to small, not wholly developed babies who go through
a long period of dependency before they're even able to eat solid food
or toddle, much less pick up a hoe and work the fields.

The burden of rearing such helpless offspring falls overwhelmingly
on the mother, and for her it's a fantastically expensive proposition, in
more ways than merely the hours and energy devoted to the job. The
number of calories a new mother expends producing milk after she gives
birth is actually greater on a month-to-month basis than the amount she
spent growing the baby during the pregnancy itself. It takes more than
100,000 calories to feed a newborn for just the first four or five months
of its life, which is nearly three times the 36,000 calories a woman of
average weight has on hand at any one time in terms of body fat.
There's a reason new mothers are advised to indulge themselves in milk
shakes and other high-calorie treats when they're nursing, since so much
of what they consume hangs around in their bodies just long enough to
be reprocessed into nutrients for someone else. Of course, in the pre-
industrial era, milk shakes were unheard of, and humans were often just
one failed harvest away from starvation. The same conditions prevail in
much of the developing world today.

And that's only if all the kids are healthy. But what if they aren't?
What if, as with the chicks, there's a frail or sickly baby in the family?
Should the mother continue to pour resources into what's likely to be a

failed reproductive enterprise, or should she let the weak newborn die and concentrate on its siblings? For our species, the answer is usually easy: save the baby. Indeed, far from giving up on a sick or special-needs child, parents often double-down on their investment in its care, devoting time and money to keeping it alive that may exceed by a large measure what they spend on their healthier offspring. That drives nature nuts. There is no rational reason any species should behave this way, but reason isn't at work here, and we take justifiable pride in the way our compassion can trump our survival drives. In other, subtler ways, however, we're a lot more calculating and a lot less compassionate than we know.

In 1999, anthropologist Edward Hagen of the University of California, Santa Barbara, conducted a controversial study arguing the provocative premise that postpartum depression (PPD)—which strikes about 10 percent of new mothers—may be less an affliction than a sort of cunning adaptation. PPD goes beyond simple melancholy, which most new mothers may experience, and instead becomes a deep, disabling gloom, one often accompanied by loss of interest in the newborn and even thoughts of harming it. In the case of a mother with a nonviable child, this is just what evolution would want, since the condition would paralyze the mother into discontinuing feeding and other care—in effect, cutting the baby's lifeline and cutting her own genetic losses in the process. That unlovely idea caused the paper to generate a lot of heat and meet a lot of resistance at the time it was published, and Hagen has not pursued the topic since. Still, he amassed a lot of data that make at least a credible case for his premise—in part simply by ruling out most other possible explanations for PPD.

For one thing, hormones, which are one of the first places people look in trying to explain various kinds of depression, appear to play at best a secondary role in the postpartum variety. Levels of progesterone, estrogen, prolactin, and, significantly, cortisol—a stress hormone—often remain within the same range for depressed and nondepressed mothers.

Similarly, socioeconomic factors such as occupational status, education level, the number of other children in the home, and even the mother's marital status also do not closely correlate to maternal PPD. Yet if anything ought to send a new mom into a funk, you'd think being out of work, undereducated, or unwed would do it.

The two big things that do correlate with postpartum depression are the amount of child-care assistance the mother feels she is getting from the father, and the health and viability of the infant. When either one is lacking, PPD is statistically likelier to appear—and the baby is statistically likelier to get less care. "Mothers with PPD mother less," Hagen wrote. Their depression informs them that "they have suffered a reproductive cost and that successfully motivates them to reduce this cost."

Such withholding of resources doesn't always mean a mother is actually giving up on the baby. In the case of a nonsupportive husband, she may simply be going on what Hagen called a "labor strike," forcing Dad to step up his game or risk losing his own genetic investment in the child. In the case of the nonviable baby, Hagen does believe that evolution may be trying to drive the mother to let go. The voices of the mothers who were quoted in his paper certainly suggest that.

"I would be going along and being okay," said one woman, "and then I would get up to that changing table and in a matter of seconds my mind would have started with, 'Oh, the baby is going to fall off the table. I don't care if she falls off the table.' Why did I think that I don't care? Of course I care." Of course she does—but evolution doesn't.

With such behavior baked into our genes, the sibling brood ought to be nothing at all like the close and nurturing thing it usually becomes, but more like a team of rivals, a childhood-long battle, with life itself often the thing being fought over. This is especially so, since parental selectivity continues well after babies are out of infancy.

Both across history and across cultures, for example, girl children have traditionally ranked lower in value than boys, and have been treated accordingly. While such a sexual caste system is now seen as morally indefensible in much of the world, natural selection does help explain how it got started. In general, girls don't hunt, they don't go to war, and while they do breed, it's in a comparatively limited way, with nine months of gestation followed by a long period of nursing, during which ovulation usually stops. Throughout human history, only the most prolific mothers have turned out nine or ten children in a lifetime—and most give birth to far fewer.

A male, on the other hand—particularly a young male—is nothing short of a reproductive machine, with every mating theoretically able to produce a child, and many matings with many partners possible in a single day. The eighteenth-century Moroccan ruler Moulay Ismaïl is said to have fathered 888 children with his 500 concubines. Genghis Khan, the Mongol emperor who ruled much of Asia during the twelfth and thirteenth centuries, makes Ismaïl look practically barren. A 2003 analysis of the Y chromosome of 2,123 men now living across the former Mongol empire suggested that there are 16 million males living today whose line stretches back to the great conqueror—or 1 out of every 200 males now on the planet. Since all of the other men living in Genghis's time are thought to have about 20 male descendants currently at large in the world, that means Genghis outperformed them by a factor of 800,000. At some level, all parents are hardwired to want a child like Genghis who will mass-produce the family genes so successfully, and no female could ever qualify for the job. "In terms of genetic payoff," says Catherine Salmon, professor of psychology at the University of Redlands in California, "a son is going to be a much better bet than a daughter."

Human culture has only widened that value gap. The custom of a dowry, essentially a bribe to a groom to take a marriageable daughter off her birth family's hands, imposes a burden on parents every time a girl is born. Somewhere, fifteen or twenty years down the line, they're going to have to come up with a cow or a horse or a sum of cash to pay off the eventual husband, lest the daughter remain unwed and dependent. A newborn boy, on the other hand, will not only not use up the family's wealth but generate some of his own. While the general death of the dowry along with a host of other cultural factors have eliminated much of this primal bias in the West, in parts of the East it's only grown stronger.

When an overpopulated China introduced its one-child-per-family policy in 1979, the national gender balance between boys and girls was roughly fifty-fifty. By 2000, there were about 124 births of boys being recorded in China for every 100 girls, and young males under the age of twenty exceeded young females by a whopping 32 million. The missing girls were simply abandoned, given up for overseas adoption, or, with the advent of modern pregnancy screening techniques, aborted. Neighboring India, even without a one-child policy, was little better. "In 1980, a paper in the journal *Science* looked at amniocentesis rates in India in tandem with abortion rates," says Mock. "It was two hundred to one against daughters."

Gender and health are not the only variables that can raise or lower the perceived value of one sibling compared to another. Age plays a powerful role, too. Firstborn favoritism is a very real thing, and family psychologists have offered a lot of theories to explain it—most having to do with the sheer novelty of becoming a parent for the first time, and the inevitable habituation that comes from repeating the experience again and again. That is surely part of it, but biological economics explains the rest.

Every calorie, dollar, and hour parents spend to feed, raise, and care for a child is a calorie, dollar, and hour the parents are never getting back. Corporations refer to such investments as sunk costs—revenue devoted to product development that will pay off only if the product succeeds. Sunk costs are a powerful motivation for those companies to keep their attention focused on the line of merchandise furthest along in design and development. Sports teams, whose product line is human athletes, do the same thing: A pitcher who's spent three or four years in the minor leagues and is almost ready for the majors will be a lot less likely to be traded than a recently drafted rookie. It's that way with families, too.

"There's a kind of resource capital that parents pour into firstborns," says Ben Dattner, a business consultant and organizational psychologist at New York University. "They build up a sort of equity in them. If a child has to be sacrificed—due to poverty or famine, say—it's very rare that any society encourages taking resources from the firstborn. It's almost always the second-born who is sacrificed."

Children, at least very young children, ought to be oblivious to the biological bookkeeping that drives parents to behave the way they do. The parents, after all, are often wholly unaware of it themselves. But if parents are genetically programmed to pick and choose among their kids, the kids come equally programmed to fight to be the chosen ones.

In that sense, they compete no less vigorously than animal siblings—and in many ways compete much harder. Animals, after all, have little more than instinct fueling their competitiveness; humans have emotion—jealousy, resentment, outrage—and that can turbocharge even the mildest rivalry.

Of all the kids in a growing family, it's once again the oldest who stands out in terms of feeling most acutely the competition for resources. Firstborns have it awfully good in the early part of their lives—borne along by their parents' doting care and liking that just fine. When a younger brother or sister comes along, all that changes. Dattner is a psychologist who has read deeply in the literature of sibling dynamics, but when he describes the trauma singletons experience when they're suddenly presented with a baby sibling, he quotes an unlikely authority: Cindy Crawford, ex-supermodel and the mother of two.

"Crawford once observed that if you want to know what it's like for a firstborn when a little sister or brother joins the family," he says, "try to imagine a woman whose husband tells her, 'Honey, I've got a new, better-looking wife coming along and you'll be moving to a room down the hall. But don't worry, I'll love you both the same and there's plenty of room for all of us.'"

Terrible as that sounds, it's actually worse for the child than for the hypothetical wife. A displaced spouse at least has the power to up and leave. Single children who suddenly find themselves merely one of a pair are stuck with their new, reduced station. Psychologists call what the firstborn goes through in these situations "dethronement," and it's an experience that can leave scars for a lifetime. Author and family researcher Judith Rich Harris, who wrote *The Nurture Assumption: Why Children Turn Out the Way They Do*, likes to cite the case of Pulitzer Prize–winning novelist John Cheever, whose older brother Fred suffered from depression and alcoholism—conditions that Cheever believes had their roots in his own arrival in the family.

"He was happy, high-spirited, and adored," Cheever wrote about his brother, "and when at the age of seven, he was told that he would have to share his universe, his forebodings would naturally have been bitter and deep. . . . His feeling for me was always violent and ambiguous—hatred and love—and beneath all of this must have been the feeling that I challenged him in some field where he excelled—in the affection of his parents."

Cheever is likely wrong about the causes of his brother's alcoholism and depression—two clinical conditions with a complex mix of genetic and environmental variables—but not about the profound resentment his own arrival probably caused his brother. What's more, in the hothouse of a small family, Cheever himself probably felt that anger coming his way every day—and he returned it in his own fashion, with his fiction often featuring conflict between brothers, some of it violent. In a 1977 interview, the year after his older brother's death, Cheever's daughter conducted an interview with her father and asked him a very candid question: "Did you ever want to kill Fred?"

Cheever responded with equal directness: "Well, once I was planning to take him trout fishing up at Cranberry Lake, which is just miles away from everything in the wilderness, and I realized if I got him up there he would fall overboard, [and] I would beat him with an oar until he stayed. Of course, I was appalled by this."

In most families, things never get this serious. When the firstborn is very young—say, three years old—the arrival of a baby sibling commonly leads first to the nuisance behavior known as regression, with the older child reverting to a period of infantile behavior. Toilet-trained kids suddenly return to bed-wetting; kids who have moved beyond the bottle or the sippy cup suddenly want to go back. In the child's mind—at least the unconscious mind—this makes perfect sense. It's all the diaper changings, feedings, and bathings the baby needs that are taking so much of Mom's and Dad's time. If you once again need the same care, you'll once again get the same attention.

Behavior such as regression is unheard of in species that breed in litters or even in twos and threes, since the mother gives birth to a single, same-age group all at once and by the time she's ready to do it again, the first brood is grown and gone. Among the few animals that breed single babies with long periods of dependency, however, self-infantilizing by the older sibling is more common. Jane Goodall, who has spent decades in the wild with chimpanzees, has often observed regression behavior in the troops she studies as a female with a newborn finds herself having to push away a newly clingy firstborn. When regression fails, aggression follows, with firstborn chimps handling baby siblings in ways that could pass for rough play, except that the baby is clearly having no fun.

"It's not until female chimps are eight or nine years old that a mother will let them hold and care for a baby sibling," says Salmon. "Even then, they're standing by and will snatch the baby away if the big sister gets rough or careless."

Human children are no different, and how they will treat a baby sibling is no less age dependent. Small children think nothing of snatching a toy from a smaller toddler sib. Babies who have just learned to get up on their feet are often knocked squarely back off them by an older brother or sister. In the weekend war room of our family's playroom, my brothers and I may have worked out a strategy to keep Bruce out of harm's way, but that doesn't mean we didn't sometimes try to inflict that harm ourselves, as our mother discovered one day when Bruce was barely a toddler and my other brothers and I were two, three, and five. She passed by the living room to find Bruce playing absently on the floor while the rest of us stood menacingly on a chair above him, looking for all the world like we were going to pounce. She had no idea if that was our intention—and I certainly have no recollection of the moment—but she didn't wait to find out, sweeping into the room, scooping up Bruce, and taking care that we never played with him unsupervised again until we were all a little older.

In our case, the firstborn of our brood, Steve, was actually a little bit past the age at which he should any longer have posed such a physical threat. Four years old is about the time that most children are not only less menacing to babies, but actually starting to become solicitous of them—helping to feed them, cooing at them, sometimes mimicking the baby talk that was directed at them not so long before. "Among hunter-gatherers," says Salmon, "four was about the age at which a child was fully weaned and no longer needed the resource of Mom in order to eat. When you're not competing with your baby sibling, you're less likely to try to hurt it."

Few modern mothers would nurse a baby anywhere near as long, and most four-year-olds have plenty of other sources of nutrition beyond breast milk. But the survival imperatives of the ancient world take a long time to catch up with the customs of the contemporary one, and first-borns will cling to Mom until their genes tell them it's safe to let go.

When the age difference between siblings opens up beyond four years—the six-, seven-, and eight-year gaps that sometimes occur when parents either have an unplanned child or decide late in the reproductive game that they'd like to have just one more—older siblings adjust much more easily. They are still utterly dependent on their parents, but they have also begun to chafe at that dependence, pulling away or looking put out if Mom tries to kiss them in front of their friends or if Dad tries to hug them when he picks them up at school. What the new baby needs—the constant nuzzling attention of a hovering pair of parents—is precisely what bigger kids don't want. "By seven years old," says Salmon, "the separation process has begun." That's not always so easy for parents to experience.

When my younger daughter, Paloma, who is now seven, was in kindergarten, she would leap into my arms and hug me good-bye when I dropped her off or picked her up at school. By the time she reached first grade, she'd put such childish things behind her and would grant me only a demure peck as she was saying good-bye—taking care to do it out of sight of her classroom. When my wife dropped by the school early one afternoon on an errand and surprised Paloma in the cafeteria, she was greeted with similar coolness. Later that night while getting ready for bed, Paloma—exhibiting the predictable ambivalence of a child experimenting with independence and not knowing quite how she feels about it—burst into tears over what had happened and promised my wife she'd never turn down a hug in school again. That, of course, is a promise she won't—and can't—keep.

For Paloma, this growing-up process is tough enough, but for our older daughter, Elisa, now nine, it's a little more complex. The very maturity that impels children to edge away from Mom and Dad comes with other familial burdens—specifically helping to care for the younger sibs. Alloparenting—the custom of aunts, uncles, grandparents, and other adults participating in the rearing of a child—is practiced only fitfully in the United States, and generally doesn't go much beyond babysitting or looking after the kids while the parents take a rare weekend trip. Here as well as everywhere else in the world, however, big siblings, who are present all the time, are forever being drafted into helping to care for little ones—even if it's merely in such small-bore matters as shoe tying, coat zipping, or assisting with homework. In Africa and other places with more traditional cultures, the responsibilities are much, much greater—and the relationships among siblings are much, much different.

Tom Weisner, a professor of psychiatry and anthropology at UCLA, has conducted extended studies of families in multiple cultures to observe parenting practices and, specifically, the role siblings play. One of his most in-depth projects was a long-term survey of forty-four nuclear families in Kenya, made up of roughly 400 people, or nine individuals per family. He found that not only do older brothers and sisters do more work to help raise little sibs than their counterparts do in the West, but that they actually do *most* of the work. "Siblings care directly for each other," Weisner says. "Parents serve as the indirect managers of a socially distributed caretaking system."

That's partly a result of the economic system in parts of traditional Africa, with jobs often seasonal and requiring parents to travel in search of them. Rather than uproot the entire family, they leave the big kids in charge of the little ones while they're away earning a living. Even when cultures live more fixed and settled lives, however, a tradition of sibling alloparenting remains. Weisner has found that to be particularly true in Polynesia and Hawaii, both lands with long agricultural histories predating industrialization, and both lands in which older brothers and sisters are still expected to do some heavy lifting to help rear younger ones. This not only eases the burdens on the parents, it also leads to stronger lifetime bonds among sibs—sometimes in ways Westerners would find inexplicable.

"In Polynesia," Weisner says, "it would be an expected or valorized part of life for a married couple to live apart from one another and live

with siblings. In the United States, we've de-emphasized the sibling relationship relative to other relationships, particularly the parent-child
relationship and the romantic relationship. But what if your mythology,
movies, bedtime stories, and commercials were about siblings and how
they do things together and have fun?" Brothers and sisters raised in
these cultures still fight and tease and fiercely compete, they just do so
less—and alloparenting is part of the reason. "It isn't a cure," Weisner
says, "it's just another solution."

President Barack Obama's close, or at least cordial, ties with his
sprawling web of half siblings may be less a result of alloparenting—he
grew up without any siblings around at all—than of the multiple cultural
legacies that helped shape him. Born in kin-conscious Hawaii, with a
father, half siblings, and other assorted relatives in Kenya, he got a double dose of family-centric training. Obama did not even meet his half
sister Auma until 1982, after their father died, but as he wrote in *Dreams
from My Father*, the connection was immediate. "I knew at that moment,
somehow, that I loved her. Even now I can't explain it; I only know that
the love was true, and still is, and I'm grateful for it."

The president's relationship with his older half brother, Malik, is
similarly close. The two never met until 1985, when Barack was twenty-
four and Malik was twenty-seven. Nonetheless, they stood as best men
at each other's weddings, and the little brother made a point of bringing
his fiancée to Kenya to introduce her to his big brother before getting
married—a gesture of familial respect not common among half sibs who
did not share their lives at all when they were children. Like many Ken-
yans, Malik considers extended family members who do not live in the
home country "culturally lost," though close kinship bonds with those
living overseas can help honor the ideal of the family all the same.

Of course, parents don't have to live in Polynesia or space their kids more than four years apart to foster intimacy and reduce competitive tension in the home. The mere fact of having more than two children can actually contribute to less rather than more conflict—at least in that critical period when a new baby is getting integrated into the family. In the same way that parents habituate to the successive arrivals of newborns, becoming slightly less enthralled with—or at least slightly less consumed by—the birth of each, so do siblings themselves. In a sense, says Richard Zweigenhaft, a professor of psychology at Guilford College in Greensboro, North Carolina, that's because each sibling is born into what is essentially a different family.

"My older sister was born into a family with no siblings," he says. "I was born into a family with an older sister. Every subsequent child comes into a different situation."

That, certainly, was how things were in my home. I never knew what it was like to be an only child, and so I had nothing to miss. I barely remember not having a little brother, either, since I was just sixteen months old when Garry was born. If the psychologists are right, however, at some level I did resent his arrival. I do remember Bruce's babyhood—I was nearly two and a half when he was born—and what I recall of it I enjoyed, partly because by then I was surely used to the loss of my last-born status. What's more, I was just old enough to find Bruce cute, to enjoy hearing him struggle to pronounce my name when he began to speak—though it seemed indistinguishable from the way he pronounced Steve's name. That may have said something about the interchangeable roles his two biggest brothers played for him (Steve's and my names sound nothing alike, after all). Garry, who was Bruce's closest playmate and full-time roommate, he learned to address by name quickly and clearly. We may have all been part of the same brood, but we already had very different roles and histories in it.

Dattner takes a business consultant's view of the same idea. If a family is a corporation and Mom and Dad are the co-presidents of it, they're going to take one approach to running a small operation and a different one to running a larger one. And the employees will notice. "Each child takes up a proportionate share of the parents' attention," Dattner says. "It's going to be harder to go from 100 percent to 50 percent, than it is to go from 50 percent to 33, or 33 to 25." By the time kids get down to the single-digit percentages of truly large families, communal living and distracted parents are all they ever know.

In the course of this, the siblings are forced to take a corporate perspective of their own: No matter when they joined the payroll, they're now part of a joint enterprise. The job of the entire team is to keep the operation running smoothly and peacefully. That, they will soon learn, is much harder to do than they could have possibly imagined.

THREE

The Outbreak of Hostilities

Why Siblings Fight and What to Do About It

I knew enough not to tangle with Steve. As older brothers went, he was not especially menacing. He liked to read; he liked to write; he loved listening to music and could get lost for hours in my mother's collection of Broadway soundtracks. He was breathtakingly bad at sports—the kind of bad that rises almost to the level of performance art—and his lack of agility made him equally bad at anything approaching physical combat. I saw him angry plenty of times, but I never once saw him throw a punch at a friend or a schoolmate—as much because of any innate pacifism, I always assumed, as because he simply had no idea how to do it effectively.

All the same, he was an older brother, with all of the authority and capacity for menace that that implied. He could tease mercilessly, he could provoke diabolically. He was bigger and stronger than I was, and even with his limited pugilistic skills, he was not above the leap-and-pummel strategy older siblings routinely use to keep younger ones in line. To that extent, I was intimidated by Steve—at least until the day I decided to take a stand. It was a strip of balsa wood that gave me my chance.

Woodworking was never much taught or valued in my family. My father was good with his hands, but in the precise and pointillist way of, say, a jeweler or a fly-fisherman. He could assemble a model solar system in a cardboard box that was accurate down to the Saturnian moonlets, but hanging a door or building a bookshelf was another matter entirely. When my father did finally decide to work in wood, it was thus no surprise that balsa wood was his medium of choice. Sold in sheets and planks—to the degree that anything that was three feet long and less than a quarter of an inch thick can be fairly called a plank—it could be cut with heavy scissors instead of a saw and pieced together with straight pins instead of nails. Still, the stuff had strength and it had twang and I took special pleasure in watching my father build a lovely—and perfectly useless—birdhouse with it, one that was fine on a mantel but would not have survived half a day in an actual tree with an actual bird. Steve and I decided we'd like to work with balsa wood, too, and my father bought us some, which we stored under Steve's bed when we weren't using it.

One night, not long before going to sleep, I was playing on the floor of our room when Steve returned, having just taken a bath. He dropped his towel to put on his pajamas and I looked up to see my older brother's bum a few feet in front of me. I was six, Steve was eight, and in all the years of a shared bedroom and shared baths, I'd seen his rear almost as much as I'd seen his face. But it had never been positioned just so before—and certainly never with a light, springy, whip-cracking strip of balsa wood just within reach of my right hand.

I loved Steve; I admired and even feared Steve. More to the point, I respected him—and not just him but his office. He was the oldest of the four of us, and that entitled him to deference. And yet his butt, the balsa wood, and a fleeting moment of opportunity had come together in front of me—a moment needing only courage on my part. That perfect convergence would, I knew, vanish in an instant. In a great flash of carpe diem folly, I whipped my hand under the bed, grabbed the wood, hitched back my arm, and swung.

What I remember most about that moment was the wonderful thwacking sound that followed the swing—a sound that, no doubt, has been embellished by the years. I remember, too, Steve wheeling around, locking his eyes on mine, and in a fraternal flash sending me a complex, unspoken message. He was astonished by what I'd done and—truth be told—he was a little impressed by it. "You've got moxie," his expression said, "but you're going to have to pay for it." My return look, I suspect, conveyed just two words: "Of course."

I covered up and Steve attacked, administering a harmless if humbling pounding perfectly suited to my crime. With that, the natural hierarchy was restored. I was reminded of the primacy of his position—but he was reminded that more and more he'd be called upon to defend it. It was one of a thousand such balance-of-power maneuvers we'd already traded in our years together—and it was one of thousands more still to come. And that was precisely how things were supposed to be.

It's no surprise that families are fantastically complicated things—a scrum of people and personalities crowded together under a single roof for eighteen or twenty years and expected to get along there. By some measures, it's a wonder they survive six months. Even that, however, doesn't quite capture all the complexity at play. Most of the time, we think of a family as a single emotional organism—a mom and a dad and a group of children, moving and acting as a mass. But there are a lot more people—or, more specifically, a lot more relationships—in any one household than you think.

Every individual in your family has a separate, one-on-one relationship with every other individual, each of those relationships representing a discrete, stand-alone pairing. All families are made of many such pairs—or dyads—and just how many of them there are in a single home is a matter of simple arithmetic. Psychologist Jennifer Jenkins of the University of Toronto begins many of her studies of family dynamics with a statistical device called a correlation matrix. The formula seems opaque:

$$k(k - 1)/2 = x$$

But it's actually a very simple thing, with k standing for the number of people in a family and x for the number of dyads. If your family has 3 children and 2 parents, that means there are 10 one-on-one relationships playing out at any one time. Dad has his own relationship with each child, Mom has her own, and Mom and Dad have the marital bond. Add to that the relationship between child number one and two, child number two and three, and child number three and one. In a 4-sibling, 2-parent family there are 15 such dyads. The 6-child Brady Bunch had 28; the original Kennedy clan, with 9 children, had 55; and Bobby Kennedy, who grew up to have 11 children of his own, had a household with a whopping 91 dyads.

Every such pairing in any one family has strengths, intimacies, and challenges that are peculiar to it, and this is particularly so in the case of siblings. The relationship between, say, two middle-born sisters will be very different from that between a firstborn son and a second-born son, a firstborn girl and a fourth-born girl, and on and on. "We used to think of families as a kind of unified environment," says Frank Sulloway, psychologist, science historian, and author of *Born to Rebel: Birth Order, Family Dynamics, and Creative Lives*. "But your relationship with any other family member is different from your sibling's relationship with that same member. It's different because you have a different history. You can almost argue that there is no such thing as a shared environment; the family is instead a series of micro-environments."

As with all environments, each of these can develop its own climate and ecology, and this is particularly so when it comes to the onset of storms. Parents who are asked how often their children fight will predictably answer with exasperated absolutes: "Constantly," they'll say. "When do they *not* fight?" Unscientific as these responses are, the fact is, they're surprisingly accurate. Indeed, parents who lament what seems to be the almost hourly outbreak of hostilities in the playroom may actually be lowballing things.

Psychologist Laurie Kramer, who, in addition to her teaching work at the University of Illinois, directs research at the school's Family Resiliency Center, was among the first to try to put a hard number on just how often siblings fight, visiting homes and observing brothers and sisters at play. With the cooperation and connivance of the parents, she has concealed microphones in kids' bedrooms—or even on an article of their clothing—and retreated to another part of the house to listen in as they go about the complicated business of growing up together. The results surprised her.

During a forty-five-minute play session, Kramer found that the average pair of children in the three- to seven-year-old age group engage in more than 2.5 conflicts. That factors out to 3.5 every hour, or one every seventeen minutes. And by conflict, Kramer doesn't mean a single-volley remark or an aggressive physical bump that goes unanswered. She means extended conflict—at least three sequential hostile exchanges. When you add the smaller pokes and provocations, the count climbs even higher. A related study by psychologists Michal Perlman of the University of Toronto and Hildy Ross of the University of Waterloo focused on sibs from two to four years old and found that in that age group, hostilities break out an astonishing 6.3 times per hour—or one fight every 9.5 minutes. A well-regarded study from as long ago as 1980 found that fully 82 percent of siblings had engaged in some form of physical violence against a brother or sister in the course of the preceding year, and that 40 percent had hit a sib with an object of some kind.

Bradley McKay, twelve, and his brother Pete, nine, are growing up on Chicago's North Side, and have successfully achieved something of an interpersonal trifecta when it comes to fighting: They're siblings, they're boys, and they're close in age. Pete estimates that he fights with Bradley about two-thirds of the time they're together—which fits comfortably inside the range Perlman, Ross, and Kramer observed. Their mother, Donna, marvels at how little it can take to spark hostilities. "They fight about almost everything," she says.

The bill of particulars Pete cites against his brother confirms that. "Whenever I get the remote first, he screams and tells me to change the channel," he says. "He seems to call me stupid and fat for no reason. And when we play board games, he accuses me of cheating when I'm about to win. Once he pulled my tongue. I get hurt a lot." Bradley, not surprisingly, denies the charges: "Anything he says about me, if it isn't positive, is a filthy lie."

The McKay boys are hardly alone in finding nearly any grievance a sufficient reason to fight. When I was a child, Steve and I almost came to blows because he inexplicably wanted to name a new stuffed puppy he'd been given "Brittany"—a name he no doubt overheard from TV or an adult conversation, and one I considered far too snooty for any plush toy that was going to live in our room. When Larry Stone, now a national baseball reporter for the *Seattle Times*, was small, his older sister knew she could elicit a reaction simply by fixing her eyes on him during dinner and refusing to look away. "Mom," he'd cry, "Esther's gazing at me!"

For all these everyday provocations, however, the most common casus belli among siblings is property. Small children have almost no control over their world, and what little they do have concerns their possessions. They understand early on that toys that are presented to them belong to them, and while kids are perfectly willing to encroach on the property rights of another, they can't abide someone else trespassing on theirs. "In one of my papers," says Catherine Salmon, of the University of Redlands, "we found that 95 percent of younger siblings and 93 percent of older siblings mentioned that the taking of property was a major problem in their relationship. It's a very important part of the development of personal identity—the idea of 'What's mine is mine and what's yours is yours.'"

Hildy Ross has conducted longer-term studies of children in the two-to-four age group and then returned to observe the same kids when they're four to six, and for all the maturing that goes on in that critical span, she has found that they barely budge when it comes to the fierce assertion of control over their own belongings. Actual violence in the defense of property—the toddler with a toy who is approached to share it and instead clunks the other child on the head with it—might diminish with age, but defending what's theirs by other means doesn't.

Yet the very sensitivity to property rights that drives so much conflict also carries the seeds to its solution. Encouragingly, studies by Ross and others have shown that even without the intervention of a parent, when a battle over property breaks out and is successfully resolved, the settlement usually favors the rightful owner—almost as if the encroaching sibling feels innately wrong and is more inclined to back down than the aggrieved sibling. That's not the case all the time, of course, and Ross concedes that it helps a lot when the rightful owner also happens to be the older child. But older or younger, the owner wins far more times than would be explained simply by chance.

Close behind property as a trigger for sibling war making is the general concept of fairness. The English language is filled with idioms expressing this simple ideal: We seek a square deal, a level playing field, a fair shake. Things get divided even steven, fifty-fifty. We exhort one another to stick to a bargain, to do the right thing. That's a whole lot of vocabulary for so straight-up a concept, and it's a measure, perhaps, of how deeply rooted fairness is in our DNA. Research conducted by numerous scientists, including Samuel Bowles, a professor of economics at the University of Siena and a faculty member at the Santa Fe Institute, has shown that the part of the brain that lights up when we encounter something we consider unfair is the same that lights up when we feel disgust—meaning we recoil from the very idea of inequity in the same way we recoil from a rotten egg or putrefied meat. And this is not a concept that arose late in human development; it's the brain's insula that is the seat of disgust, a deeply buried region far below our vaunted—and comparatively modern—cerebral cortex. Human impulses don't get much more primally encoded than that, and this same sense of equity may have played a key role in the formation of civil society itself.

In 1971, sociobiologist Robert Trivers of Harvard coined the term "reciprocal altruism" to describe the bilateral flow of goods and favors that undergirds any social system. Primitive humans who shared their food when their neighbors had none would have been a lot less inclined to do so if they weren't reasonably sure their neighbors would provide for them when they were wanting. The man who lends his hammer to a neighbor today does so with the unspoken expectation that he can come asking to borrow a ladder tomorrow. Without that understanding, the original favor would never be performed—and a cooperative culture wouldn't coalesce. We may not like assigning such cool and reductionist motives to so sublime a concept as human generosity, but it's an inescapable part of what drives us all.

This is no less true in the home, but here a small child's sense of what's fair and what's not goes beyond the favor-for-favor, good-deed-for-good-deed arrangement of reciprocal altruism, extending to pretty much any transaction at all that involves a brother or sister. The cupcake must be cut precisely in half or the child who got stiffed will howl. An 8:00 p.m. bedtime is perfectly all right with one sibling unless the other sib gets 8:15—in which case a grave injustice has been done. Birthday presents, weekly allowances, tooth fairy money—all get counted up and compared. Often, the very idea that something inequitable is taking place is far more important than the substance of that something. The cupcake grievance may have some merit, since every quarter-inch that gets added to Child A's half must, by definition, be subtracted from Child B's. But the little brother with the 8:00 p.m. bedtime did not have to give up fifteen minutes in order for his big brother to stay up till 8:15. When sibs grow up, they may realize the fundamental pointlessness of these arguments on principle, but when they're children, the issues seem very, very real.

Wynne Wong-Cheng, a thirty-four-year-old elementary school psychologist living in Van Nuys, California, remembers how her big sister, Wileen Wong, now thirty-six, would lean on their mother to be stricter with Wynne—even though the way their parents treated one sister had no real impact on the other. "I got away with things with my parents, and I know that upset Wileen," Wynne says. "Even with little chores my parents asked us to do, I didn't have to follow through on them. Also, I was a picky eater and she wasn't, so even though our parents tried to make us eat everything on our plates, I didn't have to. Wileen was always reminding Mom to set limits on me, but I knew how to work it. So she would say to my mom, 'It's not fair that she gets away with these things.'"

Young siblings can—and should—be forgiven some of this behavior, since the hard fact is that they're not capable of much else. Fairness is a complicated concept, and children are limited in their understanding of it, applying it bluntly, broadly, and without exceptions. "Siblings tell their parents about something that the sibling has done wrong—she is talking with her mouth full, she spilled her milk," says Hildy Ross, "things that don't really affect the child's own well-being, but enforce the family rules."

Ultimately kids do start to learn that fairness is a more flexible concept than that—that there's plain fairness and situational fairness. A first-grader may get angry when he comes home from school and finds that his big sister, who was sick and had to stay in bed, got to watch cartoons all day. By third grade, he may still grumble, but he'll also understand that the circumstances of the day mitigate the perceived injustice. That transition from "Unfair!" to "Unfair, however . . ." may not seem like much, but it's a big developmental step—one that parents eagerly wait for their kids to take.

Squalls that break out over fair dealing or toy sharing are tolerable, if maddening, but things get a lot more serious when screaming turns to physical fighting. Psychologists and family experts are not speaking lightly when they call sibling relationships the most abusive in most families, all the more so in an era in which spankings and other kinds of corporal punishment that parents once imposed are increasingly understood to be a mistake, and have become far less socially acceptable in any event. That often leaves kids as the only hitters in the house, and studies as far back as 1980 have consistently found fights between siblings to be the most common type of family violence.

"I did a longitudinal study of adolescent siblings once," says psychologist Lew Bank, of the Oregon Social Learning Center. "I thought it would be interesting to ask a group of younger siblings—who were on average about sixteen years old—what's the best thing your sibling ever did with you and what's the worst thing. We had to stop asking the question in the first week of the study because there were so many reports of assault and even rape. It was a high-risk group of kids, but still."

Clearly, even the worst sibling relationships rarely take so dark a turn, but the mere fact that the capacity for such ugliness exists is a reminder of the powerful feelings that can be at play. The first thing parents need to do when faced with brawling kids is to determine what's a real fight and what isn't. A lot of sibling wrestling and hitting is just a form of kabuki combat designed to test limits and recalibrate the balance of power—the very thing that motivated my balsa-wood whack and the pummeling that followed. Psychologist Eleanor Maccoby of Stanford University has written extensively about the value of what she labels rough-and-tumble play, a form of relatively harmless hitting, shoving and wrestling that takes place among all children, but particularly among boys. In most cases, the point of the sparring is to gauge the other boy's strength and willingness to fight.

My brothers and I routinely made nighttime trips to the emergency room for stitches or splints that resulted from too-rough games gone painfully awry. In the era when we were growing up, our appearances in the hospital were met with rolls of the eyes or even a smile as a nurse would check her chart to see how frequent our regular visits had become. Today, the nurse's eyes would narrow instead, and a call would surely be made to child protective services to make certain that all the bloodshed wasn't a product of parental neglect or abuse. But if the era has changed, the nature of boys hasn't, and when my extended family recently met in an otherwise orderly restaurant in Los Angeles for a too-rare gathering of the clan, it was no surprise when no sooner had we arrived than two of my nephews—brothers aged five and three—dropped to the floor, wrestling. The parental cries of "It won't seem like so much fun when one of you gets hurt" as they pulled the boys apart were exactly the same as they were when I was little, and the risk of injury was exactly as great. But as in the past as well, both parents had a pretty good idea of what was behind the brawling—and it clearly wasn't hostility.

Among sibs, this probing for weaknesses starts even earlier than the three-to-five age group. Part of the purpose of Ross's study of small children at two-year intervals was to determine how firmly fixed dominance patterns are and what it takes to change them. In one experiment in 1994, she observed a sample group of two- to four-year-olds, noting which ones were aggressors and which were conciliators. Typically, it was the older siblings who threw their weight around and the younger ones who tolerated it. Ross returned in 1996 and observed the same subjects, looking to see if their dynamic had changed. Significantly, she found that aggressive older siblings remained aggressive as long as the younger sibs accepted that that was the natural order of things. In the relative handful of relationships in which the younger sib pushed back, the older sib usually chose not to push harder but instead to retreat a bit. The relationship became less hierarchical, if never one of true equals. "If the second-born stood up for himself," Ross says, "the aggressor stood down."

Real fights fueled by real anger do break out, of course, and even the most benign rough-and-tumble does operate on the knife edge of trouble. One way to distinguish the difference is what happens not when the weaker—usually younger—party pushes back, but instead signals surrender. If the hostilities immediately break off, the fight was probably harmless. If the aggressor persists, any rough-and-tumble deal that did exist has been broken and something more is going on. Parents may not always be able to see where the line exists in any particular bout, but the sibs themselves do.

"Children recognize the difference and get angry if the boundary is crossed," writes child expert Judith Harris. "After a bout of rough-and-tumble play, children continue to play together. After an aggressive encounter, they go their separate ways."

Brother-on-brother brawls may be the most common form of sibling combat, but that's not to say that fights of the sister-sister or sister-brother kind don't play out, too, sometimes with equal ferocity. Among the three possible sibling gender pairings—boy-boy, girl-girl, and girl-boy—it's actually the girl-boy matchup that includes the most physical provocation, though with overwhelming frequency it's directed at the sister by the brother, and just as much so when the boy is the younger of the two. Older brothers—whether by natural inclination, social training, or both—usually go easier on little sisters. Little brothers are not so constrained, which makes it a good thing that they're also not very powerful. Physical fighting between younger brothers and older sisters may break out often, but it rarely lasts long, both because the sister does not have much interest in it and because she has the size and strength to stiff-arm her attacker away. To the extent that a big sister does rise to the combat bait, she often does so creatively.

Actor Jake Gyllenhaal was once asked if his big sister, Maggie, also a Hollywood star, ever beat him up. His answer: "Depends on what you call beating up. She performed the musical *Cats* for our parents and she made me lick milk from a bowl while she sang, which was, in a way, abuse."

Much worse than sister-brother fighting is sister-sister, and it can carry a special edge. Among boys, strength and size are pretty much everything. Among girls, things are subtler. Before the blows, there are usually words, and those words can cut. There's a lot of truth to the stereotype that girls are generally better at intimacy skills than boys are, and parents and teachers observe that fact every day. During a parent-teacher-student classroom party when my daughter Elisa was in second grade, she clunked her head on something and wailed inconsolably for a minute or two. As I comforted her, I noticed two of her friends—both girls—hovering a few feet away, unseen by Elisa. Their hands were knitted worriedly and their faces crinkled with empathic pain. It was sweet and real—and it was wholly outside of my boyhood experience. I got clocked by something and cried plenty of times when I was Elisa's age, and if any of my male peers were even aware of it—much less worried about it—I surely didn't notice.

But there's also a downside to what girls share. Boys, even brothers, may never get to know one another at the deep and granular level at which their private fears and closely guarded vulnerabilities are held, but girls exchange those secrets readily, and often use that openness to build shared trust. Sometimes, however, they exploit that intimacy. The more knowledge you have about the other girl, after all, the more you can turn it back on her when you're angry. "Because girls know each other so well," says developmental psychologist Judith Dunn, of King's College in London, "they can be devastating teasers and bulliers. They know just what upsets the other."

Indeed, I saw that same flip side of empathy play out in a very dramatic way in 2008 between Elisa, who was seven at the time, and our then-five-year-old Paloma. That year, a construction crane collapsed near Second Avenue in New York City, killing seven people and crushing a midtown brownstone. I, my wife, and Paloma happened to be on the other side of the avenue when it occurred. The sound was deafening, and the sight of the crane tipping forward and destroying the house was horrific. Worse for those standing nearby was the sudden stampede of people running from the scene as a smell of leaking gas rose from the rubble—a stampede in which we quickly found ourselves. I scooped up Paloma so that she wouldn't get trampled underfoot, and we all raced along as fast as we could until we made it clear of danger.

The experience, not surprisingly, stayed with Paloma and for weeks afterward caused her no shortage of sleepless nights. She confided in Elisa—who was in a weekend class at the time and missed the drama—that she could not get the thought of cranes out of her head. Elisa listened to and consoled her little sister and was a source of true comfort. Yet when the girls found themselves in an argument over the course of the following days, she would sometimes tease her by finding a way to work the word "crane" into the conversation. When my wife and I would reprimand her, she'd innocently insist that she meant the bird, not the machine. More than once, Elisa's needling led Paloma to take a swing at her—and a shoving, hair-pulling fight would break out. Such gratuitous taunting, of course, is hardly gender specific, and brothers are capable of the same unpleasantness. But a boy who was troubled by something like Paloma was would also be more inclined to suck it up, tough it out, and never mention it out loud. If you don't expose your vulnerable neck, no one's ever going to bite it.

Certainly, when girls are older, they're more empathic than they are at seven, and a sister who witnessed a tragedy the way Paloma did would get only sympathy from the other sister. But during the course of an argument, it's less certain that the same two girls wouldn't find other, subtler weak spots to exploit—a boyfriend problem, an academic setback, even a body-image issue—and that things couldn't then turn physical all over again. "The studies of physical fighting between kids that are based on playgrounds talk about boys' aggression and minimize girls'," says Dunn. "But that is not so when you look at girls who also happen to be sisters. In those cases, they can be incredibly aggressive physically—and that aggression is exhibited in a way that isn't typically described for girls."

If sibs come factory-loaded for fighting, they come equally well equipped with an impressive set of peacemaking skills. That's critical both for their emotional development and for the maintenance of their relationship—to say nothing of the sanity of their parents. Not only can't Mom and Dad forever be brokering cease-fires among the siblings, their efforts may not even be worth all that much: Peace imposed from the outside is never as lasting as the kind that's hammered out between the parties themselves. It's not always easy to spot the tools sibs use to settle their disputes, particularly since they're usually subtler than the ones they use to wage war. In 2009, psychologists Holly Recchia and Nina Howe, both then at Concordia University in Montreal, conducted a multipart study designed to look more closely at this aspect of the sibling dynamic.

Recchia and Howe recruited a sample group of several dozen sibling pairs and then divided them into three age groups: four to seven, six to eight, and seven to ten. In the first part of the study, they instructed forty-five of the pairs to select a recurring conflict in their relationship and gave them ten minutes to sort it out. A discreetly placed video camera recorded their conversations, but otherwise the kids were left entirely alone. This, of course, could be a prescription for a full-blown war, but the kids did much better than expected.

The average negotiation lasted just two minutes and four seconds before the siblings emerged and announced they'd resolved their differences. Of the forty-five pairs, twenty-nine reached a solution that the researchers termed a compromise—the gold standard of conflict resolution, with both parties giving up something and both getting something in return. Ten reached an agreement that was a straight-up win-lose arrangement—a zero-sum settlement in which one sibling prevailed completely, but to which both sibs at least agreed. Only four were termed a standoff, with no agreement at all reached. And only two were what the researchers decorously labeled "unproductive," and what parents would label "a meltdown."

Certainly, the way kids behave in the controlled setting of the laboratory with a flock of scientists hovering outside the door is very different from the way they behave in the free-fire zone of the playroom, and any number of them might have reached an agreement only because they knew the grown-ups expected them to. This is a version of what's known as the Hawthorne effect, named for industrial experiments conducted at the Hawthorne Works manufacturing plant outside of Chicago in 1924. In those studies, researchers wanted to determine how various levels of light affect employee efficiency, but the results proved useless. The workers improved their performance during the studies—seeming to validate the methods being tested—but as soon as the experimenters left, productivity returned to what it had been. The boost in performance was not in response to the improved work setting, but to the mere presence of the observers.

Recchia and Howe were mindful of the Hawthorne effect and concede that it may have played a role in their research. But what they were most interested in was not whether the kids they observed reached a resolution, but how they reached it. That was the real variable measured in the study, and that was much less likely to be influenced by the presence of the scientists. The techniques the siblings used, the researchers found, were often dependent largely on their age.

The older the kids were, the more inclined they were not just to make their arguments, but to provide justifications for them. As with kids' understanding of conditional fairness, the difference between "I want this toy" and "I want this toy because . . ." is a very big one. The sooner that at least one sibling learns it, the more rational the arguments are likely to be. Kids in the older end of the study group were also better at generalizing their resolution beyond the immediate conflict and applying it to future ones that might come up. Children do this all the time when they're playing—inventing bits of a game on the fly and codifying it with the declaration, "From now on, the rule is . . ." Applied to in-family arguments, that same skill goes a long way toward avoiding the *Groundhog Day* phenomenon that occurs when the same fight comes up again and again. Build up a body of such laws and before long you've got a sort of ad hoc civil code.

The problem with such age-specific skills, of course, is that often—indeed, most of the time—children are arguing back and forth across developmental lines. The older child who's learned the art of justification and rule generalization must try to reach a resolution with a younger child who's nowhere near that point. And the younger child must try to make a case with an arsenal of argumentation weapons far less sophisticated than the older one's. Yet many of the siblings in the study proved adept at adjusting to this disparity, calibrating their arguments to the age and maturity level of the other. A child in the middle group—the six-to-eight category, for example—was more likely to use justifications and explanations when bargaining up to a sibling in the seven-to-ten group than down to a younger sib in the four-to-seven group. "Siblings may be more motivated to express their point of view if they think the listener will understand and benefit from it than when they will not," the researchers wrote.

With such instinctive abilities to feel their way to peaceful play, kids often do not need their parents' sometimes clumsy intervention. But that's not to say it's a good idea to go too far in the leave-them-be direction, and not just in order to prevent someone from getting killed. A venerable—if questionable—bit of child-rearing wisdom is that some arguments between siblings are staged mostly to get the grown-ups' attention. In the constant competition to stand out in the brood, there is nothing like being wronged by a brother or sister and then having a parent side with you to give you a temporary edge. With that in mind, when a conflict breaks out, some child-care experts argue that a parent may be smart not to take the bait and instead to let the kids sort things out on their own.

Maybe. But parents do need to take a more selective approach, always looking closely at what the conflict is about and just which siblings are involved. Not only will this prevent a younger, weaker child from getting pounded by an older, bigger sibling should the fight spin out of control, but it can also help kids who do have some peacemaking skills to use them more effectively.

The second part of Recchia and Howe's two-step study involved telling the same sets of siblings to address another conflict that regularly occurs in their relationship, but this time with a parent acting as mediator. Once again, the kids were given ten minutes to wrestle with the problem and come up with some resolution. With an adult in the room, it took longer to reach a consensus, with the average time of negotiation more than doubling—from two minutes and four seconds to five minutes and twenty seconds. Some of the additional time was, no doubt, consumed by the parents themselves. Moms and dads are notoriously verbal in their dealings with their kids, with lots and lots of counsel to dispense—some of it worthwhile, some of it not, but all of it time consuming. In this phase of the experiment, however, the kids themselves also seemed to be doing more talking—and, significantly, more thinking.

With the guidance of a parent, the siblings were able to reach compromise slightly more often—32 times compared to 29. The less desirable win-lose solution (with one child getting everything and the other getting nothing) occurred only 6 times in the presence of an adult compared to 13 times when the sibs were on their own. There were 11 standoffs in the just-kids negotiations, compared to 7 with a parental arbitrator.

When the researchers looked deeper into their results, they found additional reasons to be pleased. With parents present, the siblings were also better able to maintain a present- and future-oriented focus rather than relitigating past battles—the "You always get the toy!" phenomenon. The parents also showed an instinctive sense for how not to get pulled into an argument at the children's level. When one sibling would complain, "That's not fair," the most common parental response in the study was "You both think it's not fair," or some variation on that idea. A child who feels wronged is not generally inclined to consider that the other child feels the same way, and while a parent pointing out that fact is hardly guaranteed to make an impression, in the absence of the parent, the observation never gets made at all.

Most important, on those occasions when a compromise or some other solution was entirely impossible, the parents in the study at least served as a safety net. Those who were ultimately forced to take sides almost always did so on behalf of the child in the weaker negotiating position. Typically that was the younger child, but sometimes it wasn't, as a comparatively passive big sib can sometimes be overwhelmed by a comparatively aggressive little one.

The parents in the study were no more immune to the subtle hand of the Hawthorne effect than were the kids, of course—indeed, they might have been even more susceptible to it, since adults are far likelier than kids to know what good behavior looks like and to mimic it for the benefit of an observer. But the mere fact that they did know that—that when they were forced to think about the most effective responses to their kids' fights they made the right choices—suggests that more rather than less parental intervention can be helpful in the home.

Children—by their age, nature, and lack of life experience—will always be domestic anarchists, though the older they get, the more civilized they become. That's a fact that moms and dads—long since socialized into the ways of conflict avoidance and peaceful resolution—often forget. There is genuine wonder in the voice of a parent who asks, "What did you *think* would happen when you touched his toy?" or "Why must you always tease her when you know she gets upset?" But the thing is, the child often didn't think in the first case and truly doesn't know in the second. If children needed as long to learn, say, the concept of gravity as they do to learn how to get along with their brothers and sisters, no amount of Mom or Dad pleading "but you know that egg will break if you drop it" would suddenly give them a full under-standing of Newtonian physics.

In the laboratory of sibling relations, brothers and sisters do come to learn up from down—that fights can be negotiated and regulated and eventually avoided altogether. And parents do have the power to facili-tate that learning—at least some. And in the years it takes for the kids to acquire the skills they need, Mom and Dad can take at least some comfort from knowing that along with the learning can also come a measure of gentleness, empathy, and deeper familial love.

"Competition and conflict will always happen," says Shirley McGuire, associate professor of psychology at the University of San Francisco. But, she promises, "warmth, cooperation, and trust will hap-pen, too." That goal may sometimes seem elusive, but it's one that's manifestly worth pursuing all the same.

FOUR

Who's on First?

The Mysteries of Birth Order

It could not have been easy being Elliott Roosevelt. If the alcohol wasn't getting him, the morphine was. If it wasn't the morphine, it was the struggle with depression. Then, of course, there were the constant comparisons to big brother Teddy.

In 1883, the year Elliott began battling what was then known as melancholy, Teddy had already published his first book and had been elected to the New York State assembly. By 1891—about the time Elliott, still unable to establish a career, had to be institutionalized to deal with his addictions—Teddy was U.S. Civil Service commissioner and the author of eight books. Three years later, Elliott, thirty-four, died of alcoholism. Seven years after that, Teddy, forty-two, became president.

Elliott Roosevelt was not the only younger sibling of an eventual president to cause his family heartaches—or at least headaches. There was Donald Nixon and the loans he wangled from billionaire Howard Hughes. There was Billy Carter, hawking beer and talking loose and trying to intervene with the U.S. government on behalf of the pariah state Libya. There was Roger Clinton and his year in jail on a cocaine conviction. In the book *A Treasury of Great American Scandals*, author Michael Farquhar cites similar cases even earlier in history: Randolph Jefferson, the younger brother of Thomas, was widely seen as both reckless and clownish, forever at the edge of bankruptcy as a result of one ill-considered business deal or another. One of the president's slaves captured the general perception best when he said, "[Randolph] was one mighty simple man." Orvil Grant, little brother of Ulysses, conspired with Secretary of War William Belknap to solicit kickbacks from the sale of trading posts in the West, and was eventually called out for it by General George Custer during a Senate investigation.

In fairness to all of the little sibs whose big brothers land in the Oval Office, it can't be easy being a runt in a litter that includes a president. But it couldn't have been easy being Billy Ripken, either, an unexceptional major league infielder craning his neck for notice while the press swarmed around Hall of Famer and elder brother Cal. It couldn't have been easy being Dom DiMaggio, with his .298 career batting average for the Boston Red Sox and his seven selections to the All-Star team, glittering achievements by any measure, until they're compared to those of big brother—and New York Yankee—Joe.

Of all the things that shape who we are, few seem more random than the simple timing of our birth and how it compares with the timing of our siblings'. Maybe it's your genes that make you a gifted athlete, an accident of brain chemistry that makes you a drunk instead of a president. But in family after family, case study after case study, the roll of the birth-date dice seems to have an odd and arbitrary power all its own.

For families themselves, this comes as no surprise. There are few extended clans that can't point to the firstborn child with the heir-apparent bearing who makes the best grades, keeps the other kids in line, and, when Mom and Dad grow old, winds up as caretaker and executor, too. There are few that can't point to the lost-in-the-thickets middle-born or the wild-child last-born. And hard data support those everyday observations. Firstborns are disproportionately represented in Ivy League colleges, with one study revealing that 66 percent of incoming students were the oldest in the brood. This has knock-on effects later in life, with the exceptionally well educated similarly dominating white-shoe law firms and investment banks. The firstborn edge applies even extraterrestrially: Twenty-one of the first twenty-three U.S. astronauts were firstborns or only children. By contrast, last-borns are looser cannons, less educated, and statistically more likely to live the life of an artist or a comedian, an adventurer or entrepreneur, a GI or a firefighter. And middle children? Well, they can be a puzzle—to families, scientists, and themselves, for that matter.

Even when people aren't actually siblings, we sometimes can't help but see them that way. There was always an odd brotherly quality to Bill Clinton and Al Gore's partnership, with Clinton the flashy, popular, slick-talking big sib, forever eclipsing Gore, his studious little brother—unless of course you saw Gore as the disciplined and industrious firstborn and Clinton as the troublemaking baby. Ringo may have been the oldest Beatle, but he came across as every bit the goofy youngest. Paul and John seemed to battle for the firstborn crown, while George filled the role of the quiet middle-born. Buzz Aldrin, the second man on the moon, is seven months older than Neil Armstrong, the first. But if the men were brothers, would there be any doubt that the serious, sober Armstrong was the big sib, and Aldrin—with his product endorsements, bit parts on TV shows, and goofy turn on the prime-time hit *Dancing with the Stars*—was the little one?

Across the landscape of the behavioral sciences, real insights into human interactions usually require rigorous studies and decades of double-blind research. The power of birth order, by contrast, is something we always seemed to feel before scientists ever got into the game. "There are stereotypes out there about birth order, and often those stereotypes are spot-on," says Delroy Paulhus, a professor of psychology at the University of British Columbia in Vancouver. "I think this is one of those cases in which people just figured things out on their own."

But science is catching up, and what it's revealing about the power of birth order is surprising even believers. According to a widely reported 2007 study by Norwegian researchers, firstborns are generally smarter than any siblings who come along later, enjoying on average a 3-point IQ advantage over the next eldest. The second child, in turn, is a point ahead of the third. Three points may not seem to amount to much, but consider that just 2.3 IQ points can correlate to a 15-point difference in SAT scores, which makes an even bigger difference when you're applying to, say, Stanford or Yale with a 690 verbal score and are going head-to-head against someone with a 705. Once you have that academic leg up, there's no telling where it can lead.

"Take a person who just manages to squeak into Harvard and the other one gets into some lesser college," says the University of California's Frank Sulloway, the widely accepted wise man of birth-order research. "The one who gets into Harvard meets a charismatic teacher and gets a summer job in the lab and gets taken on as a grad student and goes on to have an amazing career in science and wins a Nobel Prize. All of that can be a cascading effect that comes from a relatively modest difference."

Behavioral scientists call such phenomena "threshold effects"—the seemingly inconsequential variable that leads to big results—and while

Sulloway is surely overstating the case here, birth-order science is filled with similar examples. Studies in the Philippines show that later-born siblings tend to be shorter and weigh less than earlier-borns. Think the slight height advantage Peyton Manning, the six-foot five-inch quarterback of the Indianapolis Colts, has over Eli, his six-four little brother, who plays the same position for the New York Giants, doesn't help when they're trying to throw over the outstretched arms of a leaping lineman? The brothers' lifetime stats certainly say it does.

More than the sibs' careers are affected by birth order; their very health may be, too. Surveys show that younger siblings are less likely to be vaccinated than older ones. Kids with at least two older siblings are 50 percent likelier than other children to have been taken to an emergency room with asthma-related breathing problems, according to a study from Columbia University's Mailman School of Public Health— probably due to increased exposure to infectious agents brought into the home by the bigger sibs. Second and third children also have a higher risk of diabetes than their firstborn sibs, with a 43 percent increase in cases for every five years of maternal age at birth.

As for the health-and-longevity disadvantages of being the eldest child? Not many, with the very significant exception that firstborns seem to run a greater risk of coronary heart disease. In a study conducted at a major cardiovascular rehab unit in Milan, Italy, firstborns represented 46.7 percent of all patients, yet they made up only 29.3 percent of the surrounding population. But even this undeniable downside may be a result of the eldest kids' generally privileged lot. "The family context frequently orients them along a perfectionist path," said Dr. Maurizio Ferrantini, head of the rehab unit. "[This gives] them a determined, competitive, winning and aggressive attitude—aspects frequently seen in subjects with a type A personality."

It's pointless, of course, for a later-born to be too resentful of a first-born's advantages, since many of them are unavoidable. You can hardly blame the eldest themselves for the fact that they're born into a home with fewer child-borne pathogens than the younger ones experience. And if it's maternal age that's behind additional child health concerns, such as the increased risk for diabetes in younger kids, well, you can't fight the simple arithmetic that makes Mom a little older every time she has a kid. Even the IQ advantage may be inevitable: Eldest kids get at least a year alone with their parents, which leads to a no-distractions period of intellectual stimulation. Firstborns are also needed to mentor and tutor their little brothers and sisters—whether it's help with home-work or merely shoe-tying—activities that are thought to have brain-boosting powers of their own.

But these natural advantages are reinforced by culturally invented ones, too. It's the oldest princes, after all, who inherit the castle, the land, and the crown. Younger princes get smaller sinecures and token respon-sibilities and spend their adult years, often as not, living the life of the dilettante. This can lead to trouble—and down through history it has. Britain's Prince William, first in the line of succession to the throne after his father, Charles, gets his turn, has had a largely scandal-free young adulthood, while his little brother, Harry, has been snagged in serial embarrassments—boozing, pot smoking, wearing a Nazi armband at a costume party, and describing a fellow soldier who happened to be Pa-kistani as "our little Paki friend." The British press tut-tuts at the inci-dents, but rarely evinces any surprise. Little royals have always been a handful, after all.

Among the nonroyal masses, firstborns are likelier to inherit the family business, control the family's wealth, and be fawned over not just by mothers and fathers but by grandparents, aunts, and uncles, too—for whom that child is often the first baby of the new generation. While most parents will resolutely deny that they have a favorite child, the family scrapbooks, home movies, and other mementos tell a very different story. Says Laurie Kramer: "When a second child is born into a family in which there already is another child, we know they take fewer pictures and their photo albums aren't as complete."

My home reflected that perfectly. In the days of the eight-millimeter movie camera and home-editing machine, my father was a ferocious amateur moviemaker, shooting thousands of feet of films of Steve and painstakingly cutting, pasting, and editing them into finished products. He did the same with me, though the final library was decidedly smaller; with Garry it was smaller still. By the time Bruce came around, there was little footage shot at all, except for a few short rolls of unedited film that remained forever stored in the little yellow boxes in which they came back from the developer. (Our mother, with a more even hand and a greater appreciation for the signal such disparate archiving could send, was the one who handled our baby books, keeping them up to date until we reached seven—the prescribed age then for how long such record keeping should go on—and practically counting pages to make sure no one boy's book was longer than any other's.)

Still, familiar as all this sounds to anyone who grew up in a multi-child home or is raising kids in one, not all scientists are sold on the idea that birth order is as all-fired powerful as it seems. Stack up enough anecdotal maybes, and they start to look like scientific definitelys, but perhaps they're not. There are doubts about the methods used to study the birth-order phenomenon, the objectivity of the scientists who come into the field, even the reliability of the reports from the sibs themselves. For many behavioral psychologists, there's simply a reluctance to heap so much significance on any one variable when so many other X factors—income, education, culture, divorce—shape our personalities.

"We like structure, we like clarity, and birth order is beautifully clear," says psychologist Aaron Wichman of Ohio State University, a birth-order doubter, who nonetheless concedes its appeal. "We know astrology is ridiculous, but tons of people like it. Well, birth order is more plausible than astrology." If the best thing you can say about any science is that it's more reliable than reading horoscopes, then it can hardly be a discipline worth studying. But such skepticism does not prevent more and more researchers from being drawn to birth-order research, and as they are, their findings—and the debates over them—continue to grow.

The puzzle of birth order has intrigued scientists for a long time—though in the early going the work was bungled badly. One of the first investigators to try to prove the birth-order effect was Sir Francis Galton, the nineteenth-century British anthropologist, geographer, and statistician who was best known not for pursuing those noble sciences but for inventing one that was decidedly ignoble: eugenics. It was his belief that the human species was ultimately perfectible—or at least improvable—if only people with desirable traits would marry among themselves, producing offspring who would carry on their genetic gifts and crowd out less desirable individuals. From there it's a short leap to more pernicious ideas about racial supremacy and nations of supermen, and while it's hardly fair to blame Galton because evil men later made that leap, it's not unfair to charge him with playing a significant role in getting such thinking started. In a review of a biography of Galton, science journalist Dick Teresi once described him as a "comical British bonehead," which is about the kindest thing people say about him these days.

Still, Galton seemed to get one small thing right. In his seminal 1874 book, *English Men of Science: Their Nature and Nurture*, he sought to determine the innate traits that highly accomplished scientists (or at least highly accomplished male English scientists) share. The work runs thick with eugenic muck about "purity of breed" and the lower classes as a sort of societal "residuum," and even about the hair color and body type of the scientists' parents and what this may say about the accomplishments of their offspring.

And then, amid all this hooey, came a nugget of science: Among 99 scientists sampled in one part of his study, Galton found that 26 were firstborns, 22 were only children (effectively firstborns), 36 were the middlings, and 15 were the youngest. "The elder sons," he wrote, "have, on the whole, decided advantages of nurture over younger ones." Their parents, he went on, treat them more like companions than like children. The firstborns, in turn, were likely to get more attention and better nourishment, which is particularly important in families of modest wealth, and this makes them "more likely to become possessed of independent means."

Hold your nose at Galton if you like—and indeed you should— but here he was onto something, and nearly a century and a half later, similar numbers continue to back him up. Catherine Salmon of the University of Redlands reports that a firstborn's allowance at any given age is likely to be higher than that of younger siblings when they reach the same age. Similarly, parents with limited income are more likely to invest in a computer for the oldest and let the younger sibs get by with scrounged or borrowed machines. And when it comes to paying for college, parents without the resources to educate the whole brood will most commonly invest in the firstborn—even if a later-born shows a greater aptitude for learning. Indeed, when Salmon tries to recruit subjects for her sibling studies, she often has to go beyond the college campuses that usually serve as such a good source of volunteers, since even in the modern age, the schools tend to be overstocked with firstborns. "Parents try to direct their investment evenly," she says, "but most of the time it's not going to turn out that way."

A poll of corporate heads conducted by Vistage, an international organization of CEOs, takes this further, showing what the later-life implications of such early-life privileges can be. According to the survey, 43 percent of the people who occupy the big chair in boardrooms are firstborns, 33 percent are middle-borns, and 23 percent are last-borns. Steve Ballmer, CEO of Microsoft, is the eldest in his family. So is Charles Schwab of the eponymous commercial investment house; so is Michael Bloomberg, CEO of the Bloomberg news service and, effectively, of New York City, too. And so are—or at least were—the CEOs of companies as diverse as Avon, Medtronic, TD Ameritrade, Koss, and 1-800-FLOWERS.

Sandra Black, an associate professor of economics at UCLA, has found that firstborns in general earn more than later-borns, with income dropping about 1 percent for every step down the birth-order ladder. Eldest siblings are disproportionately represented among surgeons and MBAs, according to Stanford University psychologist Robert Zajonc. And a recent study found a statistically significant overload of firstborns in what is—or at least once was—the country's most august club: the U.S. Congress. "We know that birth order determines occupational prestige to a large extent," says Zajonc. "There is some expectation that firstborns are somehow better qualified for certain occupations."

That expectation begins the moment firstborns emerge from the womb—the pampered princeling in what was until that moment a childless home. No parents are quite as giddy as first-time parents, nor quite as inclined to see their child as uniquely perfect, gifted, and deserving of their emotional and material resources. Such a belief can quickly become self-reinforcing as the flood of parental attention produces a fitter, smarter, more confident firstborn, leading Mom and Dad to invest even more in that child. Kids who come along later are hardly left with table scraps and parental indifference, but they do find themselves in a home in which they have to compete with not just any older child but one who's been bred and tended like a hothouse rose. It's no wonder the little sibs often fail to measure up.

The ferocity with which the Kennedy brothers fought to achieve great things, sometimes at lethal bodily risk—diving into crowds unprotected, speaking before audiences that on occasion were not just hostile but downright menacing—was often attributed to a decades-long quest to meet an impossible standard that Joe Sr., their larger-than-life father, had set for them. But the more compelling standard still might have been set by Joe Jr., the big brother who had been raised from the cradle to be president and then died during the Second World War, leaving an idealized legacy that could never be clouded by scandal or failure, and instead only grew shinier and less attainable with time.

As firstborns are growing up, they repay the parental favors they receive with loyalty. One of the reasons eldest kids tend to inherit the family business, for example, is that they're usually the ones who have shown the most interest in it. "Firstborn siblings have an incentive to accept their parents' worldview and excel along a dimension that is deemed important in their families," says NYU's Ben Dattner. "They defer to their parents and become comfortable with the idea of operating within an existing structure." Firstborns also take on the so-called kin-keeper role—the sibling who assumes the task of organizing the reunions, gathering the extended clan for a funeral or birthday, even writing the family genealogy.

"The literature has always said that females are more inclined to be kin-keepers," says Salmon. "But when I'd ask people to come do their family trees for me, I found there was a birth-order effect, too." How pronounced that effect was usually depended on the particular subjects Salmon was studying, but again and again the kin-keeping behavior among firstborns did rise to a level that made it through the statistical noise and into the region of experimental significance. That's the gold standard for any behavioral research, and in Salmon's studies the data usually delivered. When the rule doesn't apply—when the eldest shows little or no interest in kin-keeping behavior—there are often intervening variables that have scrambled the birth-order effect in other ways. A firstborn with health problems or emotional or behavioral issues, for example, will often cede the duties of the eldest to a second-born. Similarly, in families with a tradition of sending some of the children to boarding school, it is typically the firstborn who gets first crack. When that happens and the other kids stay home, those kids will become better family historians simply because they spend more time as an active part of the extended clan.

If eldest children recognize that they get more than their fair share of the family perks, it doesn't escape the notice of the younger sibs that they get less than theirs. And while the firstborns are not inclined to rock the comfortable boat in which they find themselves, the later-borns are forever trying to capsize it. This isn't so easy when being younger also means you're smaller and weaker—a fact that firstborns exploit to their advantage, using what sibling researchers call a high-power strategy. "If you're bigger than your siblings, you punch 'em," Sulloway says.

But there are low-power strategies, too, and one of the most effective ones is humor. It's awfully hard to resist the charms of someone who can make you laugh, and families abound with stories of last-borns who are the clowns of the brood, able to get their way simply by being funny or outrageous. Birth-order scholars observe that some of history's great satirists—Voltaire, Jonathan Swift, Mark Twain—were among the youngest members of large families, a pattern that continues today. Faux bloviator Stephen Colbert—who yields to no one in his ability to get a laugh—often points out that he's the last of eleven children. My youngest brother followed that pattern as well, and even spent the first decade of his career in theater, principally pursuing character roles in comedies and musicals. The younger of my two daughters similarly seemed to know very early how to use subtle tools, such as an arched brow or a change in inflection, to mine the most laughs from a moment. And while a theatrical temperament may be as much an accident of birth as anything else, the traits children develop fully and the ones they let languish are more a matter of choice and circumstance. In the case of most last-borns, humor is usually a trait that gets a lot of exercise.

Other forms of artistry also get a workout, and here the later-borns may wind up happier than the eldest. My father was the older of two boys, and was deeply invested in winning the approval of their father. This brought him repeated frustration—particularly when his plans to assume control of the family business were aborted just before his graduation from college. My father's little brother, Richard, was spared much of this and had the breathing room to develop his own skills and choose his own career. He eventually chose journalism and later became a prolific author of both novels and historical nonfiction. Two of his books, *Simple Justice*, about the landmark 1954 school desegregation decision, and *The Paper*, a history of the *Herald Tribune*, were nominated for the National Book Award. A third, *Ashes to Ashes*, a history of the Philip Morris company, won a Pulitzer Prize in 1997. Would any of that have happened if he had been a firstborn? I have no idea. I do suspect that if he had the chance to replay his life and run that experiment, he'd wisely decline.

Part of being an artist is having a keen sense of human behavior, and here, too, do last-borns benefit. Personality tests show that firstborns tend to excel on the dimension of temperament known as conscientiousness—a sense of general responsibility and a tendency to follow through—while later-borns score higher on what's known as agreeableness, or the simple ability to get along with people. "Being born later contributes to kids' learning how to interact within a family, and that leads them to being more effective interpersonally in a lot of situations," says Richard Zweigenhaft of Guilford College, who did the work that revealed the overrepresentation of firstborns in Congress. "Think about it: If you have to negotiate with an older sibling who's bigger, stronger, maybe smarter—at least in that five-year-olds know more than three-year-olds—then you'd better find some ways to maneuver, and it may be through your interpersonal qualities."

Even more impressive is how early younger siblings develop what's known as the theory of mind. Very small children have a hard time distinguishing between the things they know and the things they assume other people know. A toddler who watches an adult hide a toy will expect that anyone who walks into the room afterward will also know where to find it, reckoning that all knowledge is universal knowledge. It usually takes a child until age three to begin learning that that's not so—and effectively applying that insight to all situations takes longer still. Even now, Paloma, my seven-year-old, will occasionally begin a story about something that happened at school with a bit of phrasing like "You know that cabinet near the door where my teacher puts the pencils?" Um, no, I don't—and I don't have any way of knowing. Elisa, my nine-year-old, would be much likelier to begin the same story with the informational statement "There's a cabinet near the door where our teacher puts the pencils."

For children who have at least one older sibling, the theory-of-mind insight usually comes earlier and develops faster, and if the studies are correct, Paloma will fully outgrow her ingenuous assumption of universal knowledge at a slightly younger age than Elisa did, simply because she's grown up with a big sister and has found it helpful to be able to intuit her thoughts. "When you're less powerful, it's advantageous to be able to anticipate what's going on in someone else's mind," says Sulloway.

Later-borns, however, don't try merely to please other people; they also try to provoke them. Zweigenhaft conducted a study in the late 1990s of a group of protesters who were staging labor demonstrations every Sunday at a Kmart near his campus. At some point, a faction of the group decided to engage in civil disobedience in order to press their grievances further, even if it meant being taken into custody. Zweigenhaft and a student from one of his classes interviewed the protesters and found that the later-borns were likelier than the firstborns to be part of that more militant subgroup. "It was a statistically significant pattern," says Zweigenhaft. "A disproportionate number of them were choosing to be arrested."

Such high-wire living extends to the boardroom as well. Dattner has found that when later-borns become CEOs, they approach their work very differently from the way firstborns do. Eldest sibs do best when they're making incremental improvements in their companies: shedding underperforming products, maximizing profits from existing lines, and generally making sure the trains run on time. Later-born CEOs are more inclined to blow up the trains and lay new track. "Later-borns are better at transformational change," says Dattner. "They pursue riskier, more innovative, more creative approaches."

Dattner points to Andrea Jung, the firstborn CEO of Avon, who has been with the venerable company for sixteen years but has not reinvented it in any significant way—and never intended to. Instead, she has focused more on such unsexy details as operational efficiency—cutting waste and organizational redundancies—as well as advertising and marketing a proven line of products. Microsoft CEO Ballmer, also an oldest child, has won deserved plaudits for turning what was once a start-up company into a global juggernaut. But he has also been second-guessed for perceived stodginess, regularly upgrading an existing inventory of goods and services, but rarely coloring outside those lines in a way that allows the company to do anything truly transformative anymore. It's this, critics say, that continually leaves Microsoft playing catch-up with more innovative competitors such as Apple and Google. Second-born George Soros, by contrast, earned his multibillion-dollar bankroll in part by taking very big risks with very big hedge funds.

"He bet $10 billion against the British pound in 1992," Dattner says, "and he made $1 billion from that one transaction." For all that, Soros describes his older brother, a successful industrial engineer, as "the real brains of the family." That might be true, but it's Soros himself who is the guts.

Later-borns are willing to risk not just their companies but their health and safety. All siblings are equally inclined to be involved in athletics, but studies have shown that younger ones are likelier to choose the kinds that can cause injury. "They don't go out for tennis," Sulloway says. "They go out for rugby, ice hockey." Even when siblings play the same sport, they play it differently. Sulloway has collaborated on a study of 300 brothers who were major league ballplayers, and his preliminary findings revealed that older brothers gravitate toward positions that involve less physical danger—handling put-outs at first or chasing down fly balls. Younger sibs are the ones who put themselves more directly in harm's way—crouching down in catcher's gear to block an incoming runner, say.

George Brett, the fiery Hall of Fame third baseman who played for the Kansas City Royals, had more innate talent than his older brother Ken, a pitcher of middling gifts who played for the Red Sox, Pirates, Angels, White Sox, and Phillies. But George also had a more fiercely competitive temperament, which surely accounted at least partly for the success he enjoyed—and that big brother Ken didn't. Paul and Lloyd Waner, infielders who played for multiple teams from the 1920s through the mid-1940s, are the only pair of brothers in baseball's Hall of Fame, and show similar tendencies. Lloyd, the younger of the two, was somewhat taller, but he weighed only 132 pounds, which even then was small for a major-leaguer. He maximized what he had, though, making a career as a successful slap hitter who learned the game well, connected with the ball when he had to, and collected 2,459 career hits—well shy of big brother Paul's 3,152, but still impressive. So tough an out did the Waner brothers prove to be that they became known by the nicknames "Big Poison" and "Little Poison." The monikers suited them well even if, in some retellings, the roots of the name came from a Brooklynite mispronouncing the word "person": "Them Waners!" the fan is said to have exclaimed. "It's always the little poison on thoid and the big poison on foist."

In a 2009 study published by the *British Medical Journal*, investigators at St. George's Hospital Medical School in London found a similar birth-order effect among soccer players. Surveying fourteen clubs in one nationwide division, they found that the average number of siblings a goalkeeper had was 1.1; for defenders it was 1.8; for forwards it was 2.0.; for midfield players it was 2.4. The lower the number of siblings, of course, the likelier that a player will also be the firstborn. The investigators did not speculate about what was behind the relationship between birth position and field position, but goalkeepers may have things a little bit safer than players navigating the high-speed traffic in the middle of the field—again, consistent with the firstborn's greater taste for risk avoidance. Salmon even sees a similar risk-related pattern at amusement parks. "The firstborns are usually afraid of the crazy rides," she says. "The last-borns are willing to fling themselves in midair." That's another trait that was in evidence among my brothers and me, and is now turning up in my younger daughter, who loves roller coasters, and my older daughter, who loathes them.

As different as older and later-born siblings can be, in some ways the gap does close over time—but only between the firstborn and the very last born. The sibs at either end of their parents' procreative arc, after all, usually have something in common: At some point, they're the only child at home. They are thus the sole recipients of Mom's and Dad's attention, caregiving, and, sometimes, money, and that tends to bind them more closely to the family as a whole. Certainly, a firstborn experiences that parental attention very differently from the way a child who is, say, fifteen and the last one left when the bigger kids leave home.

Indeed, the fifteen-year-old may actually want little to do with the parents—which is often the way things are with adolescents. But if the parent-child relationship is even a moderately good one, it's likely to become better still in these later years. It's probably for this reason that kin-keeper studies show that many last-borns are eventually as knowledgeable as firstborns when it comes to family genealogy, and may even be as conscientious when it comes to planning family events.

And what about middle sibs—the ones who never get this total-immersion parental love? Do they wind up less devoted to their families? Research says they do—in a thousand little ways. In one of Salmon's studies, for example, she surveyed whom teenagers call for help when they get into car accidents and found that first- and last-borns typically call their parents, while middle-borns call a friend. In another, she recruited more than 100 college students who occupied different spots in their families' birth-order hierarchies and played them recordings of political speeches. In some of the tapes, the speaker addressed the audience using kinship terms, such as "my brothers and sisters," or spoke of the nation as a vast family. In others, terms of nonfamilial comradeship were used instead—"my friends" or "my fellow Americans."

All such terms may have passed out of political vogue—"my brothers and sisters" sounds odd to contemporary ears, and "my friends" can sound strained and overly familiar——but they have a long history in electoral politics and may still have the power to move us at an unconscious level. The key is which words suit which listeners. Salmon found that first- and last-borns were much more inclined to react positively to the politicians who chose kinship language, while middle-borns were drawn toward appeals to friendship. "Middle-borns don't see their families as great sources of support, and so they don't react to terms that invoke those relationships," Salmon says.

If middle sibs seem ambivalently connected to their families, it's partly because their very roles in those families are equally unclear. The youngest in the family, but only until someone else comes along, they are both teacher and student, babysitter and babysat, too young for the privileges of the firstborn but too old for the bemused tolerance given the last. Middle children are expected to step up to the plate when the eldest child goes off to school or in some other way drops out of the picture—and they generally serve when called, becoming what's known as "functional firstborns." The 2007 Norwegian intelligence study showed that when firstborns die, the IQ of second-born stand-ins actually rises a bit, a sign that they're performing the hard mentoring work that goes along with the new job. Most middle sibs, however, are stuck for life in their center seat, and that may exact a psychological toll. Sulloway cites research showing that the U-shaped distribution of family resources—with the oldest and youngest at some point getting 100 percent of their parents' time and care and kids in the middle always getting less—is paralleled by a U-shaped distribution of self-esteem, with the middle kids again exhibiting the lowest.

The phenomenon known as de-identification may also work against a middle-born. Siblings who hope to stand out in a family often do so by observing what the older child does and then doing the opposite. If the firstborn gets good grades and takes a job after school, the second-born may go the less disciplined, more ambling route. The third-born may then de-de-identify, opting for industriousness, even if in the more unconventional ways of the last-born. A Chinese study in the 1990s showed just this kind of zigzag pattern in homes (at least those that did not obey the country's unpopular one-child policy), with the first child generally scoring high as a "good son or daughter," the second scoring low, the third scoring high again, and so on. In a three-child family, the very act of trying to be unique may instead leave the middling lost, a pattern that may continue into adulthood.

This is not always the case, of course, and, depending on the talents and temperament of the child, being lost in the middle can actually be a good thing. The late Wendy Wasserstein, a Pulitzer Prize–winning playwright, was the middle child of three and, in a *New York* magazine story about power siblings, once said, "My talent was to accommodate larger personalities and observe; solid early training for a playwright."

For Wasserstein, birth order was not destiny, and that can be the case for other middlings, too. Anthropologist Margaret Mead used to describe the kind of position a middle sib occupies as the pivot role in a family, and as demanding as it can be, it pays dividends. In the same way that middle managers in an office are often more interpersonally effective than the top dogs because they must learn both to defer to superiors and oversee subordinates, so, too, do middle sibs become more socially supple. This certainly seems anecdotally true. When parents describe the behavior of one of their kids with phrases like "Never been a bit of trouble" or "Always the easiest of the group," it's usually the middle child they're talking about. Someone who knew my brothers and me well once described Garry, the archetypally easygoing middle child, as "the white sheep of the family."

With such a complex body of evidence seeming to prove the power of birth order, it's easy to conclude that the science is by now a slam dunk. Perhaps there's more to explore in terms of the implications and specifics of the findings, but the broad ideas are no longer open to serious question. That, however, is nowhere near the truth; indeed, plenty of investigators believe that the real research hasn't even begun, largely because the vast body of work that's been conducted so far has been conducted all wrong.

One of the biggest problems, they argue, is that there is a whole constellation of other factors that shape emotional development, and some of them are so powerful that birth order might not get a chance to exert any leverage at all. The difference between growing up in poverty and growing up with privilege, for example, is surely a lot more defining than whether you happen to be a firstborn, a third-born, or even an only child. The same is true for education: An oldest child and a middle child who both finish high school and go on to college are going to have a lot more in common than a graduate and a dropout who both happen to be firstborns. Gender is a powerful wild card of its own—indeed, perhaps the most powerful, one that's generally thought to account for at least twice the variance in a person's temperament that birth order does. Culture, country of birth, the health of the family, and the presence or absence of a father in the home may all take precedence over birth order, too.

"Human behavior is multiply determined, it's complex, and there are a bunch of different things that are affecting people," says Zweigenhaft. "I would say birth order is a player, but I don't think it's the most important player."

In an era of nontraditional families, your birth order may not even be a fixed thing. Zweigenhaft once asked the students in his psychology class where they fell in their family's hierarchy, and got some surprisingly vague responses. "One girl couldn't answer," he says. "She said she was the firstborn child of her biological parents, but her parents adopted an older child, and she suddenly became the younger child. In the past, many people came from intact families, but now a lot of people are from single-parent families, blended families; they're being raised by divorced parents, gay parents, remarried parents."

Even in an unchanging family in which birth-order lines are firmly established, things can get jumbled. In a 2005 study, investigators at the University of Birmingham in Britain examined the case histories of 400 abused children and the 795 siblings of those unfortunate kids. In general, they found that when just one child in a family is abused, the scapegoat was usually the oldest, which would obviously break the close bonds the parents and the firstborns typically share. But the same rupture also occurs if a younger child is the one who's taking the punishment, as the oldest turns from parental ally to protector of the brood. At the same time, the eldest may pick up some of the younger kids' agreeableness skills—the better to deal with irrational parents—while the youngest learns some of the firstborn's self-sufficiency. Abusiveness will "totally disrupt the birth-order effects we would expect," says Sulloway.

The age gap between siblings is also a key variable. Sibs who are two years apart relate in very different ways from those who are four or five or eight years apart. Kip Gould, a publisher in New York City, and his wife, Joan Dineen, an architect, are the parents of kids who take that variable to an unusual extreme. Aiden, their oldest son, is twenty-three; Devin, the next eldest, is twenty-one; and Blythe, the youngest, is just eight.

"The boys were fifteen and thirteen when Blythe was born," Gould says. "Devin seemed fascinated that here was this little thing to love, Aiden seemed less interested, but we didn't say to either one, 'It's time for you boys to take care of your little sister.'" Now that both sons are out of college and Blythe is in fourth grade, their relationships are strong, but not in a traditional way. "It's not the same as siblings who are closer in age," says Gould. "It's more like an uncle-and-niece relationship."

Birth-order studies that fail to take into account the size of the family present problems of their own. The 1 percent reduction in income that each child down the age line earns as an adult tends to flatten out as the brood gets bigger, with a smaller earnings gap between a third and fourth child than between a second and third, and a smaller one still between the fourth and fifth, and on and on. The posited link between IQ and birth order may also be mitigated by family size. In small families with just two or three kids, parents do much of the tutoring and mentoring that are key to what the Norwegian researchers believe helps drive the intelligence of firstborns. In bigger broods, older kids pitch in more and are likelier to reap whatever IQ benefits there are to be had. "The good birth-order studies will control for family size," says Bo Cleveland, associate professor of human development and family studies at Penn State University. "Sometimes that makes the birth-order effect go away; sometimes it doesn't."

Research by psychologist Aaron Wichman of Ohio State University casts further doubt on the IQ work, suggesting that maternal age is actually a bigger driver of a child's intelligence than birth order, since the younger a mother is when she starts her family, the less education she's likely to have had. That often means less intellectual stimulation for the kids during the critical period in which their analytic skills, vocabulary, and study habits are developing. Even the simple experimental precaution of administering two IQ tests to kids instead of one—the first when they're seven or eight years old and the second when they're thirteen or fourteen—sometimes makes the birth-order factor disappear, since this can correct for misleading findings that result from a smart child happening to have a bad day.

But the most grievous flaw in birth-order work, according to the critics, may be that the majority of the research is what's known as between-family studies—comparing the firstborns in one family with those in dozens or hundreds or thousands of others, and then doing the same with second-borns, third-borns, and so on. That's worse than comparing apples and oranges, the skeptics insist. It's more like comparing apples and shoes. Between-family studies may minimize or simply ignore the manifold socioeconomic differences among families in favor of the single variable of birth order, producing results that are interesting but ultimately worthless. The alternative to between-family work is what investigators call in-family studies, a much more painstaking process requiring an exhaustive look at a single family, comparing every child with every other child, and then repeating the process again and again with thousands of other families. Eventually, you may find threads that link them all. It takes a lot longer to reach your conclusions, but they may be a good deal more reliable.

"I would throw out all the between-family studies," says Cleveland. "The proof is in the in-family design." And why don't more birth-order researchers use that method? One reason, Cleveland believes, is a sort of unintentional bias. Birth-order researchers select into the field in the first place because they find the science compelling. They may be naturally disinclined to believe in an investigative method that could prove they've been wasting their time.

The debate over birth order will, of course, never be entirely settled. Family studies and the statistics they yield are cold and precise things, parsing human behavior down to decimal points and margins of error, which is how solid science is supposed to work. But families are a good deal sloppier than that, a mishmash of competing needs, moods, and clashing emotions, better understood by the people in the thick of them than by anyone standing outside. A firstborn alternately laboring with the burdens that come with the position and enjoying its fruits, a middle-born struggling for recognition, a last-born riffing and joking for laughs and love—all live very particular lives and have very particular emotions and histories. No psychologist is going to have much luck questioning those experiences. That won't stop the scientists from looking for answers in their own way—and it won't stop parents and siblings from looking in theirs.

The Golden Child

Favoritism and Its Consequences

Families are often compared to palace courts, and that's as fair an analogy as any: There's an unmistakable king and queen, there's a collection of princes and princesses, there is competition and intrigue among that younger generation worthy of the czars and the Windsors. Comparisons to the animal kingdom work, too—with the tooth-and-claw battle for resources among the young and the life-and-death struggle for genetic advantage. But the best analogy may be to a corporation. It's not just the top-down command structure that makes the parallels so apt, or the constant jostling to win the favor of the boss man or boss woman in the corner office. It's the way those chiefs often play favorites with the tribe. The family has its birth-order hierarchy, just as an office has its organizational chart and seniority rules. But in both venues, there's often one subordinate who somehow sidesteps that structure and, through a mixture of charm, charisma, or a thousand other qualities, becomes the best beloved among what is supposed to be a team of equals.

By almost any measure, Garry should have been the favorite in my family. For one thing, he was gorgeous. With his fine and symmetrical features, he seemed oddly too beautiful to be a boy—an observation the obstetrician made the moment he saw him. "A waste," he clucked, only half-jokingly. When Garry's first, feathery crop of hair grew in, it was not Steve's and my sawdust brown or Bruce's fiery red but a bright platinum blond—wholly suited to his fanciful, found-in-a-cabbage-patch look.

There is not a parent on the planet who would admit to favoring a beautiful child over one less beautiful, but scientists aren't constrained by the same pretense of impartiality, and long-standing bodies of work point to the human species' deeply wired bias for the lovely over the less so—at home, in the workplace, and certainly in the dating market. It's something we all know intuitively and goes back to what psychologist Catherine Salmon calls the "general heuristic that things that are attractive are healthy and good and smart."

But Garry had more than his looks going for him. He was a serenely agreeable child—one who, even as a newborn, seemed to cry only when it was strictly necessary and to quiet down as soon as his immediate needs were met. As we were growing up, he quickly became my favorite playmate, in part due to his fertile imagination—an imagination he was perfectly content to explore by himself. In his hands, an empty soda bottle—plus a little tap water and a drop of red food coloring—became a potion or a poison or whatever else suited his fantasy play. The rest of us would watch him as he got lost in the narrative he'd invented and then go scurrying for empty soda bottles of our own, which never quite had the magic Garry found in his. When it suited him, he'd invite us into his game, and there we'd find the fun.

For all this, however, Garry wasn't the favorite. For my father, it was

Steve—a selection made mostly on the basis of primogeniture. "Heir apparent" was the term my father used, and while I didn't know what it meant, I was pretty sure it didn't apply to me. For my mother, the favorite was Bruce—and that, in a way, was my father's doing, too. Before Bruce came along, my father had had it with baby making, and hadn't planned on adding another child after three so close in age. He learned that a fourth was on the way when Garry, the third, was only four months old. When Bruce did arrive, my father made his new son's accidental station clear in the most primal way he could—which for him meant an even freer hand with corporal punishment, on at least one occasion administered when Bruce's crime was little more than crying in his crib or toddler bed before going to sleep. When a criminally reckless babysitter gave Bruce a slug of the prescription drug phenobarbital to get him to go to sleep one night—knocking him out for a day and a half—my father acceded to my mother's demands to fire the woman, but only grudgingly.

My mother matched my father's negative bias toward Bruce with a fiercely protective positive one, and when Bruce later acquired the last-born's signature gifts—a bright wit, a natural charm, and a sharp theory of mind that made him innately empathic—the love match was set. When my parents split up and my father left the house, the special attention he had paid to Steve left with him, and Bruce assumed the favored role alone.

My parents were hardly unique in having a favorite offspring. Indeed, what would have made them remarkable would be if they hadn't. It's one of the worst-kept secrets of family life that every parent has a preferred son or daughter—and the rules for acknowledging it are the same everywhere: The favored kids stay mum about their status—the better to preserve the good thing they've got going. The unfavored kids howl about it like wounded cats. And on pain of death, the parents insist that none of it is true. The larger the family, the more acute the problem—simply because there are more aggrieved children. In a two-child home, there's a good chance the parents will split their preference, and while the firstborn may forever nag Dad to admit that the baby was his favorite and the second-born may resent Mom because she favored the oldest, both at least know what it is to be someone's number one. But simple arithmetic means that in a three-, four-, or five-child family, there will be at least one, two, or three who will always feel like a second choice.

Study after study has illustrated this point, and the numbers they've produced are compelling. Katherine Conger, at the University of California, Davis, assembled a group of 384 adolescent sibling pairs and their parents, visiting them three times over three years. During those sessions, she questioned them all about their relationships with the other family members and interviewed the kids alone about their sense of well-being. To see how the family interacted as a group, she also video-taped them as they worked through sample conflicts. Overall, she concluded that 65 percent of mothers and 70 percent of fathers exhibited a preference for one child—in most cases, the older one. What's more, the kids were aware of exactly what was going on and, in Conger's study at least, accepted it with surprising equanimity. Typically, they would look for a reason for the parental preference—the gender or age or temperament of the favorite child—and simply choose to live with that reality. Reports Conger: "They all say, 'Well, it makes sense that they would treat us differently.'"

But just because favoritism is everywhere doesn't mean it's as easy to understand as it seems, or that there are universal truths about which kids will be tapped as the best loved. The father-son bond is the stuff of legend—unless it's the father-daughter one that's the rule in your family. A mother innately understands her daughters—unless the girls turn out be an utter mystery to her and she adores one of her boys best. Being the unfavored child can be a blow to a child's ego, while being the favored one breeds confidence and self-esteem—unless it's the other way around. No matter what, kids who do suffer for their status—favored or unfavored—will remember it for a lifetime.

"My mom didn't like my older sister and did like me," says Roseann Henry, a magazine and website editor and now the married mother of two girls. "Everyone assumed I had it great, except that my sister tortured me pretty much all the time—and really, what affects daily life more for a kid: the approval of a parent or the day-to-day torment of an older sister? Personally, I can't remember a single instance of my mother's theoretical approval, but I could repeat word for word some of the fat jokes I got from my sister forty years ago. Now excuse me," she adds, presumably joking, "I have to go get a Krispy Kreme."

Henry is hardly the only adult who's found favoritism a mixed bag of perks and punishment, guilt and rewards, nor is she the first to find that the memories of those experiences don't simply go away. If the parental habit of assigning different values to different children in a single brood can cause such pain, it's a wonder it ever became such a firmly established part of human nature.

As with so much else, the favoritism impulse begins with the parents' own survival needs—the biologically narcissistic act of trying to replicate themselves through succeeding generations and thus ensure that they live on even after their technical death. This impels Mom and Dad to tilt in favor of their biggest, healthiest, prettiest offspring on the theory that those kids will be more reproductively successful than others. Whether we want to admit it or not, that is the same kind of reductionist, bottom-line strategizing that drives the crested penguin to kick her smaller egg out of the nest and the black eagle mother to watch idly while her bigger chick rips her smaller one to ribbons.

Humans, however, do bring more to the game. Under black eagle rules, for example, the very fact of my father's antipathy for my baby brother ought to have doomed him in my mother's eyes, too. A child who's already being ill treated by one parent has hurdles to overcome just getting out of childhood in one piece, much less making it to a procreative adulthood. Best for a mom with years of child rearing ahead to cut her losses now and focus on her other chicks. Yet not only did my mother not push Bruce aside, she gathered him closest of all.

Compassion—a feature not wholly unique to humans but seen a lot more commonly among our species than among any other—was clearly at work here. But so were some practices we do share with nonhuman species. In her elegant book *Mother Nature: Maternal Instincts and How They Shape the Human Species*, anthropologist Sarah Blaffer Hrdy cites work conducted with coots, a species of black-and-white waterbird common in Europe and the Americas. Unlike other birds, coots don't pour most of their parenting efforts into their strongest chicks but rather play a different probability game, spreading the care and the goodies around in the hope of maximizing the raw number of offspring that survive. This can mean not just remembering to treat the youngest and weakest of your offspring equally but favoring them, since they're the ones that need the most help.

In case the mothers forget which chick is the youngest (coots do all look remarkably alike), nature provides an unmistakable cue in the form of a bit of fancy red plumage on the babies' heads. Newly hatched birds don't have the colorful tuft for long, but for the period they do have it, they become irresistible. Mothers with a nest full of babies will deliberately steer extra food to the reddest head in the bunch, reckoning that that chick needs the most care. It is surely just a coincidence that Bruce, the baby in our nest, was a redhead, too, but my mother's protectiveness of him was not that different from the mama coot's, both in terms of her instinct to provide special care and in the way Bruce's cuteness encouraged that impulse. The chapter in Hrdy's book that deals with the coot is called "Why Be Adorable?" and the behavior of both human and animal moms answers that question neatly.

There is, however, another, much darker side to parental favoritism, and Hrdy reports on studies that powerfully document that as well. The late William Skinner, a University of California anthropologist, specialized in research on Chinese and Japanese cultures, and was particularly struck by parenting practices during feudal Japan's Tokugawa shogunate, from 1603 to 1868. Like many other cultures, the Tokugawa Japanese had a strong preference for male heirs, prizing their long reproductive potential and the leadership roles they could be counted on to assume in the extended family. A child who was not just a son but a firstborn son ought thus to have been of special value. Yet when many Japanese hit the procreative jackpot this way, they'd do something unexpected to that eldest boy: They'd kill him. The family's goal was not so much to have a firstborn male as to have the fittest possible male. Paradoxically, that meant hoping for a daughter first, someone who, as Hrdy says, would become "a handy little allomother who could help her parents rear their primary heir so he could grow up to be a model son." So culturally valued was this daughter-first-son-second—or *ichihime nitaro*—model that few people worried much about the infanticide that it sometimes made necessary.

The *ichihime nitaro* tradition was, surely, the most extreme example of favoritism imaginable: Few sibs would rank lower in a family's hierarchy than the girl raised to serve her younger brother or the boy killed at birth to make such an arrangement possible. And few would rank higher than the son for whom the killing was done and the sister was conceived in the first place. Still, the extremes of the feudal East do bracket the practices of the modern West, and we are susceptible to some of the same biases that drove *ichihime nitaro*, particularly when those biases are based on gender.

The oft-seen pattern of parents with cross-gender preferences in their kids—the dad who's all but helpless in the face of his daughter's charms, or the mom who adores her eldest son—is one very good example. Such favoritism patterns hardly exist in every family, but they're more common than we may think, as Salmon discovered in a 2003 study published in the journal *Human Nature*. "I asked subjects to list which child in the family was their mother and father's favorite," she says. "Overall, the most likely candidate for the mother's favorite was the firstborn son and for the father, it was the lastborn daughter. You would think fathers would favor their sons—they certainly do a lot of things with them, like play sports and video games—but in terms of things like emotional closeness, there is a tendency for them to dote on their little princess. Meanwhile, mothers tend to dote on their firstborn sons."

Studies that have dug deeper into this preference have found that what parents find most appealing about their opposite-sex favorites is often different from what we'd expect. It's not just the frilliness of a little girl that appeals to Dad, or the uncomplicated love that can come from a boy that delights Mom—though these stereotypes are frequently part of it. And while Freudians would raise the Oedipal specter—with a dark sexual subtext running beneath cross-gender preference—modern studies have marginalized that factor, though it sometimes does play some role. Instead, what parents seem to value most in their opposite-sex children are the traits that, paradoxically, are associated with their own sex—the sensitive mom who goes gooey over her son the poet, or the hard-knocks dad who adores his tough-as-nails daughter. Narcissism, again, may play a role in this. It's not always easy for a father to see himself replicated in a daughter or a mother to see herself in a son. But if the kids can't look exactly like you, they can at least act like you—and you'll love them more when they do.

Gender can be an especially powerful variable in determining favoritism in three-child families. As a rule, first- and last-born children have a better shot of being at least one parent's favorite than middle kids do. In all-boy or all-girl families this is especially so, since the middle child stands out neither by birth order nor sex. That's also the case in families in which the gender sequence is, say, boy-boy-girl or boy-girl-girl, since the middle child is still not unique. Shifting the sequence slightly, however—to boy-girl-boy or girl-boy-girl—may change everything. In these cases, the uniqueness of gender may trump the usual appeal of the oldest or youngest, and at least one parent may favor the middle sib.

"If you have a child who is different for any reason—especially being the only girl or only boy," says Salmon, "that child is going to get extra attention and investment. This takes away from the negative aspects of being in that disadvantaged birth-order position."

My wife, Alejandra—the middle child between two brothers and in many ways the de facto oldest—is a very good example of this phenomenon at work. Born in Mexico, the three sibs were raised largely by their divorced mother, who was (and still is) the costume director of the Instituto Nacional de Bellas Artes in Mexico City—essentially Mexico's Kennedy Center or Metropolitan Opera. The kids would often go straight from school to the theater, where they would settle into the red velvet audience seats to do their homework while waiting for their mother to finish her workday. The boys showed little interest in the costuming arts, but after a childhood spent watching the great ballets and operas take shape, my wife did—and grew far closer to her mom in the process. Ultimately, and unsurprisingly, she also became something of a mother pro tem, looking after her little brother when no adult was around, and serving as a conduit to her older and more private big brother. It may be too much to say she was the favorite—Mexico, more so than the United States, remains a patriarchal place, and an oldest son is still a thing to be highly prized—but as the sole girl, she was and remains the one with the closest and easiest ties to her mother.

Whichever child becomes the favorite, once the patterns are established, they're awfully hard to break. There are not many kids who spend their first ten years as Mom's or Dad's best-loved child and then fall to second place, though adolescence can sorely test even the strongest parent-child bonds. Still, favoritism does have some flexibility to it, depending on what are known as family domains—the different venues or situations in which family members operate. And those venues are numerous. There's what happens inside the home and what happens outside it, what happens at the dinner table or on the soccer field, on vacation or in the living room, and the shifting locales can lead to shifting preferences. The ex-jock dad who favors his athletic son may be driven to distraction by the boy's restless energy when it comes time to read a book or simply have a conversation. When Dad is looking for thoughtful parent-child bonding he may thus turn to his daughter. Over the long course of an entire childhood, the son may still come out on top, but the daughter will get enough emotional nourishment that the overall disparity may not wind up being terribly significant to her.

"Large-scale favoritism patterns are pretty stable," says Corinna

Jenkins Tucker, an associate professor of family studies at the University of New Hampshire. "But there are definite differences by domain. Maybe Mom gave a son more love, but she spent more time playing games or reading books with her daughter. That winds up being okay for children. It becomes a problem when there is a child who isn't favored in any area at all."

Children themselves are not passive players in the favoritism sweepstakes—and they often fight ferociously to change the existing arrangement. The Kennedy family, again, is a case study in how this plays out. Joe Sr., the patriarch of the clan, was often away from home, but when he was around, he took the opportunity to remind all of the kids that they were expected to compete aggressively with one another in all things—particularly sailing and other athletic pursuits. He made it clear they were in the game not for the fun but for the victory, and Kennedy kids who were found wanting in their effort were made to eat in the kitchen.

What made things harder for most of the kids was that Rose, the mom of the brood, openly favored Joe Jr., the oldest child. John, the second boy, was willowy and even frail compared to his big brother. According to *The Kennedy Obsession*, a 1997 book by John Hellmann, Rose referred to JFK as "impish"—which is not how you want to be seen when you're battling for approval and dominance. John forever hurled himself into competition with Joe—fueled in equal measures by desperation and resentment. The two once engaged in a bicycle race in opposite directions around the house. Predictably, they collided—and predictably, John came out the worse, winding up with twenty-eight stitches. Joe Jr. walked away unhurt.

Kids growing up in less of a familial pressure cooker generally find other ways to balance the favoritism scales a bit. You can't do much about your gender or your birth order, but you can learn to make the most out of the niche you've got. The non-favored daughter who talks film with her movie-loving mother may have come by her own love of the cinema naturally—or she may have come by it strategically, knowing that that was one way to win some extra maternal attention. The same may be true of the son who learns to like watching football even if he's not naturally drawn to it, reckoning this will net him some bonding time with his father on Sundays, despite the fact that the rest of the week Dad clearly favors his daughter. In this sense, kids are a bit like tree leaves, sorting themselves out so that they grow in a shaft of light not blocked by the leaf above.

"Siblings are devilishly clever," says Frank Sulloway of the University of California, Berkeley. "Much smarter than psychologists. They figure out every way to compete within the family. They are constantly trying to fine-tune their niche to squeeze the maximum benefits out of their parents."

Sons and daughters learn to game the system on a more day-to-day basis, too, flipping blatant favoritism to the shared advantage of all the sibs. In these cases, the favored child may be a willing accomplice, agreeing to ask for favors from Mom or Dad that a less loved sib could never manage. "They'll say to one another, 'Why don't you ask Mom if we can go to the mall because she never says no to you,'" says Conger.

While all the sibs can reap small-scale benefits from such ploys, the larger issue for psychologists—to say nothing of parents themselves—is what the long-term damage of favoritism may be. Can you go through your entire childhood looking enviously at the crowned prince or princess across the dinner table and not begin to wonder if perhaps you're somehow less worthy? Do you carry that uncertainty with you even when you've moved into the larger world in which confidence and self-worth are critical to getting ahead? And what about the favored sibs themselves? Do they arrive at adulthood with a sturdy ego and a happy sense of their own value? Or are there hidden downsides to being the golden child, ones that don't seem evident when the prizes are being bestowed but slowly reveal themselves outside the home—and exact their own price?

Not all psychologists agree on just what the impact of favoritism is, but as a rule their advice to parents is simple: If you absolutely have to have a favorite—and you probably do—you're right to try to keep it to yourself. Psychologist Victoria Bedford of the University of Indianapolis has studied favoritism extensively, looking at the impact of what she calls LFS (least favored status) on children's relationships with other family members, self-esteem maintenance, socialization, and later functioning in the world. No matter how she broke down her data, it all told her the same thing. "My main conclusion was how horrible favoritism is on siblings," she says flatly—and sibs themselves often agree.

Charles Dickens wrote painfully—and, of course, poignantly—about his own LFS experiences. His childhood dream, as he described it in autobiographical essays, was to grow up to be a "learned and distinguished man," and he was devastated when it seemed he'd never get the chance. His parents had enough money to pay for schooling, but not for both him and his older sister, Frances. They made what was, in the nineteenth century, the uncommon choice of educating the girl in the family, sending her to the Royal School of Music. Charles went to work in a bootblacking factory. Hard as that was for him, the most acutely painful part of the experience occurred when he was required to attend a ceremony at which his sister was presented a scholar's medal for her fine academic work.

"I could not bear to think of myself," Dickens recalled, "beyond the reach of all such honourable emulation and success. The tears ran down my face." Even as a highly celebrated adult, he never fully got past the experience. "My whole nature was so penetrated by the grief and humiliation of such considerations that even now, famous and caressed and happy, I . . . wander desolate back to that time in my life."

Sulloway, who covers Dickens in detail in his book *Born to Rebel*, writes about those observations: "This autobiographical fragment forms the basis for *David Copperfield*, which Dickens once described as 'a very complicated interweaving of truth and fiction.' For Dickens, the response to being abandoned by his parents was to become obsessed by the problem and its diverse remedies."

(Dickens, to his credit, bore his disappointment and resentment over his upbringing with grace, and did not allow it to affect his love for Frances. She married and later had a physically disabled son, who became the model for Tiny Tim in *A Christmas Carol*. Frances died of consumption in 1848, at age thirty-eight. Shortly before her death, Dickens visited her at her sickbed. He was struck by the courage and strength she exhibited as she faced death and that night wrote to his friend, the essayist and historian John Forster, about the experience: "I asked her very often, if she could ever recall anything that she could leave to my doing, to put it down, or mention it to somebody if I was not there; and she said she would, but she firmly believed that there was nothing— nothing. Such an affecting exhibition of strength and tenderness, in all that early decay, is quite indescribable. I need not tell you how it moved me. I don't know why I write this before going to bed. I only know that in the very pity and grief of my heart, I feel as if it were doing something.")

Favoritism dramas play out among sibs who don't achieve Dickensian fame. Bob Strozier, a writer born in Georgia in 1940, was the oldest sib in a three-child family that included a younger sister and brother. Unlike many firstborns, he was not the best loved—and he learned it early and painfully. "When my younger brother, Chuck, was a teenager, I was wildly jealous because he was a football player and had girlfriends and was the apple of my father's eye—all the things I thought I should be," he says. "At first I thought I was measuring up on all counts, but then I gradually felt I wasn't. And the more my stock seemed to fall, the more Chuck's rose."

Even before the brothers' teen years, Strozier had the sense that he was being displaced, and found creative ways to express it. When his younger brother contracted ringworm at age five, he received the then-accepted treatment, which was radiation to the scalp. Not surprisingly, that would kill the parasite—and also cause the patient's hair to fall out. "I used to sit with him in my lap and pull clumps of his hair out," recalls Strozier. "Then I told him I'd found a hole in his head and that it would have to be filled with hot lead." He adds: "We're still speaking."

Clare Stocker, a research professor in developmental psychology at the University of Denver, has amassed evidence showing that unfavored children may turn their disappointment not only outward, in the form of aggression toward the first-tier brother or sister, but inward, in the form of privately suffered emotional turmoil. She studied 136 sibling pairs from one western U.S. city and its suburbs (leaving the city unnamed in her paper to encourage subjects to participate and to be candid), then returned to observe them again two years later, and once more two years after that. Over that period, she found that kids who felt less loved than other siblings were more likely to develop anxiety, low self-esteem, and depression. Unable to understand those feelings, much less cope with them effectively, some of the subjects would begin exhibiting behavioral problems. That would lead parents to crack down on them, only widening the apparent gap between the kind of treatment Mom and Dad were meting out to them and the kind being lavished on the favored child.

None of this is good for the unfavored sibs, but it's the low-self-esteem piece that worries some psychologists most. Children learn life-time lessons about their own value almost from the moment they're old enough to understand a parent's tone of voice, which is one of the reasons even the most frustrated moms and dads are so often reminded that while it's all right to express anger, exasperation, and disappointment to a child, they should carefully avoid such demeaning expressions of emotion as contempt, disdain, or disgust. Most parents do manage to stay away from using such heavy emotional cudgels, but subtler, less voluntary slights are harder to eliminate entirely. There are, however, ways to compensate for them.

Patricia East, herself an identical twin and now a developmental psychologist and researcher in the department of pediatrics at the University of California, San Diego, School of Medicine, stresses that parents' goal should not be to treat all of their kids identically. That's not only impossible, it's unwise, since every child has a particular temperament and set of qualities that have to be dealt with in particular ways. Rather, the objective should be differential but fair treatment that, East says, plays well to kids' "unique qualities, their emotional optimism, their happiness. It would be ideal if parents recognized these things and then parented according to the individual child's aptitudes and personality."

Even without thinking about it much, parents are often very good at doing just what East recommends—signing the artistic child up for a drawing class, enrolling the athletic child in soccer camp. Similar attention to particular strengths can be paid around the home. It may be impossible not to get frustrated at the child who is not a natural student and is forever trying to dodge homework, but it's not impossible to balance that with applause for the same child's woodworking gifts or fashion sense. Harvard may not be in the future, but a carpentry business or design school could be.

The manifold damage that can be done to an unfavored child throughout the long slog of childhood is easy enough to imagine and understand. Harder to fathom are the ways the best-loved son or daughter can suffer, but they're very real as well—and they go far deeper than merely the resentment a first-tier child such as Roseann Henry felt from her second-tier sister. The biggest risk may be that when you spend your early life enjoying the huzzahs of your parents, you may be entirely unprepared for a larger society in which the family hierarchy and value system don't apply and you're just one college student or young adult out of many. There's nothing wrong with a puffed-up child learning a little humility—indeed, it may be essential to social and professional success. But what happens when favored kids don't learn it? What happens when an outsized ego resists being brought down to size?

The story of the family prince struggling with adulthood is a repeated theme in both drama and history. Arthur Miller's *Death of a Salesman* is about more than the tragedy of its lead character, Willy Loman, as he loses both his livelihood and his dignity. It's also about the crisis of his sons—particularly Biff, the older of the two—who grew up on a steady diet of paternal praise, only to find that others play by very different rules, expecting laurels to be earned before they're bestowed. When, as an adult, Biff at last learns the hard truth, he blames not himself for his failure to achieve what he'd dreamed of achieving but his father, for making him temperamentally ill equipped to do so.

"I never got anywhere because you blew me so full of hot air I could never stand taking orders from anybody!" he shouts.

"The door of your life is wide open!" Willy protests.

"Pop!" Biff answers. "I'm a dime a dozen, and so are you!"

George W. Bush also bumped up hard against the difference between the adoration of his parents and the more exacting demands of the larger world—and indeed his parents themselves exacerbated the problem. In January 2000, when Bush was fighting for his political life in the New Hampshire presidential primary, both of his parents came to the state to help. "This boy," Bush Sr. proudly told the crowd, "this son of ours, is not going to let you down."

The assurance fell flat both because voters like to think of their prospective presidents as more than somebody's boy and because a beaming father's faith in his favorite child is by definition a blind and unreasoning thing—something everybody but the father himself usually realizes. Some of Bush Jr.'s own problems as president—his prickliness at being challenged, his inability to come up with an answer when a White House reporter asked him if he could think of a single mistake he'd made during his first term—were characteristic of a favored son who has never adjusted to being seen any other way. As family expert and author Judith Harris puts it, the first-among-equals status conferred in the home "doesn't travel well."

(Presidents, admittedly, can be poor case studies—albeit very tempting ones—because their mere pursuit of the office implies an ego so overweening as to be borderline unhealthy almost by definition. Still, the particular weaknesses they exhibit in office are usually unique to their backgrounds. Bill Clinton, who yields to no man in the presidential neuroses derby, did not receive the ego pampering a young Bush Jr. did at home or in school—where, as he writes, he was forever being teased for being the chubby boy in the band. That he successfully compensated—indeed overcompensated—for this is a matter of historical record. Still, entitlement was not one of the hurdles he had to overcome to get there, and his desperate need to be adored even by his enemies came not from the expectation that he would be popular—but that he wouldn't be.)

Favored sibs have other burdens to carry well before adulthood—among them a sense of guilt. It's hard not to feel pleasure at the preferential treatment that keeps coming at them from Mom and Dad, but it's hard not to feel sympathy for brothers and sisters who are denied it. Jeremy Dunn, twenty, a college student raised in Pacific Palisades, California, experienced just such mixed feelings about his younger sister Ellen, seventeen. Jeremy was their father's favorite and he and Ellen were painfully aware of it. The unbalanced treatment the kids received got even worse when their parents were divorcing and the natural stresses of a fracturing family were expressed in their father's occasional outbursts of anger—particularly when they were directed at Ellen. That made Jeremy feel even worse for his sister. He would respond by coming to her defense, and she recognized the effort he was making.

"I remember specifically our dad would start yelling and blow up at me, and my brother would always try and steer his anger away from me," she says. "I always appreciated it. He was very protective of me. Then I felt guilty because [my father] would be screaming at my brother." It's a neat trick when a single parental act—openly preferring one child over another—can leave both kids with a guilt burden to carry. Jeremy and Ellen spun that experience into greater closeness as they got older, but things could just as easily have gone the other way.

One thing that does make even the most blatant favoritism easier to take is when there's a defensible reason for it and all the kids understand what it is. Perhaps the most extreme example of this is when one child in the household has special developmental or physical needs. Children with Down syndrome or autism certainly require a particular kind of care and attention, including extra applause for skills learned and tasks performed well. Kids with physical challenges—everything from grave conditions such as muscular dystrophy to milder problems such as common scoliosis—will require more time and attention from parents, and that time and attention will necessarily be subtracted from the fixed amount they have to give their other kids. Even the most tolerant siblings won't always accept this immediately and at some point will begin to feel that, healthy or not, they deserve their full share of care, too. Talking about the situation openly is the best and most direct way to limit resentments or hurt feelings. "Parents should give reasons the differential treatment is important so kids can try to perceive and understand why it's fair," says Shawn Whiteman, assistant professor of family studies at Purdue University. "Research suggests that differential treatment may have no negative effects when children understand why."

Kids are also surprisingly good at understanding that an older sibling will enjoy certain prerogatives that younger sibs don't get—though this can admittedly be a harder sell than when illness or disability drives the disparate treatment. What's more, the very fact that the older sib does such trailblazing usually means looser rules and somewhat earlier privileges for the younger ones. Parents may be beside themselves with worry the first time their firstborn goes to school or heads off to camp or gets behind the wheel of a car. By the time the second or third or fourth kids are doing it, they've habituated some and everything is more relaxed.

"What comes first is more salient," Whiteman says. "The age at which kids get privileges will look the same in terms of trajectory, but for second-borns, everything occurs earlier. It is a hidden aspect of birth order."

One of the best things about favoritism conflicts is that they usually do fade in significance as children grow older. "Usually," of course, is not the same as "always," and childhood resentments may never be entirely forgotten. Life issues such as which child becomes the caretaker of aging parents or which is bequeathed the most in the will can often become occasions to fight old wars and relitigate old grievances.

Still, in the best of circumstances, even those battles can be fleeting. For every sibling bond damaged by parental favoritism there are many more brothers and sisters who do ride out the storms of childhood and make it to adulthood with their love—and their humor—intact. Even into middle age, my brothers and I—including Bruce—continue to try to coax our septuagenarian mother to concede that Bruce was her favorite son. And honoring the code of maternal *omertà*, she continues to deny it. Age can make even the stoutest defenses slip, though, and one day she and I were recalling a long-ago school talent show that—like so many talent shows when we were children—starred Bruce. My mother beamed throughout the performance, and I glowered throughout it.

"Why were you so mad?" she asked when I reminded her of the evening. "Because he was my favorite?"

"Aha!" I cried.

"What?" she responded.

"You admitted it! Bruce was your favorite!"

She looked at me innocently and blinked. "I have no idea what you're talking about," she said. It's her story—and she's sticking to it.

SIX

Breaking Up

Brothers, Sisters, and Divorce

Steve was the only one in the kitchen the night the fist came through the window. There was no sound of shattering glass. The pane—one of four small ones in the door—had broken a week before and we had temporarily covered the opening with cardboard. That did a serviceable job of shutting out the early winter chill but it was little protection against a burglar. Crime, however, was not something we thought about much, this being suburban Baltimore in 1961, and housebreakers never troubled our block. Still, our home now did appear to be under assault—and by someone who knew what he was doing. The hand swept the remaining cardboard away and then reached straight down, manipulating the lock and chain. Steve—who was nine years old and had come down to the kitchen on some pre-bedtime errand—stood staring, too frozen by fear to do anything else.

After an instant, he found his voice, unrooted his feet, and tore up the stairs, calling out to all of us that someone was breaking in. Garry,

Bruce, and I heard his cry and ran into our parents' room, just as Steve arrived there. From downstairs, we could hear a rattling in the kitchen and then, horrifyingly, the door banging open. Our mother was home alone with us, and while she seemed alarmed, she seemed oddly not to be afraid—or even terribly surprised. She ordered the four of us to go back to our rooms and stay there. We did as we were told, darting across the hall just in time to see a male figure in an open black overcoat sweeping up the stairs and heading toward her room. It was our father— windblown and looking furious. He carried a folded sheaf of papers with a pale blue cover in his hand.

That was the first we'd seen of him in weeks. Our parents' marriage had always been volatile, but in the past year it had come wholly undone, with more fighting, more distance, and a general sense of menace in the air. There was talk of separation, then talk of divorce, and finally the talk turned to action and our father moved out. The two of them played out the early stages of their divorce proceedings the way they'd played out too much of their eleven-year marriage—which is to say loudly, badly, and with a pointless stubbornness that served no discern- ible end. My father made it clear that he wanted the divorce proceed- ings to be heard in New York, where he longed to return. My mother wanted them heard in Baltimore, where she planned to stay. The first to serve papers on the other would win. Of such small things are dramas— and traumas—made.

Over the previous week, my brothers and I had hunkered in the house with our mother as a series of process servers—dark, stocky men in fedoras and overcoats—rang the bell and pounded on the door. The shades were kept drawn and the doors were kept locked, and under no circumstances were my brothers or I to let anyone in or acknowledge that our mother was at home. Finally, my father—whose keys no longer fit the locks—did what the process servers could not legally do, break open the door and storm upstairs to deliver the papers himself. From the bedroom I shared with Steve, I heard my parents' door slam open and then slam closed and the two of them proceeding to shout. Finally, the door swung open again and I heard my father's footsteps approaching. He suddenly appeared, out of breath, in our doorway. All I perceived—or at least all I've ever recalled—was the black, Batman-like billow of his overcoat.

"I love you, boys!" he barked.

There was a terrible incongruity between the words he spoke and the tableau that surrounded them, and I had absolutely no response for him. I looked frantically around my room, but I couldn't say for what. I'd taken a shine to nature toys lately and my eye fell on a plastic model I'd just built of an odd little marshland bird called a hoopoe. It was a delicate thing, an interesting thing, and I suppose I reckoned it might have the power to appease.

"Do you like my hoopoe?" I asked my father.

I don't recall if he answered my question, or even heard me. Instead, I recall him sweeping from our room and into Garry's and Bruce's and from there, too, I heard, "I love you, boys!" Then he was gone.

My brothers and I fell into a shell-shocked silence. I have no recollection at all of what happened after that, and years later my brothers remember little more—though Steve does recall that our grandparents were sent for and they came by and did what they could to try to settle us down. It is perhaps a measure of the ugliness of the night that we all seem to have erased any part of it that we could. What we do remember is more than enough.

. . .

Divorces come in a lot of flavors. There are amicable ones and acrimonious ones, quick ones and protracted ones. There are divorces that require the division of land and fortunes, and those that call for nothing more than loading half the furniture into a moving van. No two bust-ups are exactly alike, except in one respect: They can all be murder on the kids.

Children are often the collateral casualties of even the most civilized separation. Parents may tell themselves that they're shielding the kids from the worst of things—that they're answering all their questions, helping them explore their feelings, and otherwise following the guidance of the child-rearing books—and maybe they are. But that doesn't mean the experience isn't going to be lousy and hard and scarring anyway. It just means it might be less so.

Spouses who are parting are sometimes surprised by this fact—by how little they can do to protect their kids completely from the upheaval—but they shouldn't be. Of all the different two-person dyads in the home, it's the mom-and-dad unit that's easily the most important. The spousal partnership is what psychologists call the "executive function" of the family—the management suite through which stability is established and policy is made. Eliminate it—or even temporarily disrupt it—and the entire enterprise is shaken. "When the parents are getting along," says family specialist Mark Feinberg of Penn State University, "the system is more coherent. When they're not, it's not."

And when that happens, the kids feel the effects fast and first. Children are particularly susceptible to injury in such a volatile atmosphere because their minds are works in progress. Just as environmental toxins such as lead and mercury do more damage to the young, developing brain than they do the fixed, adult one, so, too, do emotional toxins have a more destructive impact on an unformed psyche. Just how any one child is affected depends in part on age—the small child who most needs reassurance that the world is a safe and stable place instead learns just the opposite; the adolescent boy who needs a firm male hand as his adult identity is beginning to form is now denied it. But if all kids suffer differently, none of them escapes unscarred—and that's particularly bad news in the United States and other Western nations, simply because divorce is so common here.

If you believe the common wisdom, about 50 percent of American marriages eventually break up. While that's a handy and universally cited data point, it's also misleading, if only because there are so many different ways to crunch the numbers. Widely accepted surveys from the U.S. Centers for Disease Control do show that there are currently 7.1 marriages and 3.5 divorces for every 1,000 Americans, which brings you in almost exactly at the fifty-fifty mark. The problem is that the number of divorces is not the same as the number of individuals who *get* divorced. The bust-up rate for first marriages, for example, is about 41 percent. For second marriages it's 60 percent; the third time around it's 73 percent. One serially marrying man, therefore, can account for nearly all of the divorces in his 1,000-person population group, but only three out of the seven marriages. There will still be four more men who get married and stay married—putting the per-groom divorce rate at just 20 percent.

So many other X factors can determine the number of divorces in any sub-population—age, income, education, ethnic group, geography, family history, and more—that most social statisticians despair of ever distilling out a single figure that captures the whole nation. Still, no matter what the precise numbers are, it's safe to say that it's been a long time since divorce lawyers in the United States suffered any shortage of business.

For children in households heading for the courts, the storms usually begin long before the first papers are filed. Unhappy homes are turbulent homes, and that instability typically goes on for years before parents finally give up and split up. One of the first things they may do as their marriage is coming apart is try to recruit the kids to their end of the sinking ship. Initially, this alliance building may be done subtly and often unintentionally.

A wife who's becoming fed up with her husband's short temper may be justified when she tells a child, "Don't bother Daddy when he gets home; you know how angry he gets." But the child—who may or may not be the usual object of that anger—gets a powerful message anyway: Dad is bad news. Mom may be perfectly happy to let that interpretation stand. The father who comes home from work to a harried mother who's been with the kids all day and then gives piggyback rides all around may—inadvertently or not—be sending a very loud message of his own: *Dad's fun! Mom's mean! (And remember that, kids.)* In a stable marriage, Dad would also take pains to give Mom props for how hard she works and to remind the kids that anybody would be fed up at the end of a long day of domestic labor. In a dying marriage in which parents don't speak much anymore, he may simply let the kids draw other conclusions and may even make a more overt gesture such as shooing Mom out of the room as he takes over. That can be read as either a welcome way of telling her that she's off duty at last, or a less benign signal to the kids that he's protecting them from her nasty mood—with marital context, again, being everything.

Before long, these passive alliance strategies can give way to dangerously active ones. If it's always been an open secret that Mom favors the older daughter, Dad may work harder to win her loyalty or, in the alternative, may line up more closely with the youngest son. If Dad has been cracking down on the oldest son because of his grades or his behavior, Mom may be more inclined to give him a break, even exchanging a wink or a reassuring look during a father-son contretemps. *I understand,* it says. *He doesn't.*

"Certain pathogenic patterns begin to appear," says psychologist Thomas O'Connor of the University of Rochester Medical Center. "Parents begin to enlist a child as a confidant or an ally. Now you have a split in the family. At that point, not only isn't the marriage working out, the family as a whole isn't, either."

My brother Bruce, as my mother's manifest favorite, had a natural— and reciprocal—allegiance to her, and would rarely tolerate hearing her spoken ill of. He certainly couldn't do anything about whatever our father might say or think, but he was quick to defend her if one of us had just been the object of a maternal reprimand or punishment and returned to the playroom muttering angry or seditious sentiments. Steve was powerfully drawn by the magnet of my father's favoritism, and though he was far less free to act on it once our parents separated, he was clearly the weakest of the allies in our mother's camp.

Garry and I, as middle children, were the only chips still truly in play and we felt the pull in different ways. I was close enough to Steve in age to envy the paternal attention he received, to say nothing of the dangled offers of visits to New York, and was easily swayed by the idea that as I got older I'd get the same. Garry was an even softer touch. A toy junkie almost from birth, he was a sucker for anything that beeped, whirred, lit up, blew up, or could be ridden, shot, thrown, flown, launched, assembled, or cuddled with. That's a lot of bait with which to attract a child, and one evening after our parents separated and our father had moved out, the four of us and our mother came home from an after-noon out to find the living room piled high with boxes of gift-wrapped toys—four piles, one for each boy. It was the holiday season and though our father had already sold his toy business and begun training to be-come a stockbroker, he had arranged for gifts to be delivered from an-other local store. My mother's housekeeper—who had not been enlisted in the plan—was serendipitously there to let the deliverymen in.

The four of us gaped—Garry nearly swooned—and my mother glowered. She knew a naked bribe when she saw one, declared the toys off-limits, and phoned the store, ordering them to take everything back. We all experienced our own degrees of grief and denial as the delivery-men came and cleared out the bounty, though if Garry could have clung to their legs as they were leaving, I suspect he would have. As it turned out, even that drama was not sufficient to shake any one of us loose from our mother's camp, but nor did it win her any points—and it did win our father sympathy and gratitude.

The pathology in a divorcing home doesn't stop with the building of alliances. Next comes what psychologists call triangulation—and if that sounds unsettlingly political, it's because it is. In triangulating families, the stable alliances that start to form between parents and select kids are joined by more transitory alliances of convenience. A child who has thrown in his lot with his father may suddenly cozy up to his mother if Dad is refusing to let him use the car that night. A daughter who favors her mother may tactically—and temporarily—play the Dad card when she and Mom aren't getting along. That kind of thing happens in stable families, too, but in unstable families, it's much more common, and both parents in a collapsing home are particularly vulnerable to it. The last thing either one of them wants is to be the less favored parent of all the kids, and both are thus a lot easier to manipulate. "When alliances and triangulation emerge," O'Connor says, "the entire family system has gone bad."

It's not easy to measure the different psychic wounds such a broken system inflicts on the kids—at least not with any empirical certainty—but lots of good studies have tried. One of the most comprehensive was conducted in Canada by investigators at the University of Alberta and published in 2005. Sociologist Lisa Strohschein and others analyzed data collected in a sweeping survey of 17,000 Canadian children—from infants to eleven-year-olds—that ran from 1994 to 1998. The investigators looked for early signs of mental distress such as anxiety, depression, and antisocial behavior, and tried to determine what was behind those conditions. Consistently, they found that children whose parents divorced during the survey period were at much higher risk than other kids of developing all of these emotional problems—and the symptoms, significantly, usually began well before the parents actually split up. Indeed, in many cases, the kids' behavior and moods actually improved after the divorce, since the uncertainty and the daily spousal warring were at least over, and a stable—if often sadder—home life could begin. One implication of this is that a common reason parents give for not ending an unhappy marriage—that they're staying together for the sake of the kids—can be misguided.

Children of divorce suffer in other ways. An ambitious British-Canadian study published in the *Journal of Divorce and Remarriage* broke down some of the less discussed but distressingly common symptoms kids exhibit as their parents are splitting up. According to the study, as many as 80 percent of children become preoccupied with the idea of their parents' separation, often to the exclusion of other things; 53 percent try to cope with that ruminaton by pretending that the divorce hasn't taken place; and 42 percent suffer significant concern about the custodial parent, usually worrying much less about the parent who has actually left the family. Most painfully, 25 percent of kids blame themselves for the divorce. That problem turns up most frequently in the three-to-five age group—or precisely the age at which kids may in fact have the least power to influence the conduct of the misbehaving adults around them.

The emotional drama of divorce plays out only within the kids' psyches or between the parents and the kids, but also in the relationships between the brothers and sisters themselves. O'Connor is fond of quoting the opening lines of *Anna Karenina*—"Happy families are all alike; all unhappy families are unhappy in their own way"—and that's never truer than when siblings are watching their own households dissolve.

Of all the blows sibling relationships sustain during the divorce, the worst occur as a result of custody battles. It's hard enough when separating parents start arguing over weekends and summer vacations, leaving the kids to watch as their calendar is carved up. It's much worse when the animosity is so great—and the pre-divorce alliances are so entrenched—that different children actually wind up living with different parents. This kind of live property division, with the family being broken up like a shared dinette set, is less common than it used to be, in part because so many studies of children in divorced or foster homes have shown how vital it is for brothers and sisters to be housed together, and many judges have heeded those warnings. This is smart for several reasons.

For one thing, children whose parents separate may feel an acute sense of longing for the noncustodial parent, a life change that can often push their still-undeveloped coping skills to the limits. That pain will only be exacerbated if they must absorb the loss of a full-time sib as well. What's more, shared trauma is, as a rule, milder trauma, and a complete complement of empathic siblings will typically bear the pain of a divorce much more easily than the individual components of a smaller broken group can.

Those truths are straightforward enough, but they weren't always well appreciated by the courts or by families. My parents separated for good when Steve was ten, and Garry, Bruce, and I were seven, six, and eight, respectively. My mother was awarded full custody of us, and my father, who moved back to New York as he'd wanted, was granted only weekend and holiday visits. That seemed about right, given the uneven and sometimes explosive brand of parenting he practiced— and I suspect he felt the same way. But the divorce had dealt his ego a hit and he began a years-long campaign to change the custody arrangement so that Steve, at least, could come live with him. Finally, he prevailed, and when Steve was fourteen, he moved to New York and was installed in a boarding school north of the city from which he would visit my father on weekends. My father, meantime, had fully relaunched his life, opening his own brokerage firm and, more disconcerting to us, remarrying.

I had weathered my father's departure dry-eyed and, I think, in stride. But Steve's was a different matter. I could write him daily, talk to him often, and see him during vacations, but the sibling unit was something I'd always considered inviolable. When a quarter of it was carved away, I grieved the loss terribly. Steve, in his own way, did as well, though for him the separation was mixed in with the equally large loss of his parents and, for that matter, a permanent home address.

A few years later, I visited New York for the weekend and had a rare one-on-one dinner with my father. His and Steve's relationship had come to nothing in the intervening period, and Steve spent more and more time in residence at his school, until he rarely came home to the city at all. I recall my father's drinking Manhattans that evening, and while that detail may be an embellishment of memory, there was no mistaking the unaccustomed looseness of his tongue.

"I had a plan," he conceded, "and it was to get all of you." He lined up four salt and pepper shakers—one per son. "I got Steven," he said, tipping over the first. "And I wanted to get you, Garry, and Bruce away from Baltimore and away from your mother." I looked down at the saltshakers and hardly knew what to make of the disclosure. His custody battle had never been about wanting to raise us; it had been about settling a score. For that little game of retributive chess, my older brother had been snatched. I held my tongue that evening—there was nothing I could do to change things now, and I wasn't comfortable enough with my father to press the matter further anyway—but it was a nasty thing to learn all the same.

Parents don't have to be tearing at sibs so deliberately to pull them away from one another. The mere fact of divorce can do that damage all by itself. Children use their parents as models for conflict resolution, and then use their siblings as handy lab partners with whom to rehearse what they're learning. When the behavior they're observing is fractious and dysfunctional, it's hardly a surprise that the behavior they practice with one another is at greater risk of turning out the same way. "If you have a conflicted marriage, there is a view that says the sibling relationship may provide a buffer," says O'Connor. "But this is a romantic view. Where would the kids pick up the ability? If you are surrounded by conflict, how is it possible that a sibling relationship will develop that's positive, intimate, and supportive?"

That is an unusually bleak view of things, but O'Connor is not alone in taking it. Feinberg sees a number of mechanisms at work during divorce that may lead to particularly serious stress cracks among siblings.

Competition for Mom's and Dad's time, attention, and approval is one of them. Even under the best of circumstances, those resources are limited. In times of marital discord—especially when that discord is moving toward divorce—parents are even more distracted than usual and have even less energy for caregiving. What's more, it's awfully hard for them to toggle between the anger and acrimony they're exchanging with each other and the gentleness and warmth they still owe the kids. The result is often that the kids get snapped at or frozen out, too.

"Parenting is hard enough," says Feinberg. "Divorce undermines parents' efficacy and their ability to remain calm and cope well with their children. All this leaves the kids fearing that there's less affection available for them and that ultimately they may be abandoned."

Like all litter mates in such a situation, the sibs will switch into a sort of emotional survival mode, turning on one another in order to grab what little nurturing there is to be had. The longer this zero-sum battle for parental care goes on—and the more intensely it's fought out—the less likely that the wounds will heal when the crisis passes and the family settles down into some measure of post-divorce peace.

Worse than the fang-and-claw business of competing for their divorcing parents' love, siblings may also blame one another for the fact that the family broke up. It's a mercy that only 25 percent of kids who are emotionally damaged by divorce take the responsibility for the split on themselves. But some of those who don't instead direct the finger-pointing outward. Occasionally there are grounds—typically minimal ones—to make such a charge: Children with particular emotional, behavioral, or even health problems do place added strains on a marriage, and when that marriage is weak or breaking down, the extra stress may accelerate the collapse. But at worst, a child's contribution ought to be a marginal thing, and the parents, as stewards of their own union, bear the sole responsibility for what happens to it. Still, kids don't always see things that way, and when they're mourning the dissolution of their home and the family life they once knew, the temptation may be great to charge a sib with the crime. "In a lot of these cases," says Friedman, "the kids start out by thinking, 'Is this because of me?' Later they'll deflect and decide that, no, this is because of the other sibling."

Parents can correct for some of this, policing what the kids say to one another to make sure no such *j'accuse* charges are being flung, and acting proactively to insist that the kids do not turn the blame inward, either. They can also do a better job of policing themselves so that even as the spousal combat rages, they don't get too short-tempered to deal with the kids effectively. Once the household actually breaks up, parents must also be careful about how they deal with—and speak of—the now-ex spouse.

One study from Wake Forest University surveyed 500 children from 365 post-divorce families, looking for three powerful markers of emotional maladjustment: depression, behavior problems, and poor school performance. The good news from the study was that children can often adjust to a new family structure with comparative ease, particularly when custody is shared and the kids get more or less equal time living in both their parents' homes. But such a happy outcome is by no means guaranteed. In those families in which the kids had a harder go, the investigators found that the parents typically made at least one of three mistakes: They asked the children to carry messages to the other parent; they spoke ill of the other parent; and they pumped the kids for information about the other parent. By themselves, those things are comparative misdemeanors—and even understandable ones, given the emotional turmoil the parents themselves are going through. But such behavior can also strain the kids' sense of parental loyalty—which is usually stressed enough already—and create tension among the siblings themselves, who may have different views of which parent is most to blame for the divorce.

None of this means that even an ugly divorce has to damage the sibling bonds. Psychologist Shirley McGuire of the University of San Francisco has studied the myriad ways parental dysfunction can trickle down to the kids, but has given equal attention to the means by which many kids slough off that poor parental behavior, sometimes getting through divorce with their relationships actually strengthened by the experience. In some cultures, this resilience is more common than in others, and ours, regrettably, is not among the best-performing ones. The Western world's move away from sibling alloparenting—the practice of older brothers and sisters helping to raise younger children, even in intact households—has had a leveling effect on power relationships among siblings, with all of the kids essentially becoming peers on the family organizational chart. When parents divorce, it thus becomes tougher for the senior sibs to step into the breach, or at least to do so effectively.

"In other parts of the world, older siblings have a lot of responsibility in all families," McGuire says. "If a divorce occurs there, those sibs assume a caretaking role more easily and the relationships among all the brothers and sisters can become stronger. The older sibs themselves may also benefit from the sense of competence that can come from shouldering such responsibility."

Vivian Torres, now fifty, experienced the alloparenting phenomenon in a decidedly more complex way. Torres was the fifth of seven girls, and in her family, it wasn't just the sheer number of sibs that made things unwieldy, it was also the fact that they were the products of three different fathers. So much marrying, childbirth, and divorcing made the household a hard thing to manage—especially in the intervals between dads, when the most responsible sisters were tapped to play a parenting role. In the first paternal interregnum, Cheryl, the oldest, did that job.

"We considered our oldest sister a mother more than our own mother," Vivian says. This was especially so, she says, since their mother did not express love readily or well, leaving a bigger void for a sister to fill. "Cheryl contracted polio when she was seven or eight. She didn't get the vaccine and I remember her in a cast from top to bottom. She had to be home-schooled and the cast didn't come off until she was in her twenties. But she still became a caretaker for all of us."

Later, when Cheryl was old enough to leave home and the girls were once again without a father, it was Vivian who stepped forward. "I was the caretaker now," she says. "I was the cook of the family; I did the laundry. I was especially close to my second baby sister, Letitia, and sometimes I was the one who had to go rescue her at school when she got in trouble."

All of the sisters, now well into middle age, have drifted both emotionally and geographically—and Cheryl has died. But during the most challenging times, the very hardships they were facing—and the tough and creative ways in which they coped with them—had a unifying effect on them all. "We all felt like full siblings," Torres says. "We never felt like half sibs at all, even though we came from different fathers."

Siblings who are born in relatively rapid sequence may enjoy a particular kind of buffering from the worst effects of divorce. As a rule, the closer in age children are, the more similarly they process emotions such as fear, sorrow, loss, and confusion, and that can be a very good thing. A confused six-year-old, an alienated adolescent, and a high-schooler with one foot already out the door are simply not going to be occupying the same emotional terrain as kids who are all still riding the same school bus, keeping the same hours, and counting on their parents for the same kinds of care. Such children share an innate understanding of what they're all experiencing and as a result can pull together more readily. "You can observe this between twins, too," McGuire says. "The children see their parents' relationship dissolving and in effect they say to one another, 'We can stop this. We can create something different among ourselves.'"

Ellen Dunn, the seventeen-year-old Pacific Palisades high-schooler whose big brother, Jeremy, protected her from their father's temper during their parents' divorce, recalls his looking after her the same way when their home life had already turned volatile but their parents were still together. "My first memory in life was from the top stair of my old house," she wrote in an essay for her honors English class. "We lived in a beautiful white house overlooking the ocean with a winding staircase carpeted in pale gray and landing in front of my parents' room. I sat on that top stair one night with my brother and listened to the screaming coming from behind my parents' closed door. I don't remember what the fight was about; all I remember was feeling afraid. My older brother looked at me and said, 'It will be okay.'"

That is surely the most rote of reassurances, but, coming from her brother, it sounded like the truth—and Jeremy continued to do what he could to make her believe it. "[After the divorce], when we visited my father's house," Ellen wrote, "my brother and I would spend hours, just the two of us, building forts out of our bunk beds. Those forts were our safe havens." It's possible that even without such defining experiences, the two of them would have grown up to be as close as they now are—still turning to each other for counsel and encouragement and able to finish each other's sentences with an almost spousal familiarity—but the very fact of having survived the divorce wars together could not have helped but nourish that connection.

The deft way in which the Dunn kids coped with their circumstances illustrates one more salutary fact about children of divorce: Gender does not have to be any bar to the brood's surviving intact. The all-girl Torreses did it; the all-boy band in my family did, too; and so did the boy-girl Dunns. This refutes what psychologists and sociologists call the "femaleness assumption," the popular belief that it takes the presence of a girl or a woman in any intimate group to get the most out of the members emotionally, simply because females communicate more readily among themselves and encourage males to do the same.

Superficially, there is plenty of reason to believe in the femaleness assumption. The stereotype of two men spending an entire evening at a bar and one of them never thinking to mention that, say, he will soon become a father may have always been an exaggeration. But it's not too much to say that smaller confidences may go unshared between males and that even the bigger intimacies may be discussed only in passing, without much effort to plumb the deeper emotions associated with them. Similarly, there is more than a little truth to the opposite-gender stereotype—the ready empathy and remarkable intuitiveness females can display with one another. But when it comes to siblings, a shared trauma—particularly the trauma of divorce—easily trumps gender.

In a recent master's thesis on sibling relationships, Paige Herrick of Baylor University recruited 263 male and female subjects, all of whom had at least one close sibling, and asked them to describe a single experience that served as a positive turning point in their relationship—a moment that drew them close in an enduring and transformative way. The method she used to measure the impact of such experiences was a combination of essays, questionnaires, and other testing tools called the In-clusion of the Other in the Self (IOS) scale—a term that describes well the emotional enfolding between the siblings she was looking to capture. There were a lot of life incidents that scored high on the IOS scale—an illness or a sacrifice of some kind, say; for one girl it was merely the time her brother gave up playing in an important football game to be with her in the hospital. But again and again, one of the most powerful interper-sonal hinge points was a divorce the siblings experienced together.

"After my parents got divorced, we felt like we had to stick together more than we did," wrote one girl.

"My sister and I grew closer because my parents would play tug-of-war with us," one brother responded. "Also, we spent more time with each other than with either of our parents."

Another subject answered simply: "When our father left the house-hold we trusted only each other."

It's that phenomenon—that unity-through-adversity dynamic—that can sometimes make divorce such a paradoxical force for good among siblings. Yes, people who go through any crisis may sometimes emerge from the experience wanting nothing to do with the people with whom they survived it—the post-traumatic emotions causing the mere presence of other survivors to stir too many painful memories. And a certain share of kids who endure the dysfunctional mess of divorce will similarly grow up and walk away from their original families—vowing to build their own, stronger nuclear brood and to avoid as much as pos-sible anyone involved in the horror show that was their earlier life. But others who make it out of the familial foxhole alive will react completely differently—developing a deep and indelible love for the people who survived with them, one that is stronger than it was before the shooting started.

Sometime after my father's evening of breaking and entering, Steve, Garry, Bruce, and I were summoned to court to participate in one of the sessions of the custody proceedings. Wisely, we were kept out of the courtroom proper. Instead we were told we'd be seen in the judge's chambers, with no parents present to influence anything we might say. We had never heard the word *chambers* in that context before, and instead referred to where we'd be going as "the judge's clutches," a term we used without irony and that may have evinced more dread than even we realized we felt. We waited in the anteroom, wearing little suits and polished shoes, while the judge's secretaries gave us cream-filled chocolate Easter eggs to keep us busy. We ate them with differing degrees of enthusiasm.

When we entered the chambers, we sat in oversized leather chairs in front of the judge, who remained seated behind his desk. All of us had been overcoached, and Garry, whose face was streaked with chocolate, was now oversugared as well. Steve and I eyeballed him as he squirmed in his chair, his shirt and suit rumpled and untucked. The judge asked each of us what our feelings were for our parents. As instructed—and as we honestly felt—we said we preferred to stay with our mother. Garry then spoke up.

"Our mother really loves us," he piped. "But our father tries to buy our love with toys and presents, and we don't want that."

There's not a child in a million who would say such a thing and mean it, and Garry, especially, surely didn't. He was simply parroting an overheard scrap of adult conversation, one that he had been told again and again not to repeat. Steve looked at him in shock and then dropped his hand on the arm of his chair disgustedly.

"What?" Garry asked with genuine innocence. "Was that the thing I wasn't supposed to say?"

The judge may have smiled, may have frowned, may have scribbled a note—I didn't notice. We left the chambers a little while later, tired and puzzled and still cinched in our ties and formal clothes. Garry fretted that he'd done something terrible—that he'd spilled a secret that would cause all of us to be taken from our mother—and the rest of us couldn't say for sure that he hadn't. Ultimately, our mother did retain custody, and our father was awarded only visitation rights. That was the outcome we had wanted—and that even then he probably did, too, the kabuki dance of the custody battle notwithstanding. Still, it had been a miserable morning, and it left the four of us utterly wrung out. Garry's gaffe quickly became the stuff of family lore, and we would repeat it—with shared amusement—down through the years. From the safe remove of adulthood it does seem darkly funny. To the small children in the big leather chairs, it was nothing of the kind.

SEVEN

Patching Up

The Blended Family

Building a new family out of the broken bits of an old one is always hard—but it's at least easier than it used to be. Exactly what constitutes a family in the twenty-first century is a much more elastic concept than it was in the twentieth, and both courts and communities have become increasingly comfortable with a whole new set of definitions. There are families with single parents, gay parents, unmarried but cohabiting parents; there are parents who are raising children who were adopted overseas, children birthed by surrogates and carriers, children who shuttle back and forth between Dad's home half the week and Mom's the other half. Modern families have become more mosaic than portrait, and no matter how they're configured, they're being accorded a level of recognition and rights not imaginable even a few decades ago.

Still, for many parents in families that have gone through divorce, the gold standard for recovery remains remarriage—the reconstruction of a new household, with all of the traditional parts in place: one mother, one father, one set of children. There are usually two ways this can happen: the hard way and the harder way.

The hard way is the seemingly uncomplicated business of a new, childless spouse marrying into the family, taking the spot abandoned by the original, now-absent mom or dad. Maybe there's a different car in the driveway, a different set of clothes in the closet, but that's about it. You don't even have to change the number of table settings. Things, of course, are never that easy, and any stepparent who has struggled to be accepted by stepchildren knows that the process can be slow and grueling and often end in tears no matter what.

The harder way—the much harder way, actually—is when both new spouses come into the marriage trailing existing litters of their own. In these cases the commingling involves far more moving parts. Suddenly, there may be a new house with twice the number of bedrooms, twice the number of seats at the dinner table, and exponentially more opportunities for conflicts and problems. This is particularly so, since the basic arithmetic of dyads means that the number of pairs within a family grows a lot faster than the number of family members themselves. When a four-person brood grows by just two people, its dyad total leaps from six to fifteen. Add just two more, and your new eight-member family has twenty-eight possible pairs.

Such sudden family expansion means that established hierarchies are completely blown up and gender breakdowns are thoroughly scrambled. Children who were comparative strangers yesterday are sharing a playroom, a bathroom, even a parent today. Imagine collecting two groups of cats from two different alleys and locking them together in the same room. Think you'd hear some hissing?

My mother's second marriage started with more challenges than most—not the least being that the wedding took place in her bedroom.

Few people were invited, there was no photographer, and there was nothing particularly celebratory about the brief ceremony. The bride lay in bed throughout. This, certainly, was not how the day had been imagined.

My mother had been legally divorced for just over a year and her fiancé—Eddie we would call him until the moment they exchanged rings, after which we'd switch awkwardly to "Dad"—had been widowed a bit longer than that. They had been part of intersecting social circles when they were both married and, as often happens in such cases, drifted together shortly after both of them became single. It did not take them long to get engaged—a haste common in the early 1960s, when marriage still seemed almost mandatory. In fact, our father had remarried two months earlier.

The couple planned a modest, late-August wedding at a country club, followed by a brief honeymoon at a country lodge. But not long before the scheduled date, my mother contracted mononucleosis and was confined to her bed. It would have been a small matter to postpone the wedding for a month or so—the original guest list was not extensive and the invitees were all local. But the bride and groom seemed oddly anxious to press ahead, no matter what. This suggested either the sweet urgency of romance or the get-it-over-with determination of two people who had decided to do something and were jolly well going to see it through. From their demeanor on their wedding day, it was hard to tell which impulse was at work.

When the ceremony began, my mother lay propped up on pillows, with Eddie standing at her side holding her hand. The rabbi was at the foot of the bed, and my brothers and I were arrayed around it. For the four of us, the most disorienting part of the little tableau wasn't the strangeness of the setting but the presence of two other people standing with us: Eddie's children. Julie was eleven, or Steve's age; Debbie was seven, or Garry's. They would, from the day of the wedding forward, become my stepsisters. A new house had already been bought, and not long after the wedding, we would all be moving into it. I had absolutely no idea what to make of the two little strangers with whom we'd now be sharing our lives.

Julie, I guessed, was inoffensive, but she was also too chilly and buttoned up for my tastes. She wasn't particularly easy to amuse or engage, and after the casual anarchy of a house full of boys, I didn't know how to approach her—or even if I wanted to. Debbie I liked a bit better. She was eager to please and game for play. But she was also a credulous girl—easy to trick, easy to tease, an impossibly soft target for four uncivilized boys. My brothers and I had never been very predatory kids—we had neither the size nor the personalities to pull it off. Still, when a fawn like Debbie was tossed in among us, the risk was high that she was going to get mauled.

More primally, I was also vaguely troubled that the girls just didn't look like us. We were all fair-haired and pale skinned and both of them had a darker, more Mediterranean cast. All of us were also lean, and while Debbie was a wisp, Julie was on her way to pre-adolescent plumpness, which seemed alien to me. The first time we visited their house, during our respective parents' courtship, I didn't like the look of the place and I really didn't care for its smell; there was something cloying about the cleaning products or air freshener they used, and the strange scent got inextricably caught up in the larger strangeness they all represented. As an adult, I would not be proud when I recalled these biases; as a child, I knew only what I felt.

Still, the six of us were on more or less equal footing that day, dealing with the same vertiginous emotions as we watched a pair of poseur parents assume the roles that a pair of blood parents had held until only recently. The ceremony proceeded efficiently to its conclusion with no celebratory fuss. Kissing the bride was not advised, and it was out of the question for her to leave the room afterward. Instead, the children and the groom proceeded to a reception that had been relocated to my grandmother's home, just a few blocks away. It was an unremarkable event, though it was there that I tasted champagne for the first time. I found it fizzy, bitter, and generally disappointing.

It was a lot less common to inherit a pair of unfamiliar siblings back in the era when my brothers and I experienced it than it is now. The divorce rate in the early 1960s was barely half of what it is today—at least according to the admittedly imperfect methods used to calculate such things—and the increase in marital bust-ups over the past few decades has led to a commensurate increase in stepfamilies. More than 12 million children eighteen and under now live in blended homes—or about 15 percent of all kids in that age group. In the twenty-first century, the growth in that population has been especially explosive, increasing by about 1.6 million just from 2001 to 2004. It's continued at that rate since.

There are a great many X factors that determine the likelihood of any one family breaking up and recombining with another family—and even more determining if they'll do so successfully. Among the most powerful variables is ethnicity. In the United States, the lowest rate of divorce and remarriage exists in the Asian and Pacific Islander community, where only 5.1 percent of kids live in blended homes. The highest rate is among Native Americans and native Alaskans, at 17.1 percent.

African Americans, whites, and Hispanics follow at 16.5 percent, 14.6 percent, and 14.2 percent, respectively. Within all these groups, one of the biggest drivers of the divorce rate is poverty. The share of intact original families starts off comparatively high in the upper-income brackets and marches downward almost in perfect lockstep with declining wealth. According to a report by the American Prospect, a political think tank, about 38 percent of poor young children lived in two-parent households in 2000—which means that a distressing 62 percent didn't. Poverty also makes it unlikelier that any of those broken families will recombine with another and join the 15 percent in the blended group.

Regardless of differences in income and ethnicity, once families do become part of the blended population, they all face more or less the same hurdles—and those hurdles are high. The job of mixing existing families is less a businesslike combining of money, real estate, and personnel than it is a sort of organ graft. The operation may work out perfectly well, but there's also a toxic risk of tissue rejection. Indeed, our genomes powerfully predispose us to just such a failure.

Nearly all living creatures strongly prefer kin to non-kin and familiar individuals to unfamiliar ones, and there's a powerful survival incentive for such a bias. As a rule, members of your own family, tribe, or social group are less likely to want to hurt you, kill you—or for that matter eat you—than members of one outside your own. Being able to distinguish insiders from outsiders and recoil at those you don't know is one of the best ways to ensure that you stay alive long enough to contribute your own offspring to your species. There's a reason two- or three-year-old children are much more reticent around strangers than when they're two or three months old, and that's because they've reached the age at which they have the ability to toddle way from the tribal campfire and out into the larger world, where the danger lies. Best for them to learn fear then.

Determining if, and how closely, you're related to someone else is a complicated job, one that is based on more than simply getting a good look at your parents and other relatives and imprinting on their appearance. A study in a 2006 edition of *Proceedings of the Indian Academy of Sciences* by investigator Raghavendra Gadagkar cited just a partial list of species that have shown an ability to recognize even comparatively distant kin, including ants, wasps, sweat bees, honeybees, frogs, toads, mice, rats, voles, squirrels, various species of monkeys, and, of course, humans. Clearly all of these animals aren't doing this by building an elaborate mental map of Mom's reassuring face. Instead—predictably—most rely on scent.

One of the most powerful tools species use to determine affiliation is something known as the major histocompatibility complex (MHC), a region of the genome responsible for producing signature proteins that vary widely from individual to individual. MHC proteins can be detected by both smell and taste and carry a lot of important meaning. Not only do they indicate who is kin and who isn't, they also tell you who has the ability to *become* kin. Choosing a mate requires finding someone with whom you are sufficiently genetically compatible to produce healthy children. The smell of a potential partner is one way we make this determination. Part of the purpose of flirting may be simply to edge close enough to someone else to get a good whiff of that person's MHC. If sparks fly after that, one of the reasons may be that you simply like what you smelled. Flirting can eventually lead to kissing, another way of sampling MHC, since the telltale proteins are heavily concentrated in saliva. For all the romance and meaning that surround the power of a kiss, at bottom it may be nothing more than a pre-reproductive taste test. A kiss that leaves you flat may be one that tasted wrong.

Animals do not build a whole constellation of seductive rituals around MHC sampling as we do, but the purpose is still the same, and the Gadagkar study showed how precisely they can read friendly scents. Some species of social insects, for example, can detect not just the fact of relatedness but the degree, accurately distinguishing between full sisters and half sisters even when they were all raised from the egg stage together and thus had the same exposure to one another.

Other studies have focused particularly closely on the ability of mice and hamsters to make similar discriminations, since these species—as so often happens—serve as such good templates for humans. In a study published in 2005 in the UK's *Proceedings of the Royal Society*, researchers exposed 69 newborn mouse pups to the odor of various female adult mice, all of whom were lactating—a scent guaranteed to drive the hungry babies wild. Some of the adults were unrelated to the babies, some were their paternal aunts, none were their mothers. The pups' preference was unmistakable, with 54 of the 69 nursing young being drawn to the aunt more than to the stranger. It was particularly significant that the investigators chose paternal as opposed to maternal aunts, since a blood relative of the mother was likely to have many other olfactory proteins in common with her beyond mere MHC, and the baby would have encountered all of those smells during gestation and after birth. The father's kin would give off familial cues, but none the baby had ever smelled before. (The pups in this study were never allowed to be in the presence of their fathers.) A 2010 study by researchers from the University of Liverpool found a similar bias for familial MHC among baby ring-tailed lemurs, thereby proving kin-sniffing ability in the primate order, where our own species dwells. While the same skill hasn't yet been experimentally established in studies of human babies, the bias isn't hard to observe informally.

One day shortly after my wife, Alejandra, and I began dating, we spent the afternoon together while she babysat with her infant nephew, Mateo—the first son of her older brother. Mateo's mother was late returning and had not left quite enough bottled breast milk for him. It didn't take long before he began hungrily fussing—and that fussing soon turned to full-throated wailing. We had nothing to give him, but we could at least try to hold him and comfort him. Mateo wanted nothing at all to do with me, but clung for dear life to Alejandra. Finally, he latched on, mouth first, to her upper arm and stayed locked there for the better part of a half hour, furiously—if fruitlessly—nursing all the while. The analogy to the animal pups is imperfect, since my not-yet wife was by no means lactating herself. But the hickey Mateo left behind at least suggests the power of the familial MHC scent she was giving off and that I—an unrelated stranger—wasn't.

No matter how family members are recognized, the radically different ways we react to related versus unrelated individuals are undeniable. For all the scientific labor that's been expended studying this preference, the phenomenon might have best—or at least most succinctly—been explained by something known as Hamilton's rule, a wonderfully reductive principle that distills complex social behavior down to a single formula:

$$c < rb$$

This little equation, formulated by twentieth-century British biologist W. D. Hamilton, focuses on what might be the most defining feature of familial behavior: altruism—or the willingness to act unselfishly toward another person in a way that gives you nothing immediate in return and perhaps even puts your own welfare on the line. According to Hamilton, all creatures, including humans, are more inclined to behave altruistically when the cost (c) of performing an act is less than the benefit (b) to the recipient times the relatedness (r) the actor shares with that recipient. The greater the degree of relatedness is, the higher the value on the right side of the equation climbs and the higher the cost we're willing to incur. The more distant the relation, the lower the cost you'll tolerate. Animals in the state of nature make these calculations all the time and, in the complex human world, so do we. You might think twice before donating seventy-five dollars to a scholarship fund for indigent students in your community no matter how small a hardship it would work on you, but you might be willing to contribute hundreds or thousands of dollars toward the college education of a nephew or niece who needed your help. As for your own kids? Never mind mere tuition, for them you'd give up your life.

Hamilton's work has been embroidered upon much further by Harvard biologist and Pulitzer Prize winner E. O. Wilson, widely considered the leading thinker in the field of sociobiology. Wilson's theories argue that nearly all animal and human social behavior is governed by degrees of genetic relatedness, with organisms behaving one way toward individuals sharing 50 percent of their genes, another way toward those sharing 25 percent, and so on down the kinship ladder to distant cousins with whom they may have 3 percent or less in common. According to sociobiological doctrine, even so self-annihilating an act as a soldier jumping on a grenade to save a group of unrelated platoon mates could have genetic calculation behind it, since there may be just enough scraps of shared DNA in a random collection of men that the loss of 100 percent of one person's genes would nonetheless profit the dead individual genetically, provided the other men survived and went on to reproduce.

The work of Wilson, Hamilton, and others like them has by no means been universally embraced. For one thing, as with all scientists with a very powerful idea, they do tend to overstate its influence; genes are important, but they're not the whole story. What's more, even scientific absolutists recoil at the idea of such noble human impulses as self-sacrifice and familial love being distilled to a simple matter of genetic arithmetic. But no matter what mechanisms are at work, research does argue persuasively that our species is highly motivated to see the distinctions between kin and non-kin—and to act on that knowledge. As with so much else, it is with our siblings that we first demonstrate this ability most deftly.

Judy Dunn of King's College in London has observed that children as young as three who are raised with step- or half siblings somehow seem to know their comparative degrees of relatedness even without being told. In addition to straightforward observational studies, which are always the best way to conduct sibling fieldwork, Dunn has devised a simple but revealing test in which she asks small children in both nuclear families and stepfamilies to draw pictures of the members of their household and place each individual on a sort of taxonomic map. Kids, of course, are egocentric by nature and will always position themselves at the center of the diagram. What Dunn looks for is how they then array the other members of the household. Again and again, genetic connectedness seems to be the most powerful driver, with family members with whom the test subject shares more genes typically being placed closer to the center and those more distantly related getting assigned a spot farther away—even if that doesn't reflect how well they all get along. "Young children just seem to know if they are siblings or not," Dunn says. "They are very conscious of whether their parents are the same."

Not all blended families are hobbled by their different pedigrees. In many cases, familiarity and habituation can draw individuals together even if their genetic coding pushes them apart. This happens all the time even outside the family, as evidenced by the kin-like bonds that can form among soldiers or office workers or people merely out on a long survival hike together. Within families, the proximity is even closer and the phenomenon even more powerful. For blended families in particular, this can work all kinds of emotional magic.

Psychologist Mavis Hetherington of the University of Virginia, in collaboration with psychologists Robert Plomin and David Reiss, conducted a long-term investigation of 720 families called the Nonshared Environment of Adolescent Development (NEAD) study. One of Hetherington's key findings was that with each year that passes, there is less and less to distinguish the behavior and observable group dynamics of a nuclear family from a blended one. Eventually those differences seem to disappear altogether—at least judging by the behavioral measurements psychologists use. Just how long such a transformation takes is not fixed, but Shirley McGuire, a follower of Hetherington's work, conducted similar studies of her own and believes that six years is a pretty good average. A blended family that stays together for that long is unlikely ever to come apart. What's more, the bonds that are formed among stepsiblings during that six-year stretch may actually be stronger than those among full siblings, perhaps because they avoided a lot of the competition full sibs are likely to have engaged in from birth.

"There is mixed literature on this," McGuire says. "But in some cases there may be less rivalry because stepsiblings are able to say, 'You have your family and I have mine.' Maybe they are less alike and don't have the advantage of having similar personalities, but they also don't necessarily have that same feeling of competition, and that helps their relationship."

Of course, a six-year incubation period for bonding does mean that some siblings are going to get left out. Kids who were teens or young adolescents when the families first combined will grow up and leave the house before they ever get their full dose of sibling proximity. What's more, even during the years they're still around, they're likely to expend much of their emotional energy outside the home, toward their social and school peers, rather than within it—something that is characteristic of all adolescents. It's the relationships among the youngest sibs that thus benefit the most, and often the sibs themselves recognize that. In our blended home, all six children were still in elementary school, and thus none of us had even one foot out the door. Still, Bruce and Debbie—the youngest girl and the youngest boy—did seem to reach across the family divide more easily than any of the rest of us, often playing together with the natural rhythms of full sibs, instead of the forced intimacy of steps.

"Children's answers to the question [of closeness] are complex," says Professor Rosalind Edwards of London's South Bank University, who conducted a 2005 study of sib affiliation. "For them, the relationships are built through everyday communication, such as talking, playing, doing activities together, and sharing experiences." Acting like siblings, in other words, can help make you siblings.

Certainly, even six full years of greenhousing the sibling relationship is not always enough to achieve true yours-mine-and-ours collegiality. Plenty of kids can't stand their step- or half siblings' company and can't overcome that initial aversion. Others achieve a sort of friendly but cool relationship and never move much beyond it. A key variable helping to determine a family's prospects for success is the question of birth order—and how the mixing of the broods affects the existing lineups.

Blending two families is a little like shuffling cards, and in the process, familiar patterns and sequences can get completely disrupted. A second-born may suddenly be demoted to third- or fourth-born. A youngest child who's grown accustomed to the special pampering that comes with that position may be bumped up to second youngest. Worst of all, a firstborn may be busted down to second or even lower. In our family, Steve displaced Julie, who had been the oldest in her original family, and Julie, in turn dropped me from second-born to an even more ignoble third. Garry outranked Debbie by two months, helping to push her even farther down in the rankings—from second-born all the way to fifth—even as Garry himself fell from third to fourth. Certainly, the difference between positions four and five in a six-child family is far less significant than the difference between positions one and two. Still, any birth-order change can be profoundly disruptive overall, so much so that even experts in the field despair of figuring it all out.

"We don't actually have a way of quantifying it," says Frank Sullo-way, the acknowledged leader of birth-order research. "I can tell you that in the data I published in 2001, I just eliminated anyone who said their family niche was disrupted by marriage, divorce, or death. Things that disrupt families disrupt family niches, and things that disrupt family niches disrupt predictions based on birth order."

New sibling rankings require kids not only to redefine their place in the family but also to assume new responsibilities. A last-born gets away with less when the blended family has an even younger, even cuter ca-boose. Oldest siblings may like having a larger court of kids over whom they hold sway, but the members of that court may also require babysitting, help with homework, and—if the firstborn is old enough to drive—chauffeuring to and from playdates and school. It's bad enough to be put to work in the service of your own baby sibs; it's worse when your duties include caring for stepsibs imposed on you by a stepparent you may not even have wanted your blood parent to marry in the first place.

There is no fixed age difference at which the relationship between siblings becomes less one of playmates than of caretaker and charge, but a common threshold is about four years. At this age gap, the sibs' differing skill levels are great enough that the older one can often be trusted to look after the younger. The problem is, the gap is also narrow enough that siblings may still require similar kinds of attention and care from their parents. That can lead to resentment, and that in turn can lead to fighting—and in both cases things are worse between stepsibs than between full sibs.

As the age gap widens, the resentment typically eases. "Once you get more than four years apart, there is no longer any competition," says McGuire. "Ten-year-olds and two-year-olds just aren't going to compete with each other." That means that caretaking responsibilities may not only not drive sibs apart, but may actually draw them closer together, as the younger ones develop a dependency on—and an adoration of—the older ones, and the older ones, despite themselves, succumb to that unquestioning love. This can occur in both original and blended families, of course, but in the blended case it may be especially important, since it helps to cultivate sibling bonds that might never have developed otherwise.

Television and radio personality Pia Lindstrom experienced this phenomenon in a decidedly more high-profile way than most people do. Best recognized for her years as a New York newscaster, she is also known as a child of Hollywood nobility—the daughter of film icon Ingrid Bergman and the half sister of actress and model Isabella Rossellini. Lindstrom's parents were divorced when she was ten, after her mother's affair with director Roberto Rossellini went public. Lindstrom dearly loved her father and was both devastated and angered by the split.

"I felt bad for myself," she says today. "But I also thought, 'My poor father.' It was so humiliating. I admired him so and I didn't understand why my mother didn't."

Her unhappiness with her mother grew worse a year later when Bergman, who by then had married Rossellini, gave birth to Roberto, their first child. Two more children—Isabella and her twin sister, Ingrid—followed several years later. Pia heard tales of her glamorous half sibs living their glamorous lives in London and Paris and Rome while she grew up as a doctor's daughter in Los Angeles. Finally, when she was eighteen, she spent a summer in London, living with her mother and her new family. For the first time, she got to know her seven-year-old half brother and four-year-old half sisters—and fell for them completely. She returned the next summer, then the summer after that, and by the time she was in her early twenties moved in full-time and spent four years studying acting and Italian and helping to raise her little brother and sisters—alloparenting the half sibs she might have otherwise chosen to see as nothing more than the products of her mother's betrayal. Certainly, the challenge would have been even greater in a true blended family, in which Lindstrom would have had no blood ties to the younger children at all. But in both cases, the age gap can paradoxically help bridge the emotional gap, creating a rapport that is part sibling, part parental, and often, to the older sib at least, wholly unexpected.

I felt needed," Lindstrom says. "I always perceived myself as an only child and I would have loved to have brothers and sisters. Instead, I wound up feeling very maternal toward all of them. I don't know how that happened."

You can't plan an age gap in a blended home, of course, but there are other things families preparing to throw in their lots together have the power to control. The American Academy of Pediatrics has a lot of advice for parents on how best to go about the family-combining business, and a lot of research backs it up. Most important, the experts strongly counsel candor in all things. Kids who may still be getting over the upheaval of divorce and the loss of a noncustodial parent may not always react well when they're told that Mom or Dad has found a replacement mate and that a swarm of stranger sibs will be part of the mix. Still, honesty beats secrecy, and as soon as possible, children need to be told what's ahead. Presenting the coming wedding as a grand celebration, and allowing the kids to participate in it—as ring bearers, groomsmen, or bridesmaids—is a big part of this approach. In this sense, my own reconstituted family got off to a very good start, with the unlikely venue of the wedding adding an idiosyncratic detail that could have made for years of fond storytelling. It was the next steps—pretty much all of the next steps—that proved to be our undoing.

The greater natural warmth full siblings are likely to share with one another is nothing compared to the deeply instinctual preference parents have for their own blood kids. That's wholly defensible—and entirely unavoidable. Not only are remarrying parents asked to accept dependent children who share none of their genes, they're also expected to provide those kids with resources that would otherwise go to their biological offspring. Nature hates that idea.

The initial ambivalence stepparents feel toward stepkids is usually reciprocated—and the kids may actually escalate things, reacting not just with distance or indifference, but with open hostility. Here again, the age of the child makes a big difference. Younger kids—nine years old or below—generally adjust faster to a stepparent, both because their emotional needs are less complex than those of older kids and because they're more inclined to cozy up to any new adult who plays with them, gets silly with them, or otherwise pays them attention. Stepparents don't have to work very hard to put those early points on the board. Adolescents and pre-adolescents in the ten to fourteen age group are much harder nuts to crack, warns the American Psychological Association (APA). The same stepparent strategies that elicit closeness in a younger child will elicit eye rolls from a tween or teen.

The problem becomes more acute when it's the mother who's remarrying and the biological father who's absent—still the most common arrangement despite the general increase in joint-custody agreements. According to the APA, biological fathers cut the frequency of their visits with their kids by 50 percent within the very first year of divorce. That would seem to clear the field for a stepfather to take over, but just as often it simply makes the child feel more abandoned and resentful and the new dad's efforts seem more of an unwelcome presumption. This is one situation in which some adolescents and teens may actually present fewer problems than younger kids, simply because their days as part of the nuclear family are numbered. They'll either bond with their new dad or they won't, but no matter what, they'll be out of the house soon and free to find a comfortable level of lifetime closeness with both father and stepfather.

Stepparents trying to negotiate all of these issues must tread very carefully, the APA and other groups warn. They should keep themselves emotionally available to their stepchildren, but not push too hard if the kids seem resistant. This includes displays of physical affection, which can be especially fraught between stepdaughters and stepfathers, with even benign paternal gestures setting off alarms—understandable, given the fact that father-daughter sexual abuse is the commonest kind within families, and stepfather-stepdaughter is the highest within that category.

Disciplinary duties, at least for the first few years, should be compartmentalized, with biological parents serving as the real whip crackers over their biological kids and stepparents acting more like camp counselors, exercising authority but deferring to the greater power of the blood parent, says the APA. And while it's best for all parents in any kind of family to try not to let their quarrels play out in front of the kids, it's especially important in blended families, since the last thing stepkids need as they slowly acquire respect for a stepparent is a blood parent showing hostility or disrespect.

In my home, most of these rules were flouted. Our mother could be strong-willed, sharp-elbowed, and very sharp-tongued. Her new husband was a sweet enough soul, but one who could easily be rolled, and that was not a good match for her. She had left a loud eleven-year grind of a marriage and, before she knew it, had leaped back into a new one. She seemed to have little respect for the institution, her partner, or even herself for the choices she had made. All of this showed in her barely stifled sighs at her new husband's attempts to exercise paternal or spousal authority, in the snide asides she muttered more than loudly enough for all of us to hear, and—far more unjustly—in the almost equivalent disdain she showed his girls.

In response, my brothers and I went feral. We liked Eddie—he was hard not to like—but we took our cue from our mother and ignored even his limited authority. The girls got treated little better. Debbie hung in stubbornly in the face of our teasing—in part, I think, because her ingenuousness made it hard for her to see any reason she deserved to be mistreated, and she thus didn't always recognize it when it was happening. For that tenacity she earned a measure of our respect, which she deserved, even if we didn't deserve hers. Julie, who was as chilly and emotionally shuttered as she initially seemed, largely withdrew from us—joining us in games on those few occasions that we did play well together, but otherwise keeping to herself or staying mostly with her sister.

Toxic as those experiences were, they're hardly uncommon, particularly in the way children may become their stepsibs' tormentors. Ben Rogers, now a thirty-eight-year-old marketing executive in Chicago, still winces at the pain he experienced when he was six and his little sister was four, and they moved halfway across the country into the Illinois home of their mother's new husband, where three new siblings—two boys and a girl, ages ten, twelve, and fourteen—were lying in wait for them.

"For years, my stepbrothers bullied, threatened, and ostracized me," Rogers says. "Often I'd stay up all night crying in terror." He and his blood sister reacted the same way my stepsisters did, which is to say they drew closer to each other, at least initially. But perhaps to curry favor with his older stepsibs, or perhaps because of the incorrigible nature of older brothers as a whole, Rogers often found himself picking on her, too—and was often at a loss to stop himself. "I wasn't so nice to her as a kid," he recalls. "We went through this thing together but she was subjected to a lot of teasing from me. I feel guilty about it."

One mistake Rogers's family made—and one of the few my family avoided—concerned where they lived. Territoriality is a powerful thing, and no matter how much parents may stress the all-for-one ethos of the new brood, there is a natural power disparity when one half of the blending family moves into the other half's home. Regardless of how long they live there, the new arrivals will always feel slightly like interlopers and the original residents will always feel slightly intruded upon. Often, this arrangement is unavoidable, but if there's a choice—as there was in my family's case—the APA stresses that it's best for everyone to pack up and relocate to a new address to which they all have the same emotional claim. Here, too, however, parents should not push too hard. If possible, blood sibs should room with blood sibs and no one should be forced to share toys or clothes or other possessions, which serve as important symbols of identity and boundaries.

The most primal sign of a fully blended family occurs on those occasions that the newly joined spouses have a child of their own. Few things say marital permanence more powerfully than that, and while that ought to be a good thing, it, too, can be fraught. The fact that the parents will be utterly consumed by the demands of a newborn can be a source of long-standing resentment, particularly if Mom's or Dad's biological kids are still having trouble sharing them with their stepsibs. The newborn, too, faces familial challenges. Everybody's half sib, nobody's full sib, but the only one in the house with pure bloodlines running to both resident parents, the baby is in a position that is both enviable and precarious. The very fact of genetic relatedness means that hardwired bonding cues such as smell and physical resemblance kick in immediately for everyone in the house, and these are difficult for even the most recalcitrant half sibs to resist. But sibling jealousy can still erode such natural affiliation.

The best approach here, as with the planning and celebration of the wedding, is for parents to be as open as possible as early as possible, letting kids know if they think the new marriage stands a good chance of producing a new child. Even if it seems self-evident to parents that the love they'll lavish on the baby will not detract from the love they feel for the other kids, those kids need to hear that fact stated out loud, sometimes repeatedly. Inviting the kids to participate in preparations such as painting the nursery or buying baby clothes also can help. The kids should be free to decline the opportunity, and many will—particularly preteen boys, who may insist they want nothing to do with such fussy stuff—but the offer should still be made.

My own blended family never got the chance to have a blended baby—or do much else familial, for that matter. My mother's second marriage—a marriage of habit more than of romance or even convenience—ended just fifteen months after it began. At the breakfast table one morning, shortly after all six children had gone to school, Eddie handed my mother a letter he had written. It said he was leaving, that the decision was made, and that the marriage was over. It was a curious gesture—communicating by note when the two of them were in the same room—but perhaps it said something about how wholly their other lines of communication had broken down. Not long after that, the moving trucks arrived.

Steve, Garry, Bruce, and I came home from school that afternoon to find half the furniture in the house gone, as well as all of Eddie's, Debbie's, and Julie's personal effects. Unknown to us, he had also picked the girls up from school earlier in the day. The operation was clean, surgical, executed with a shock-and-awe speed that could not have been easy to pull off without a fair bit of planning.

My mother didn't seem to grieve the end of the marriage, and neither did we. We'd already experienced what it was like to lose an original father, and the loss of a genial stand-in did not shake us up much. Debbie and Julie I missed a bit more, at least in a theoretical way. Sisters were interesting and exotic additions to an all-boy brood, and my brothers and I would no doubt have grown up differently—perhaps better—if we'd gotten to know them and learned to fathom the other gender more fully. As it was, I saw Debbie and Julie only very rarely in the following years and have since lost touch with them entirely. I have no idea what kind of lives they're leading today.

EIGHT

Misguided Guidance

Drugs, Pregnancy, and Other Risky Behaviors

June de la Playa is nineteen years old and by a lot of measures she really ought to have been pregnant by now. She's the second of two girls, and for as long as she remembers, she has adored her older sister, Marta, twenty-one. The girls were raised by an aunt who looked after them well, but not in the way a true mother could have. The emotional void left by an absent mom was filled by Marta and June themselves.

"We were inseparable," June says. "We basically only had each other. Marta took care of me."

All that shouldn't spell trouble for June, but it does. Marta became pregnant when she was just seventeen—deliberately, she readily admitted. She knew early on that she wanted to be a mother and she was convinced there was no real reason to wait. June watched her sister go through the pregnancy, helped take care of the baby, and felt no particular aversion to the work. Indeed, her sister suddenly seemed very glamorous—all the more so when she left home to live with her boyfriend, the father of the child. Not insignificantly, June and Marta were born and raised in the Hispanic community in San Diego, and feel a strong sense of ethnic identity. In the teen pregnancy world, all that is a behavioral and demographic collision zone.

A girl whose older sister becomes a teen mother is statistically likelier to become more sexually active than other girls her age, with an average of up to four lifetime partners by the time she's fifteen, according to one study. She is also four to six times likelier to become pregnant herself before she finishes high school, though the numbers can vary widely, depending upon the particular study, the size of the sample group, and the population being investigated. In the Hispanic community—where big, intimate families are especially highly valued—a little sister of a teen mother will spend an average of more than thirteen hours per week assisting in baby care, compared to nine hours in the African American community and ten across all ethnicities. What's familiar becomes acceptable and what's acceptable gets copied. And that means that the four- to sixfold increased risk of pregnancy jumps to tenfold for little Latinas like June.

But June de la Playa didn't get pregnant. She had a vision for her future—she wanted to be a pastry chef—and that remained her plan. She is now in culinary school and has a part-time job in a retail store to support her education and pay her bills until she can begin her career. She dearly loves her sister and her little nephew, who is now three and a half, but she wants nothing to do with the kind of lives they're living—at least not yet.

"I never really believed in pregnancy without marriage," she says, "even when [Marta] got pregnant. I wasn't disappointed in her, but I didn't want that for myself. I guess it made me stick to my word even more."

June's decisions seem like simple and sensible ones, but the fact that they sound even a little bit remarkable is a measure of how challenging it can be for other girls in the same situation to follow the same path. It's not easy for any child to survive the teen years without making at least a few poor, dangerous, sometimes even life-wrecking choices. The teen brain is a heedless thing, able to process pleasure and temptation easily, but not yet capable of the subtler powers of judgment, reflection, and awareness of consequences. Those so-called executive functions reside in the frontal lobes, which develop slowly throughout the first two decades of life and are often not fully wired up until young adulthood.

Complicating things is the oddly bacterial nature of bad behavior. Sexual adventurousness, substance abuse, even petty criminality—all can seem thrilling to kids and teens, spreading readily among them like a contagion, with peers teaching peers and schoolmates influencing schoolmates far more persuasively than parents and teachers ever could. While any child can steer any other child into danger, not all kids have the same power to persuade. Close friends have more influence than distant ones; classmates are more powerful than weekend playmates. But in study after study, the most irresistible influencers of all are siblings.

Brothers and sisters—particularly older brothers and sisters—are permanent, live-in, total-immersion mentors, and that's not the case only with teen pregnancy. Younger brothers and sisters whose older siblings drink are twice as likely to pick up the habit themselves. When it comes to smoking, the risk increases fourfold. Drug use, truancy, and delinquency also increase in lockstep from brother to brother and sister to sister.

"Having an older sibling exposes you to things that firstborns simply aren't exposed to," says Susan Averett, who is a professor of economics and business at Lafayette College in Easton, Pennsylvania, and has studied birth order, behavior, and decision-making among sibs. "It is a different experience and you develop in a different way. The older sibling doesn't have to do anything particularly risky—it could be a PG-13 movie or an older sibling's friend who is smoking. Either way, you see things that you wouldn't otherwise have seen, and that doesn't go away. It becomes part of you, and in some ways your innocence gets taken away."

Sibling influence has its limits, of course, and probability isn't certainty. If it were, there would be no families that have both sober sibs and drinking sibs, smokers and nonsmokers, graduates and dropouts. If it were, June de la Playa would be pregnant by now. There are a lot of other variables at work, such as gender, age gap, family income, and education. Sibling influence can even flow both ways, with a younger brother or sister teaching bad habits to an older one. And even when sib-to-sib influence is at its most powerful, those influences needn't always be negative ones. If it's true that siblings can steer one another into danger, it's also true that they can steer one another out of it, playing a role that's not corrupting or destabilizing, but healthy, therapeutic, even wise. The question is which way any one sibling group will go— and the answers are never easy to determine.

Of all the risky behaviors siblings can share, it's the teen-pregnancy piece of the puzzle that's perhaps been the most studied. That's partly because it's a problem that's so amenable to intervention. Avoiding temptations such as tobacco and drugs is a job that takes a lifetime, since the substances are always there—though if you make it through your teen years without ever having tried them, it's much less likely that you ever will. But pregnancy is something that merely has to be delayed for a while—and for women who choose to marry young and have children early, the delay need not even be all that long.

The United States has done a good job of keeping its teen birthrate in check for the past generation. Currently, there are about 41.5 births per 1,000 girls in the fifteen-to-nineteen age group. That represents a decline of more than 20 percent in some demographic subsets from 1991 to 2005. The rate ticked up about 3 percent from 2006 to 2008, giving epidemiologists a few nervous moments, but it has resumed its downward trajectory since. The reasons for the happy trend are no secret: better public awareness, improved availability of contraception, and a general shift in the zeitgeist that has made delayed sex—if not complete premarital abstinence—a more fashionable choice among teens than it used to be.

Patricia East of the University of California, San Diego, has been a leader in the field of kids, sibs, and risk behavior, and much of her focus has gone to pregnancy, particularly in the Hispanic and African American communities, where the rate of motherhood among teens is generally higher than in the broader population. A great deal of this increased incidence is due to lower income and reduced educational opportunities, but family dynamics also play a role, and East and her colleagues set out to investigate that part of the puzzle. Tracking 127 volunteer girls over a six-year period, they focused principally on the influence of the two most powerful female figures in the girls' lives—their mothers and their older sisters. Some of the subject girls' moms had been teen mothers; some of their sisters had; in some cases the family had no history of teen pregnancy. The influence these differing backgrounds had was powerful—and unmistakable.

Girls in East's study with an older sister who had a baby as a teenager were 4.8 times—or 480 percent—likelier to become pregnant in their teen years themselves. If a girl's mother and sister had both been teen moms, the figure rose a bit higher, to 5.1, or 510 percent. But if her mother alone had had a baby in her teens and her sister had not, the younger sister's risk rose by just .2, or 20 percent—significant but not startling. The study suggested a lot of explanations for the results, some more obvious than others.

For one thing, to an adolescent daughter, what happens in a mother's teen years is long-ago history. It's something she wasn't around to witness herself, which dramatically diminishes its impact. What's more, the mere fact that it's part of her mother's biography makes it less appealing to a teen girl trying to establish her own identity. It's a general rule of adolescence that when you're looking for role models, you begin by considering what your parents did when they were your age—and you then do the opposite. What an older sister does is a different matter.

From babyhood, little sibs mimic big sibs and often keep right on doing so as they grow up. "Siblings train each other, they influence each other," says the University of Toronto's Jennifer Jenkins. "A person is fashioned from all these small things." That can sometimes be very good: When my brother Garry made the high school soccer team, it wasn't long before Bruce tried out and landed a spot as well. When I began running in student council elections, Garry and Bruce both followed suit. But it can also be very bad. Entering high school in the early 1970s, my brothers and I would have found it hard to sidestep the burgeoning drug culture—and the fact is, we didn't sidestep it. But our chemical experimentation began in perfect chronological lockstep— Steve first, followed by me, then Garry, then Bruce. We all quit the field in more or less the same sequence as well, with Steve and me growing out of the phase first, and Garry and Bruce following.

When it comes to teen pregnancy, the same kind of anti-mentoring is at work, too—all the more so because a younger sister has so much time to observe and learn. Marta de la Playa may have left home and moved in with the father of her child shortly after the birth of her baby, but few teen moms have so tidy an arrangement—because so few teen dads stick around to co-parent the child. Indeed, fully 80 percent of teen mothers continue to live at home in the first year after the birth, and 50 percent are still there after two years.

This means big changes for the little sister. The older girl is now doing very adult things—feeding, changing, and caring for a baby— while the younger girl is still expected to be occupied with school and curfews and other juvenile concerns. Regardless of age, siblings will always jostle for position in the nest just as they did when they were small, and when one child rises in station, the other will try to keep pace. "[The older sister] is given adult status and more power," East says. "She issues orders to the younger kids in the family such as 'You will help me with the child and babysit.' It changes the dynamic between siblings."

The only way for the little sister to attain the same rarefied position is to become a mother herself—and not only does it seem like an attractive possibility, it also becomes a somehow more tolerable one. Unless the teen mom was tossed out of the house when she became pregnant— something that does not happen often today—the fact that she's now a mother may seem to have been endorsed. "The older sister has opened the floodgates on what's acceptable behavior," East says.

Even in homes in which becoming a teen mother remains manifestly *un*acceptable after an older sister gives birth, other forces are at work to push the younger sister in the same direction. Studies like East's show that the arrival of the baby is often followed by a sort of golden period in which the whole family is smitten with the newborn and wants to stay home and help care for it. "Families become really close during the first six weeks," East says. "The sisters want to spend more time together and the mother and her teen mom daughter are getting along and everything is rosy." That, however, doesn't last.

In most families, a lot of the burden for child care falls on the teen mom's own mom, who is likely to have thought she'd long since gotten past the business of 2:00 a.m. feedings and dirty diapers and now finds herself back in the middle of it, even while trying to raise the rest of her own brood. That can be a dangerous place to be for the other kids in the house—particularly the adolescent girls.

"These new grandmothers start to be more distant from the younger sisters," says East. "The girls report that their mothers are less available, less supportive, and that they talk less and spend less time together than before." A more remote mother is one less able to keep track of a little sister's whereabouts—and a little sister who's out on her own is walking squarely into trouble.

Still, the fact remains that most such girls do manage to avoid that trouble. Even in the higher-risk populations East often studies, only 36 percent of younger girls follow their big sister's pregnancy path, which means that 64 percent don't. One key factor at work here is the age gap, with girls who are just a year or two younger than their big sisters generally facing a lower risk. The reason might be that the closer in age the younger girl is, the likelier it is that she'll have to help out with the loud, messy, smelly business of baby care. In some cases, at least, this can be enough to scare her straight—though during the golden period when the entire family is enchanted with the baby, it may have the opposite effect. What's more, close-in-age younger siblings are, as a rule, less in thrall of the older one than sibs who are, say, five or six years behind.

That makes emulating the older sib a little less appealing. "The similarity in age of closely spaced siblings precludes the kind of relationship from which modeling emerges," says psychologist Joseph Rodgers of the University of Oklahoma, who studies sibling dynamics.

That, surely, is an overstatement, as every parent who observes a little sib mimicking a close-in-age big sib knows. But what parents just as often observe is the familiar phenomenon of de-identification, which is as far from emulation as it's possible to get. The younger siblings take note of the traits and choices of older siblings and, just as they do when they look at their parents' past behavior, seem consciously to choose to go in an entirely different direction. If your big brother is a football star, you can certainly try to become one, too, so you can earn a share of the accolades and attention he enjoys. Or you might sidestep his world entirely, concentrating on music or art or at least a different sport, and thus receive 100 percent of the recognition for those accomplishments.

That's the same phenomenon that often emerges from the data when birth-order researchers study middle siblings, who may de-identify from a hardworking, A-student firstborn and instead become more of a slacker or drifter. In the case of such risk behaviors as pregnancy, the impact can be very different, and it can work in the younger sister's favor. One teen mother in a family is a drama; two teen moms may have a been-there-done-that quality about it. East conducted a five-year study of 227 families and found that, like June de la Playa, those girls who did not follow their older sisters into premature motherhood were more than just lucky; they were often consciously careful. "[The younger sister] purposely decides to go the other way," says East. "She decides her sister's role is teen mom and hers will be, say, high achiever."

None of this discounts the very proactive role the parents can—and often do—play in helping the younger sister avoid premature parenthood, even with the distractions of a squalling baby in the house. At the same time that more domestic attention goes to helping the teen mother and her baby, more disciplinary and academic attention may go to the younger sister, who is seen as the family's next, best hope for a child on the high-earning professional track.

"I've seen that dynamic at work when we go to a home," East says. "Sometimes the younger sister has been taken out of a co-ed public school and sent to an all-girls Catholic school. Other moms have been ingenious in how they have used the opportunity as a teaching moment for the younger siblings. One mom had the younger daughter watch both the labor and the birth. Another mother took her daughter out to get the Norplant patch the very day she found out the older daughter was pregnant."

Whatever methods the mothers use, they can work remarkably well. In one study of families with multiple risks of teen pregnancy, up to 80 percent of younger girls whose mothers did not monitor them closely followed their older sisters into teen motherhood. Among families in which parents cracked down, the figure was cut nearly in half, to 42 percent.

Too often overlooked in the teen-pregnancy question is the role not of mothers and sisters but of fathers and brothers. Fathers, of course, have an enormous impact on the emotional and social development of their children, but to the extent that they exacerbate the problem of teen pregnancy, it's often through their absence. More than 20 million American children—or 25 percent of all kids eighteen and younger—live in a home with only one parent, and 80 percent of those homes are headed by the mother. A single working mother has less time to supervise her children and less money for child-care assistance that could pick up the slack—which too often makes the kids de facto free agents.

Even noncustodial fathers can still play a vital role in their children's lives if they choose. A dad who lives nearby, sees his kids regularly, is always available by phone or e-mail, and backs up the mother in matters of discipline can be nearly as effective as one who lives at home. But even this happens far too rarely—as the 50 percent fall-off in paternal visitation in the first year after a divorce shows. That neglect often grows worse when the father remarries, and worse still if he has more children with his new wife. In those cases he may drop out of his original children's lives entirely.

Brothers, of course, have less responsibility to their sisters than fathers do—and they generally act on that freedom. The Hispanic community, with the highest level of little-sister participation in helping care for a baby niece or nephew, at thirteen hours per week, also has the lowest level of little-brother participation—at just seven hours. Boys in other ethnic groups do a little bit better, but not much. Across all ethnicities, brothers who have suddenly become uncles to their sister's baby tend to put in only the hours that are absolutely required of them and leave the rest to the women and girls in the house. To the credit of the brothers, having a sister who is a teen mother does not seem to make early pregnancy look more acceptable, and indeed it may make it look less so. In another study of a different mix of high-risk kids, East and a colleague found that nearly 15 percent of little sisters followed their big sisters into teen pregnancy, while precisely 0 percent of brothers fathered children while they were still in school. The boys may not do much to pitch in when a sister has a baby, but they don't complicate things further and produce one of their own.

If pregnancy were the only risk behavior siblings pass around like seasonal flu, parents' lives would be much easier than they are. But the same dynamics that drive imitative childbearing are also behind shared problems such as alcohol, tobacco, and drug use. Actually, in those areas, the behaviors among siblings are even more contagious, because both genders may be equally affected by them and, more so than in pregnancy, the influence runs from younger to older almost as easily as it does from older to younger. Of all the substances kids can abuse, tobacco is the toughest to regulate. It's both a legal product and, while its sale to minors is prohibited, the law is still widely flouted. That's a dangerous convergence of appetite and availability.

The fourfold increase in risk that younger brothers and sisters face when an older sibling smokes is a stubborn problem that endures even as the overall rate of smoking in the United States has plunged to a historic low of less than 20 percent, according to a vast sampling of 11,406 kids and young adults from age fourteen to twenty-two called the National Longitudinal Survey of Youth. A study conducted later in Australia produced the same findings, with 40 percent of kids whose older sibs smoke taking up the habit themselves, compared with 10 percent of those with nonsmoking sibs. Not only do the younger brothers and sisters follow older ones into tobacco use, they start younger, too, often lighting up shortly after the first time they see a big sib with a cigarette. In my family, in which all four boys were smokers at one point or another, this was precisely the pattern. Steve, who would sweep in for visits from prep school, having picked up who-knew-what adult habit this time, began smoking when he was seventeen. I started at sixteen, Garry was just fifteen, and Bruce drew his first lungful when he was only fourteen years old. (Quitting cigarettes was not as clean and sequential for us as quitting recreational drugs was. Garry and I have been smoke-free for many years; Steve and Bruce still struggle.)

In our case, the proximity in age was an aggravating factor, as it is with most smoking siblings. Siblings who are close in age are likelier to move in commingled social circles, in which older kids will provide contraband to younger ones. "It's difficult to imagine a twelve-year-old boy still in middle school sharing a mutual eighteen-year-old friend with his high school brother," says Rodgers. "However, if the brothers are separated by only one year in high school, this seems plausible, even likely."

That simple variable of availability is also the reason smoking moves up the sibling age ladder almost as readily as it moves down. Our family proved this rule, too: Garry—nearly seventeen months younger than me—was the first of the three junior brothers to follow Steve's smoking example. The more cigarettes he, at age fifteen, sneaked into the house, the more I, at age sixteen, was tempted to try them, until finally I succumbed.

Gender differences turn up as well. Tobacco use spreads faster from brother to brother and sister to sister than it does across the brother-sister boundary. This, again, is partly because the social circles of opposite-sex sibs are less likely to cross. But even within same-sex circles, the risk is not equivalent. Despite the historically higher incidence of tobacco use among males, brothers are a little less likely to influence one another to smoke than sisters are. Rodgers believes this is probably the result of the greater openness girls exhibit among themselves, which can be a very good thing when it comes to sharing feelings, fears, or confidences, but a very bad one when it comes to sharing cigarettes.

Drugs and alcohol follow a nearly identical contagion pattern, though the spread is a little bit slower and a little less reliable. More limited availability certainly explains part of that difference. So, too, does the fact that drugs and alcohol can be deadly in the short term, unlike tobacco, which can take decades to kill. Parents are thus more apt to watch for those substances more closely and to punish their use more aggressively, and kids themselves may fear drugs and drinking more. When one drug-using sibling does induce another to start, it may even take active encouragement—or at least endorsement.

Psychologist Elizabeth Stormshak of the University of Oregon conducted a study in which she recruited teen and adolescent siblings and instructed them to role-play on videotape. They were told to pretend they were planning a party, that some kids might be bringing drugs or alcohol, and that they should discuss whether that was appropriate or not. Predictably, when a scientist is watching and a video camera is rolling, nearly all of the subjects began by saying that, no, it was not all right and, no, they themselves certainly wouldn't try drugs, no matter what. But those first answers were not what Stormshak was looking for—and they didn't always remain the answers anyway. Sometimes the older siblings would waffle a bit—coming around to the possibility that experimenting with a substance might be all right if other kids were doing it and if they tried it only once. That quickly became the younger siblings' position, too. If the older sib remained adamantly opposed to drugs and alcohol throughout the role play, the younger kids did as well. How well the kids got along played a role, too. "When siblings are very close," Stormshak says, "that relationship becomes more powerful and meaningful and can enhance risk behavior as well."

Kids who steer their siblings into drug use are, at least nominally, steering them into criminality as well, since the substances themselves are illegal. The crimes, however, are essentially without victims—apart from the kids themselves—and the penalties, while enforced, are often not done so aggressively. But other kinds of criminal behavior—theft, assault, and drug dealing, as opposed to personal use—are nastier matters. Psychologists and sociologists closely study the phenomenon they call "delinquency training," particularly in low-income families, in which rates of criminality are the highest. A lot of the expected findings have turned up in their work. Brothers pass criminality back and forth more readily than sisters do, but girls are not immune. Opportunity and exposure are powerful variables, with younger siblings likelier to get into trouble with the law if they spend time with an older brother who has already crossed that line, or who is part of a social circle whose other members have. Some studies have also shown that brothers who have a shared history of physical violence—fighting with each other in ways that go beyond the routine blows all brothers and sisters exchange—will become accustomed to resolving conflicts as aggressively, and this will contribute to violence outside the home as well.

I got into very few physical fights with friends or other peers when I was growing up, mostly because I didn't like it and was terrible at it anyway. One of the few fights I did experience was a grueling, seemingly endless bout at summer camp with Seth Ansen (not his real name). Seth was a year younger than I was, and a bit shorter, but he was a solid plug of muscle who seemed utterly unafraid of fighting and was very, very good at it. While I used my height and reach to stay in the fight, I had no illusions about which of us was going to take the worse pounding. It was perhaps no coincidence that Seth's older brother, who attended camp as well, was also tough, combative, and something of a bully—and often scared the daylights out of me. I have no way of knowing how the two brothers worked out their differences at home, but having been on the receiving end of aggression from both of them, I found it hard to imagine they believed in negotiated settlements.

All this may have made the Ansen brothers alpha males at camp, but domestically learned violence is a much less positive commodity in adult life. A University of Florida study explored how a history of sibling physical combat also expresses itself in one of the uglier forms of social criminality: abuse or battering in dating situations (something I have no reason to believe the Ansen boys engaged in). The investigators surveyed 538 male and female college students and asked whether they had been pushed, shoved, or otherwise abused by a sibling when they were young. Three-quarters said they had been pushed or had done the pushing themselves, which actually seems low, given how commonplace sibling brawling can be. But 27 percent said that they'd been shoved against a wall by a sibling, or done the shoving themselves. An alarming 6 percent of both sexes admitted that they'd brandished a lethal weapon such as a knife at a brother or sister.

In all cases, the greater the level of sib-on-sib violence in childhood, the greater the likelihood that the same siblings would behave violently toward dates upon reaching young adulthood. Surprisingly, the rate of physical aggression was actually higher among women than it was among men, though they were more inclined to use less dangerous forms of violence, such as slapping or hitting, while the men were more inclined to punch or choke. The survey did not look at sexual assault, which is, of course, an overwhelmingly male crime. No matter the form the aggression takes, the researchers concluded that its seeds are planted early in life, and that if parents don't intervene before kids reach adolescence, it may be too late.

"After older siblings reach fourteen, they tend to gravitate to their peer group and spend less time with their brothers and sisters," said professor of health science education Virginia Noland, who conducted the study. "By that time, they've practiced these behaviors, they've per-fected them, and now they can use them quite well."

Not all sibling relationships are so troubled, of course, and far from leading little brothers and sisters into trouble, many older sibs consciously—even aggressively—steer them away from it. This may be especially so in the case of substance abuse, particularly among families living in communities where the dangers of drugs are especially pro-nounced. Frederick Gibbons, a professor of psychology at Iowa State University, tracked 900 African American families in Iowa and Georgia from 1997 to 2006, using questionnaires and observation to study the proactive role non-drug-using older siblings sometimes played in keep-ing younger members of the brood clean, and found that when the sibs do take such initiative, they can do a remarkable amount of good.

"The younger siblings won't necessarily drop friends who are using drugs," Gibbons says, "but their own use is greatly affected by whether their older sibling has a negative attitude about drugs. There is a kind of 'just say no' effect going on if it comes from the older sibling." Parents play a role here, too, of course, but what struck Gibbons is that it's often a secondary one. "Between the two—parents and siblings—the siblings' role is often the more influential one."

Such intervention can help even in the case of two problems not usu-ally included in the risk-behavior category: anorexia and self-mutilation. These conditions are heavily skewed by demographics, and tend more often to hit at the higher end of the income spectrum, and overwhelm-ingly to affect girls.

Both conditions have multiple roots, and numerous studies suggest that genes play a powerful role. Anorexia in particular also originates in self-esteem issues, some of which are triggered by growing up in a competitive family in which the afflicted girl feels she suffers by comparison to another sibling—usually a sister, and usually an older one. In this case, that big sister, while hardly to blame for the problem, can participate in its solution. In one particularly dramatic case documented by Walter Vandereycken, a Belgian psychologist, a big sister who was living away from home agreed to return for a short period and, in a sense, switch roles with her little sister, becoming a sort of willing dependent again. The older sister even went so far as to allow her mother to do her laundry for her while the little sister was now expected to do her own. Improbably, the anorexia, which had been intractable up to this point, at last began to respond to treatment. Laundry, living at home, and self-starvation ought not to have a lot to do with one another, but when the disorder arose in part from a lack of confidence or sense of autonomy, a little comparative independence can—and did—help.

Vandereycken found similarly encouraging results in a case in which the youngest of seven girls began self-mutilating, and one of her bigger sisters became involved in her therapy. The girls began to open up about some of the shared traumas in their childhood they had never discussed before, including beatings their mother had administered to all of them. In discussing the once-forbidden memories, they were able to strip them of their power. For the self-cutting sister, that proved enormously therapeutic.

"Talking for the first time in their lives about these events—feeling mutual recognition, warmth, sorrow, and pain—the sisters were able to free themselves from some traumas," wrote European psychologists Judith Dunn and Frits Boer, who also studied the case. "From that day on, [the] patient stopped mutilation."

The curative power of the sibling bond is by no means limited to such specialized cases, and sibs are increasingly being seen as an important adjunct to family therapy—or, in some cases, the central figures in that therapy. Jim Snyder of Wichita State University refers to the role of siblings in such situations as "another crowbar we can put in the crack."

That's as fair an image as any—but it also suggests a certain bluntness that captures only part of the sibling dynamic. Brothers and sisters may be good at cracking open one another's defenses and denials, muscling a wayward member of the brood into better, healthier behavior—and sometimes that's precisely the thing that's needed. But they're also good at the subtler business of gently picking one another's locks, feeling how the emotional tumblers fall, and opening a sibling up in a way no professional, or even parent, ever could. There are two parts to the idea of tough love, and well-bonded sibs can practice them both.

NINE

Running the Asylum

When Siblings Raise Siblings

L ike all of the other seniors in my high school, I was very much looking forward to graduation day. But, like all of the other seniors, I
also maintained a studied nonchalance about it. The natural cynicism of the eighteen-year-old was exceeded only by the fashionable
cynicism of the early 1970s, so we all professed not to be terribly excited
about an afternoon of ceremonial silliness that was being staged more
for our parents than for any of us. But the truth was we were very
excited—and the fact that family would be there to watch us graduate
was part of the thrill. That's what made the day particularly hard for me,
since, unlike the parents of the other 400 students in my class, mine
would be nowhere in sight.

My father had not been a regular part of the family for a decade,
though we still occasionally spoke to him on the phone and my brothers
and I visited him once a year or so. He had attended Steve's prep school
graduation in Tarrytown, New York, two years earlier, but I had no
expectation that he'd make the trip from New York to Baltimore for

mine—and I don't remember if I even bothered to ask. My mother was a different matter. I think she had planned to attend, and I suspect she would have if she'd been able to. But three days before graduation, my brothers and I had her involuntarily committed.

Technically, the commitment wasn't entirely involuntary. She signed herself into the psychiatric hospital to which we had sent her and she could have signed herself out if she'd wanted to. But the way the arrangement was sprung on her—first thing in the morning, with the family doctor and two ambulance attendants present—made it unlikely she'd resist. Plus, I suspect that at some deeper, lucid level, she knew she had to go.

For nearly all of my mother's adult life she'd had a taste for prescription pharmaceuticals. She didn't smoke cigarettes in an era in which it seemed that everyone did, and she rarely drank—something that also set her apart at a time when even pregnant women would indulge without a thought. But the clean, pure, non-caloric high of a drug was something else, and she learned its pleasures early. With four small children in the house, she never had to worry about having access to one substance or another. Somebody always had a cold or a croup, and back then cough medicine wasn't cough medicine unless it included a healthy slug of codeine. A household with so many kids could plausibly go through a lot of the stuff in the course of a year, and doctors wrote prescriptions practically on demand.

For a while I saw no sign of my mother's medicinal tippling, though things changed when she switched from cough syrup to pills. One evening during her abbreviated second marriage, I overheard her and her husband talking conspiratorially about how they were beginning to "smell airplane glue." They were smiling as they said it and seemed quite pleased with themselves. I pressed her on it and she told me they had both taken a pill of some kind, and as it began to dissolve it gave off a smell that rose back up into the throat and nose. It was just medicine and not something I was supposed to worry about.

The pill, I would later learn, was a sedative called Placidyl. It was a burgundy-colored, 500-milligram capsule that was legally prescribed by doctors, but also sold on the street as "jelly bellies." Placidyl packed a hypnotic wallop and could hit like a hammer to the head if you weren't used to it. A double dose could knock you flat and keep you that way for a long time. Since the drug was wildly addictive, multiple dosing was common.

My mother's second marriage lasted only fifteen months, but Placidyl became a commitment of much longer standing. Like all addicts, she did not take long to go from merely enjoying the drug to requiring it, and she became very good at the doctor shopping, pharmacy hopping, lies, and concealment needed to support the habit. My brothers and I couldn't always tell when she was drugged, and to the degree that we could, we explained it away. *She's tired. She's emotional. She's been divorced twice and is raising us all by herself.* There's a lot of power in those self-told fibs. I believed them as her voice got increasingly slurry and her gait became increasingly wobbly. I believed them when I'd get letters at camp written at a sloping angle in a drunkard's hand. I believed them when I'd come home from camp and her face would be a mass of bruises and cuts and she'd explain that she was simply unloading the dishwasher and bumped herself on an open cabinet door as she stood up. I'd believe her even as she would take to her bed for the evening with a little row of Placidyl neatly arranged on her night table. *They're just there if she needs them,* I'd say to myself. *She'll put them away in the morning.*

After a while, however, such denial became impossible. By the time I got to high school, our mother's day-night schedule had flipped all but entirely. She'd be up until three or four in the morning, stay in bed until one in the afternoon, and spend those daylight hours mostly drifting on the couch until the sun went down and the pills came out. Dinnertimes became sad, absurdly early 5:00 p.m. affairs, consisting mostly of deli sandwiches or Italian takeout—the better to get the household duties done and let the evening begin. My brothers and I kept ourselves on a normal school and bedtime schedule, but in the middle of the night we would often be awakened by a loud thud somewhere in the house. We'd get up to see all of the lights on and our mother's door open, but she was nowhere to be seen. We'd then begin the search for the spot she'd fallen this time, never knowing what we'd find.

Steve was away at prep school by then and Garry, Bruce, and I would handle those nighttime crises in ways entirely keeping with our developing personalities. Bruce, still our mother's most adored princeling, would hover and hand-wring and sometimes scream, doing the true—often literal—heavy lifting of getting her back to bed. I would toss about a lot of ineffectual instructions, ordering Bruce to calm down, Garry to help out, and our mother to "get in bed this very second." Garry wanted no part of the entire drama and his crossed arms and disgusted silence showed it. One night in the middle of an episode, he stalked back to our mother's bedroom, grabbed one of her pillows, and returned with it, then lifted her head and shoved the pillow beneath it. "Let her sleep there!" he barked, before striding back to his room and slamming the door.

Our mother, of course, was almost certain to die if she kept this up, and at one level or other we all knew that. There would be a car accident or a fall down the steps or simply a thud in the night from which she wouldn't awaken. And even if such a terrible end never came to pass, my brothers and I could no longer take the situation as it was.

Not long before my graduation, Garry, Bruce, and I called Steve and explained how serious things had become. He then called our family doctor. I don't know what I imagined the doctor would say, but I suppose I thought he'd promise to talk to our mother, take the pills away, and fix the problem. That was not what he said. What he said was that she was indeed in grave danger, that she'd have to go somewhere she could be taken care of, and that it would have to happen immediately—the next day, if possible. Steve agreed, called us back, and explained what was happening. He said he was on his way to Baltimore as fast as possible and, no matter what, would be there by morning. There was a bat-signal quality to the call we had made to him—and a Batman quality to the way he responded to it.

Steve arrived early the next morning as promised and we all gathered in the doctor's office along with our grandparents, who would have to sign any papers and pay any bills, since the four of us were minors. Shortly afterward, my brothers and I returned to our house, followed by the doctor and then by an ambulance. The attendants waited in the driveway while the doctor went into our mother's room, woke her up, and spoke to her. Again, we all assumed the jobs that seemed most in keeping with our temperaments. Bruce was dispatched to our grandparents' home—ostensibly to help keep them calm but more to keep him safe from the storm that was sure to break. Our mother, as we feared, went wild, screaming at the doctor, lashing out at us, threatening to grab her car keys, dash out of the house, and kill herself behind the wheel. Garry played tough, going outside and blocking her car with ours. Steve and I watched out for Garry, talked with the doctor, and fetched the ambulance attendants when it was time for them. Steve alone helped get our mother packed.

By early afternoon, it was over. Our mother was installed in a local facility under medical supervision as she began the process of detoxing from a ten-year drug addiction. No one could say how long she'd be there. We followed the ambulance over to the hospital to help sign her in. At some point after we were finished, our grandparents gave us some money for basic needs; we'd have all we needed, we were assured. They then went back to their home and we went back to ours. That night, the four of us bought some food and had some dinner and went out to a movie that none of us really watched. The next morning, Steve had to go back to New York. Garry and Bruce and I were left alone in the house. For the previous few years, the three of us had more and more been raising one another. Soon, I'd be going to college, but Bruce and Garry, just fifteen and sixteen, needed some rearing still. We had absolutely no idea what we were expected to do next.

Brothers and sisters have played a role in parenting one another for as long as multiple-sibling families have existed. The behavior starts early and happens universally: A kindergartner helps a toddler hold a spoon, a second-grader explains a game to a first-grader, an older sister minds a little brother while Mom takes a quick shower, or scolds him when he gets into a cabinet or drawer that is supposed to be off-limits.

The lines of power are typically vertical—with the bigger sibs wielding authority over the littler ones—but often they can be multidirectional, too. A middle sister fed up with a shouting match beween an older and younger brother may take them both in hand and settle them down. A fearless younger brother who thinks nothing of climbing a tree or diving off a high board may encourage a more timid older brother—and applaud him if he gives it a try. All that is part of the natural arc of siblings growing up together, and it continues into their teen years, when the same sister may crack down on her brother about getting his homework done, or the same brother may challenge his sister about what she's doing dating that slacker from her homeroom, anyway. Some of this is just pose or play, much of it isn't, but it's all a very real form of impromptu parenting.

Sibs step in to act as allomothers and allofathers to one another in all human cultures. But as indicated in the studies conducted by UCLA's Tom Weisner in Kenya, Polynesia, and elsewhere, in some places that tradition has remained a much deeper part of the culture than in others. It's the agrarian history of those lands that has usually made the difference. Farming and the related trades require big families, with all adult hands laboring in the fields, barns, or pastures while those who are too young for work look after one another—perhaps in the company of an adult who is now too old to plant or weed.

"Among the kids in families in these parts of the world, sibling care is seen as an important part of childhood," says Weisner. "It allows them to learn about child care as part of a system, a household, and a community, rather than just as an exchange between two siblings or a parent and child. The goal is that by the time you have children of your own, you know most of what you have to do. The American middle-class model is a very different one. It just does not put many responsibilities on siblings."

That's the case in most parts of America, anyway, but there are places in which the agricultural tradition and the benefits of sibling co-parenting are still being felt—and Hawaii is one of the most revealing. The native family practices of all of the Pacific islands emerged over the course of many, many generations, but those in Hawaii came under particular siege throughout much of the twentieth century as mainlanders from the United States flooded west to colonize the archipelago—a cultural swamping that only accelerated after statehood became official in 1959.

Schools, businesses, and other forms of civic infrastructure were set up with the American and European systems in mind. Classroom schedules in particular were designed to accommodate those traditions, giving little consideration to students who might also be working at home as caregivers and quasi-parents.

One of Weisner's studies tried to look at how this arrangement has affected the academic performance of native Hawaiian children compared to those descended from settlers from the mainland, and it produced some surprising results. Not only did the native kids not suffer from being pressed into service at home while also maintaining a full school schedule, they actually seemed to thrive as a result of it. Part of the benefit came from the way the brothers and sisters would play together. Nearly all play children engage in is good play, because it's all built around the idea of learning and rehearsing for adulthood. In one Hawaiian household after another, however, one of the most popular games the kids would invent was make-believe school—with the big children pretending to be teachers and the little ones students.

The game may have been merely fun, but the particular form of rehearsal it involved was especially valuable, because it kept the older brothers' and sisters' minds limber and also acclimated the younger ones to what learning in a structured, Westernized environment was all about. What's more, older and younger kids alike used the opportunity to practice a skill that too often separates native communities from an increasingly dominant settler community: language. Big brothers and sisters attending schools in which lessons were taught in standard English often came from homes in which native languages or a native-English mishmash were spoken. What they learned in class they carried home, and what they carried home they shared with their little brothers and sisters—particularly during their pretend classroom sessions.

"The native Hawaiian moms who encouraged sibling care often spoke pidgin English themselves, while the older kids were learning standard English in school," Weisner says. "In these families, the language stimulation among the siblings increased, and soon was better than the language stimulation between the mother and child. The way all the kids spoke became more similar to school language."

The learning that goes on among co-parenting siblings may yield deeper benefits than merely improving their academic performance or helping kids become better parents one day. It can also teach them primal lessons about some of the most highly valued human attributes: empathy, generosity, and even selflessness. Small children in all cultures are narcissists by nature, and why not? They know what their needs are and they know they want them to be met—and for the first year or so of their lives, that's pretty much how things go. It comes as a cruel shock when adults start saying "no," or "maybe later," or "only if you behave."

Children do slowly come to understand patience and limits and delayed gratification, but the Western model of heaping all of the caretaking work on parents, teachers, and babysitters—freeing the kids from any meaningful responsibilities for the other people in the home—does little to hasten the maturation. When bigger sibs are instead given occasional child-care responsibilities themselves, they learn what it's like to be the one who sometimes has to say no—and then to deal with the tears or tantrums that follow from a younger sib. That, Weisner says, kick-starts the kids' understanding of such higher-order attributes as empathy, patience, and communication, valuable skills for forming later relationships outside the home.

"Shared responsibility for child rearing does tend to get generalized to other situations," he says. "If you are expected to be nurturing and understanding of the needs of others—which is the definition of empathy—you're more likely to apply that ability to other relationships with other people that don't call for caretaking or direct care."

If the majority of Americans—or at least those outside of Hawaii— have not yet caught on to the distributed-care, it-takes-a-village model of child rearing, it's not to say we're a wholly lost cause. Studies of blended families do show how some older children of one parent will enthusiastically pitch in to help care for the younger children of that parent's new spouse—as celebrity Pia Lindstrom did when her film- icon mom remarried—a form of alloparenting that's good for the kids and the family as a whole, as it helps knit the two halves of the brood together more firmly. And in all families, blended and otherwise, girls do show at least a greater willingness than boys—by roughly a three- to-one margin—to step forward and help out with child care when needed. But boys generally score so low that three times close to nothing is still not very much.

If there is hope for the United States—and there is—it begins in the more recent immigrant communities. Chinese American families have generally outperformed those of European descent in embracing the distributed-care model, and the brothers and sisters in those broods typically reap all of the developmental dividends that turn up in Weis- ner's studies. Indeed, they have benefited in other, previously unob- served ways. A 2009 University of San Francisco study of 218 Chinese American adolescents found that fourteen-year-olds who help care for siblings or elderly relatives not only become more empathic and less selfish but also develop lower levels of depression later in their teen years than kids who are given no such responsibilities.

It's impossible to tease out all of the variables that could be at play here—not the least being that fourteen-year-olds who were willing to get with the family-care program might simply have been happier, better-balanced kids to begin with and would have remained that way later no matter what. But while that may account for part of the finding, the researchers believe that the rest comes the deeper sense of kinship that results from caring for other family members. That fosters a greater feeling of safety and belonging—and that, in turn, can be a powerful inoculum against depression.

African American communities similarly show greater sibling fealty than European American ones, and, according to many studies, are like- lier to exhibit an orientation sociologists call "going for kin," placing family first and cleaving tightly together, particularly in times of hard- ship. Frederick Gibbons's study of the proactive role African American brothers and sisters often play in keeping their little sibs away from drugs was a good example of this phenomenon in action and an illus- tration of how both parties—the one offering the guidance and the one receiving it—can benefit from the dynamic.

Still, among all of America's multiple ethnicities, it is Latinos— particularly Mexicans—who blow the doors off nearly all other groups. And it is the mothers who are mostly responsible. American parents think they know a thing or two about raising kids with a healthy dose of tough love, but nothing touches a Mexican mom—something I see in my home every day. My wife did not move from Mexico City to the United States until she went to college, and the sensibility of our house- hold is often more south of the border than north. Our grade-school daughters can be stubborn, strong-willed, and maddeningly rebellious, and while I often approach their acting out with a talk-about-your- feelings tolerance, my wife takes a far harder, far less flexible line. There are behaviors that are acceptable and those that are not, and there is a bright line between them. The feelings that led to a crossing of that line don't matter much in the discipline that follows. Table manners and a tidy appearance are things all parents try to teach their kids, but for many Mexican moms they're more than just goals, they're preconditions for participation in civil society. Mind your manners or leave the table; comb your hair again—properly this time—or you don't leave the house.

Such a fundamental difference in parenting philosophy predictably leads to disagreements between us, and I do have a fair body of sociological science on my side. But so does my wife. In 2010, a collaborative team of researchers at the University of California, Berkeley, and Duke University released a study of twenty-four first- or second-generation Mexican American mothers as they interacted—and often struggled—with their four-year-old children. Repeatedly, the authors found, the mothers relied on two key principles to keep the kids in line: *familismo* (a sense of responsibility to family) and *respeto* (respect for parental authority). Compared to American mothers, who often practice what the researchers call lateral reasoning—equal parts persuasion, explanation, and discipline—Mexican moms are more inclined to go straight for the rule book and tell the kids what's expected of them. In the 1,477 "compliance attempts" the researchers observed the mothers making with their kids over the course of the study, the hard-line approach worked, rarely requiring a maternal scolding or a raised voice. The title of the paper, published in the journal *Developmental Authority*, was "Commands, Competence, and *Cariño*: Maternal Socialization Practices in Mexican American Families." *Cariño*, which means warmth and affection, is the love part of the tough-love pairing.

Such a take-no-prisoners parenting style may not always be fun for the kids but, done right, it can lead to twin benefits: better behavior in the short run, and a deep sense of family responsibility and loyalty in the long run. This builds very strong ties among all of the members of a household—particularly the siblings. In the same way Mexican American girls surpass other girls in lavishing attention on the baby of an older sister, so, too, are all siblings in that community more inclined to devote themselves to one another, spending an average of 17.2 hours per week engaged in shared activities, according to one 2005 study. That easily beats the average of 12 hours they spend with parents, teachers, and any other adult. More important, it dramatically exceeds the amount of time sibs spend in shared activities in European American families— just 10 hours in a similar seven-day stretch. Mexican American and other Latina sisters tend to be closer with all their siblings than brothers are, but both genders beat those of other ethnicities.

"The Latino kids generally rated their relationships with their siblings as very close," says Arizona State University's Kimberly Updegraff, who gathered the 2005 data in a survey of families in the Southwest. "They have cultural values that highlight the importance of family support and loyalty." And, as in the African American community, it's during times of hardship that that support and loyalty are especially tested—as Davianka Lopez, a twenty-year-old resident of Southern California, learned.

Lopez is the youngest in her family—the baby sister of four older brothers ranging in age from twenty-four to thirty-three. Her parents divorced when she was small and she grew up largely without the influence of a father. From the moment the split occurred, her mother made it clear to the entire brood that many of the absent dad's responsibilities would now fall to the bigger brothers, especially the oldest, Merlyn. "My mom made sure my older brother knew that anything he did would have an impact on the younger ones," Davianka says. "She raised us to be close and expected them to be role models to the younger kids, especially me."

Merlyn embraced that role more enthusiastically than anyone might have expected. When the three older boys had grown up and left home, their mother moved what remained of the family—just Davianka, then twelve, and her brother Angel, sixteen—to Miami. The move made financial sense, but both kids were miserable there, and Davianka suspected there might be a way she and Angel wouldn't have to stay.

"I told Merlyn how unhappy we were," she says, "and he told my mother that he would take care of Angel and me because he was married and he already had kids of his own anyway. He knew I was so unhappy and not doing well in school. My mom said it was the hardest thing she ever had to do but she let us move back to California to live with him." Davianka spent the remainder of her childhood under the care of her brother, not just as a little sister, but as a de facto daughter, being fed and clothed and, for practical purposes, raised by a loving older sibling.

Such a complete assumption of a parenting role is rare for even the most devoted siblings, but the all-for-one impulse that emerges when a Latino family is in distress can nonetheless be remarkable. Patricia East's studies, for example, have looked at a range of Latino broods and come up with another unexpected finding: The sibling groups with the closest ties are often the ones being raised by a single parent. As a stand-alone data point, that's a real stunner. The absence of one parent from the household does not have to cause a family to fall apart, but it usually doesn't do it any favors, either. Among the Latinos in East's surveys, however, it sometimes did, actually improving the bonds among the members of the household who were left—probably because the very hardship the kids were all facing gave rise to an in-this-together intimacy that otherwise might not have occurred.

Divorce is not the only emergency that draws families closer this way, and Latinos are hardly the only people who can show grace in rising to such a challenge. Wayne Duvall, fifty-three, a film and television actor, experienced such a coming together when he was only thirteen and his father died suddenly of a heart attack. In some ways, death, though more traumatic than divorce, can also be a cleaner and less complicated way to lose a parent. With a permanent void where a caregiver once was—as opposed to an intermittent one that is sometimes filled by visits, phone calls, and shared custody—the need for a surrogate to step in is more acute and the willingness of younger brothers and sisters to accept the authority of an older sibling is greater.

"I was spoiled by my parents—mostly by my father," Duvall says. "When it came to chores, I could manipulate my father by saying I was tired. He would respond, 'That's okay, boy. Your brothers can handle it.' After my father died and some time had passed, a day came that I was faced with some chores. I vividly remember one of my brothers leaning down to me and saying, 'The party's over.'" That was a cold slap for a pampered child, and Duvall resisted the new order for a time. Eventually, however—fatherless but certainly not brotherless—he tumbled comfortably into it. "My brothers became my parental figures and always looked out for me after that," he says. "In some ways they still do. Even now, so many years later, they remain my best friends."

In Duvall's household, as well as in Davianka Lopez's, the lines of authority followed the siblings' ages, and that's the way things usually go after a parent is lost—but not always. In some homes, the substitute parent and chief sibling caregiver may be the so-called functional firstborn, a second- or even later-born child who takes over if the eldest is unable to assume command or for some other reason resigns the post. Gender often determines which sibling occupies this pro tem position.

In patriarchal cultures—which in too many ways continues to describe our own—a firstborn daughter may still have to give way to a second-born son in matters such as education, inheritance, or assuming control of the family business. But in matters of sibling co-parenting, the role switching is just as likely to run the other way, with a second-born sister taking the firmest hand and the rest of the brood—even a firstborn son—falling into line and accepting her domestic authority.

Power will similarly devolve to the second-born when the oldest doesn't live in the home or is simply disinclined or temperamentally unable to discharge the powers of office. All of those factors were at work in my household during our mother's growing disability. Steve had always had something of a broad, theatrical temperament, given to sweeps of mood that took him from high energy to low gloom, some-times without any calm and grounded stops in between. The back-and-forthing he went through as a child, feeling simultaneously claimed and banished by both parents, did nothing to help stabilize his gyros. There may have been no one better at parachuting in and helping out in a period of crisis. Indeed, that played nicely to Steve's self-confessed love of an entrance—which served us well on the day we institutionalized our mother. But when the ambulance had pulled away and a sort of exhausted quiet was restored, he had all he could do seeing to himself. Returning to his life as a near adult in New York was the best thing for him.

After he was gone, I was left with my little brothers and a conditional authority over them—and not a whole lot more. I did have control of my mother's checkbook—in a quaint era in which I could simply sign my name on the signature line, put the word *son* in parentheses, and explain myself when I went to the bank to cash the check for groceries or other necessities—and that helped. We maintained something of a self-enforced curfew and we did try to keep the house as picked up and neat as we could manage. Our father did not, as I recall, offer to come to Baltimore or have us up to New York, but he did offer support and sympathy of a kind. He also provided perhaps the only laugh in the whole dismal chapter. When we called to tell him what had happened—that our mother's behavior had gotten out of hand and we had made arrangements to have her taken away—he let a moment pass in surprised silence. Then he muttered, "I guess I'd better watch my step." Sometimes, in his dark way, he was not hard to like.

Sibling co-parenting is by no means always natural, nurturing, and without complications. Indeed, in some cases, families can make a complete hash of it, a problem most commonly seen after the parents divorce or one of them is widowed. A newly single mother or father is understandably bereft of company. Even in a failing marriage, it's still nice to have someone with whom to share the responsibility of child rearing. While unhappy partners often spend more time stewing in silence or openly warring than they do actually talking to each other, the lines of communication usually remain open for any conversation concerning the kids. All that vanishes when the partner does—and that makes it very tempting for the remaining parent to turn to the oldest child instead. If the firstborn is going to be pitching in with the childcare duties, shouldn't that work sometimes include participating in the parental powwows that the adult heads of the household used to practice? No—and for a lot of reasons.

When a parent is missing, younger brothers and sisters may accept the new authority of older ones, but they still want to see them as siblings—a relationship that will continue long after childhood is over. A parent who elevates a firstborn too far out of the sibling ranks disrupts the balance of the sib-sib bonds in a way that may never be fully rebalanced. What's more, it can also have an impact on the security and self-esteem of the kids who don't become the parent's confidant. Competition for Mom's or Dad's attention will become all the more intense when Mom or Dad is the only parent left in the house. The last thing that that parent wants to do now is get sloppy about how evenly care and love are distributed. "Those children who are not the confidant start to question why they're being left out," says Katherine Conger, of the University of California, Davis. "They ask, 'Why is Mom spending so much time with my sister or brother and not me?'" The answer—because you're not the oldest—is obvious, but it does nothing to ease the anxiety or reduce the tension that is mounting among the kids.

In some families, the problem starts to develop even while the parents are still together. Warren Beatty and Shirley MacLaine are celebrated for their movies but also recognized as Hollywood's most venerable brother-sister pair. They have had their unavoidable rivalries and differences, but across the arc of their multidecade careers, they've remained close. Wrote Suzanne Finstad in her 2005 Beatty biography *Warren Beatty: A Private Man*: "Shirley was Warren's best and most imaginative friend. 'I know it seems unbelievable,' MacLaine said later, 'but we played together all the time.'" Beatty, in turn, made no secret of his admiration for his big sister, once referring to her as his "first crush."

Their upbringing did not make that closeness easy. The two were raised in Arlington, Virginia, with a hard-drinking father and a too-compliant mother who often simply cleaned up after her husband. Shirley was the older of the two children by three years, and by the time she was thirteen, her mother, Kathlyn, had already begun taking her clumsily into her confidence.

"As a daughter," wrote Finstad, "[MacLaine was] privy to secrets of her mother's that were best left untold. Kathlyn took Shirley aside and told her that she would leave their father if it weren't for her and Warren." Worse, it fell to Shirley to try to stiffen her mother's spine and get her to face down their father when he acted out. "I used to say to my mother, 'Why are you being so diplomatic about this?'" Finstad quotes MacLaine as recalling. "And she said, 'Diplomacy is what keeps the world from going to war.'"

My father experienced similar things as he was growing up. His parents divorced—just as he later would—and he became both a caretaker of his little brother and a communications link between his parents. Certainly, it's not always a bad thing for a single parent to lean on a child, and when all of the kids are still at home and divorce—or the death of a spouse—does occur, there's nothing wrong with the remaining parent clearly deputizing one of them to help look after the others. Indeed, in a household in which the age breakdown among the kids is, say, thirteen, nine, and six, it would be a waste of resources not to, since the first-born is old enough to exercise real—if circumscribed—authority. But the parent should also be careful about how the authority is granted. There should be no official crowning—no explicit statement that the big sister or brother is now running the show. As the case of the Duvall brothers illustrates, sibs often fall into those new power arrangements on their own anyway. And if Mom or Dad wants to know how the little sibs behaved while the big sib was babysitting, there's no reason to huddle with that child alone. Simply asking all the kids, "So how did it go last night?" can usually yield more than enough information.

A related problem occurs when lonely parents don't lift one child up to an adult station, but demote themselves to the kids' level. The phenomenon happens more often than parents think—and sometimes quite subtly—even in two-parent homes. It's especially common when kids are entering adolescence, and the parents, seeing an empty nest in their futures, are starting to feel their years. The desire to straddle the parent-pal fence—to chase the I'm-my-daughter's-best-friend ideal—is a powerful one. But for parents who think they can pull it off, the answer from family experts is clear: You can't.

The same need for clear structure and firm family roles that is denied when an oldest sibling is too openly promoted to co-parent is equally ill served when a parent spends too much time as just one of the troops. Paradoxically, Conger says, this can lead to sibling co-parenting, too, but not the healthy kind that occurs when the kids pull together in a time of crisis. Rather, the sibs start turning to one another for guidance because a parent is, in some ways, abdicating the position. When Mom comes home wearing a new outfit she bought at the same store at which her teenagers shop for clothes and one daughter mutters to the other "What's with her?" it's a good sign that a boundary has been crossed.

Of course, there is one thing worse than growing up in a home in which the lines of parental authority are blurred or disrupted, and that's when they're blown up entirely—when a group of children find themselves entirely without a mother, father, or any other parental figure. This most commonly occurs when the parents die and there are no suitable relatives to take the kids in. But it happens in other situations— when parents become disabled by addiction or illness or even incarceration. When that happens, an entire litter of sibs is suddenly spinning free, and at that point, the state must often step in.

Foster care in the United States is governed by a hodgepodge of often irrational practices that vary from state to state, city to city, and even courtroom to courtroom. And the systems are no more consistent overseas. As a very broad rule, the more money any jurisdiction has, the likelier it is that programs are in place that will minimize the trauma to abandoned or orphaned children and give them a chance to grow up in a comparatively stable situation that won't leave too many psychic scars. But money hardly guarantees anything. Even in wealthy areas of the developed world, placement in foster homes and the transition to adoption can be an opaque or arbitrary process that takes years to play out. Supervision of new parents can be spotty or nonexistent, which too often leads to neglect or abuse. Improving the situation may take a wholesale overhaul of the way governments do things, but there is one reform that is both inexpensive and powerful and emerges again and again as a way to provide kids comfort, structure, and a natural form of ad hoc parenting even in the worst situations: Whenever possible, sibling groups should be kept together.

Much has been made—and rightly so—of the life of Annie Sullivan, the poor and nearly blind immigrant girl who grew up to be Helen Keller's teacher and companion. It was Sullivan's preternatural patience and tenacity that allowed her to open up the world to the deaf and blind Keller. But it was Sullivan's loyalty and tenderness to her little brother much earlier in life that set her apart well before she was even grown. Abused by their alcoholic father—and abandoned by him when their mother died—Sullivan, who was ten, and Jimmie, who was eight, were sent to live in the almshouse in Tewksbury, Massachusetts.

When it opened in 1854, Tewksbury was home to 2,193 indigent residents, who were looked after by fourteen employees on a weekly budget of less than ninety-five cents per inmate. By the time Sullivan and her brother arrived, in 1876, Tewksbury had, if anything, declined further. It had diversified and become part poorhouse, part hospital, and part psychiatric asylum, with little talent on staff capable of dealing with any of the residents' very particular needs.

Jimmie had always been sickly, suffering from a chronic hip infection that left him barely able to walk and always one bad flare-up away from death. Upon their arrival, he was assigned to a hospital bed and Annie to a children's ward. She, however, insisted upon staying by his side, enduring the grueling conditions in the hospital, where death was routine, odors were foul, and patients who had quietly died might not be discovered and removed until they had begun to decompose. Nonetheless, Sullivan bedded down with Jimmie every night until, six months later, he at last died. In *The Miracle Worker*, the Oscar-winning 1962 movie that told the tale of Keller's life, Helen's father asks Sullivan about her lost—and still deeply loved—sibling.

KELLER: How old was he, your brother, Jimmie?

SULLIVAN: Helen's age.

KELLER: When did he die?

SULLIVAN: Eleven years ago this May.

KELLER: And you've had no one to dream about since?

SULLIVAN: No, one's enough.

Screenwriters certainly prettify prose, and no doubt they did here as well. But no doubt, too, the sentiment was drawn from reality.

Psychologist Catherine Hamilton-Giachritsis of England's University of Birmingham has put together what's known as a best-practices manual for the European Union, providing a framework for how those countries should structure institutional care for abandoned or orphaned children, and strongly argues for keeping sibs together at nearly any cost. She recently investigated the practices in seven very different EU nations—Greece, Slovakia, Romania, Poland, Denmark, Hungary, and France—as well as EU aspirant Turkey. The initial yardstick she used in determining quality of care was the simple question of how commonly orphaned siblings in state institutions were allowed to share a room. The results were as varied as the countries themselves: Greece came out on top with an 87 percent sibling-roommate rate; Turkey finished last at 10 percent, while Denmark and France—among the richest and most Westernized members of the EU—clocked in at a dismal 25 percent and 23 percent, respectively. The other scores included Slovakia's 48 percent, Romania's 46 percent, Poland's 45 percent, and Hungary's 25 percent.

Hamilton-Giachritsis used this data and a wealth of other findings to create her foster-care guidelines, and while the handbook is long and complex, designed to accommodate a range of possible situations and complications, she does return to some simple rules. "The message is, you shouldn't be putting children of a young age—or any age—in institutions," she says, "but if you have to, there are specific things you should do. Easily, one of the most important ones is housing sibs together and maintaining sib bonds. That's the way you can limit the damage as much as possible."

Not all psychologists agree entirely. Some, such as Lew Bank of the Oregon Social Learning Center, urge a more case-by-case approach, cautioning that if the children's original family was dysfunctional or violent and an older sibling tends to bully or exploit a younger one, keeping sibs together may be precisely what the courts shouldn't do.

Hamilton-Giachritsis agrees, but only to a point. "Obviously, you have to look at cases on an individual level," she says. "Some siblings in a family are so close it would be damaging to separate them. Others might benefit from separation. But that's rare."

My brothers and I, teenagers left parentless by circumstance in a comfortable suburb in a wealthy country, in no way found ourselves in the terrible state experienced by small children in poor countries who are well and truly orphaned. We would surely have landed somewhere with other adults in our extended family, and I was bound for college anyway. Garry and Bruce and I kept a close watch on one another while we were alone, and they were present for my graduation, where they did their best to show the family's by now faded colors. As it was, our period in self-care was brief. The science of addiction recovery was still comparatively crude even a few decades ago, and our mother—like so many substance abusers of the era—was released from the hospital after just a few weeks of detox with a stern admonition to stay off the drugs and little follow-up beyond that. She promised she'd behave.

She did not, of course. That's not the way of addiction. Instead, after a relatively brief period of abstinence, she resumed her drug habit, sneaking and secreting her pills more artfully than she had before. And since she took care never to get to the same depths of sloppy, life-threatening intoxication, we were often not aware of what she was up to. She kept that subterfuge up for decades, until advancing age made it impossible for her to tolerate so much chemistry anymore. In recent years, my brothers and I have wound up as parents to our parent—not at all uncommon for sons and daughters of aging mothers and fathers, even healthy ones with a sober past. I like to think we're good at the work, though sometimes I worry we're not. That, too, is typical of most people in our position. I do know that the turbulent upbringing we had and the sibling co-parenting that was made necessary as a result is not the childhood I would have chosen for us. But I also believe that that co-parenting made us better, closer brothers—and made us better parents, too, when our time for that role came.

TEN

If You Show Me Yours . . .

Sibs, Sex, and Gender

I may have never felt so unsettled as the day I walked into the Fortune Garden Chinese restaurant in New York and noticed the striking blonde sitting at the table in the middle of the room. She was in her early twenties, with the elegant look and composed bearing of a TV anchorwoman, but without the hard edge and camera-ready sheen real newscasters have. She was beautiful, she was a complete stranger—and she was also my sister.

This was actually not the first time I had set eyes on Allison. I had met both her and her twin brother, Adam, twice before—the first time when they were newborns and I was ten years old, and then once more when they were toddlers. They were the products of my father's second marriage, born less than two years after he had gotten remarried. He had had four sons by his first marriage, his new wife had had one daughter by hers, and both of them wanted a child who would be theirs to share. They got twins.

I was thrilled when Adam and Allison were born. The familiar four-boy lineup was once again being refreshed with new talent, but this time they weren't a pair of drop-in stepsibs with whom I shared not a scrap of DNA. This time they were the blood children of my blood father—a baby brother we could gather into the all-boy band, and another chance at that rarest of birds, a sister. And unlike our stepsisters, who were gone in fifteen months, Adam and Allison would be ours forever.

Alas, forever didn't last as long as we'd imagined. My parents' divorce had been a messy business, and the relationship didn't improve much after they both remarried. There was always some sort of hostile shelling going on between Baltimore and New York, and before long, my father's new wife—a hyperprotective sort who didn't care for the idea of his previous family interfering with their new one—laid down some rules. Adam and Allison, she decided, would not be told my brothers and I existed. Neither she nor my father would speak of us in their home, and nor would Jane, her eight-year-old daughter who lived with them and who knew us all by now. When my brothers and I visited New York, we would meet my father at a neutral place like his office or a restaurant. If we called the house and one of them answered, we were to identify ourselves ambiguously—as, say, "Jeffrey, from Baltimore." If one of them stumbled across an old family photo, let them assume we were out-of-town cousins.

My father, for reasons only he could fully explain, agreed to the plan. My brothers and I objected to it but obeyed it, remaining in the shadows as our twin sibs grew from babyhood to preschool age to grade school and beyond. Over the years we'd ask our father when we might finally meet them, and over the years he'd vaguely promise that it would happen sometime in the never-specified future. It wasn't until the twins were fifteen and we were all in our mid-twenties and had moved away from Baltimore that we decided we'd had enough. Steve and Garry lived in Los Angeles, Bruce and I lived in New York, and we told my father that he had three months to tell the twins of our existence or we would. It was early May when we had that conversation. "By early August, they will know," I said. "I recommend you tell them."

He didn't. Nor did my stepmother. My brothers and I knew where the twins were attending camp that summer, and after the first week in August we wrote them both letters, introducing ourselves, telling them a little bit about each of us and giving them our addresses and phone numbers. We promised them we would always be available if they ever wanted to reach us, but we promised, too, that we would not bother them again until they were ready.

It was, in many ways, a defensible act—driven by frustration, resentment, and deeply hurt feelings. But it was also a very selfish one. Fifteen-year-olds have a tentative grip on themselves and their world, to begin with; the last thing they need is someone lobbing so big a grenade into it. The explosion from the one we lobbed was a bad one. Allison reacted the way fifteen-year-old girls do, with age-appropriate tears and drama. Adam did what fifteen-year-old boys do, which is to say he clammed up, closed off, and insisted that he was entirely untroubled by what he had learned. My father was furious; his wife was apoplectic. But my brothers and I at least kept our word and did not contact the twins again. It wasn't until six years later that Allison alone, now a college graduate working for ABC News, told my father that she was ready to meet us, and a dinner was arranged with the two of them, Bruce, and me at a restaurant around the corner from their long-off-limits home.

Once we sat down, it was well-nigh impossible not to be charmed by Allison. She was smart, she was accomplished, she was self-possessed.

She engaged me almost immediately like the big brother I was, with a bit of deference perhaps for the ten years I had on her, but a sisterly chumminess that made it clear I shouldn't count on more than that bit. That in turn made it easier for me to fall into the sibling rhythm, too. It all felt surprisingly familial and comfortable, yet I found it impossible not to be struck by how beautiful she was—and impossible not to feel a little creepy about noticing.

The evening ended with hugs, air kisses, and promises to meet again soon. Our father seemed very happy and very pleased with the way things had turned out. With five sons and only one daughter, he was so evidently proud of Allison and so enjoyed showing off the jewel of his brood that I found it impossible not to be a little touched. He never went so far as to concede that Steve, Garry, Bruce, and I had done the right thing by telling the twins about our existence, but I didn't expect him to—and I didn't need him to. Still, as I walked away, I felt a little slimy all the same, and Bruce confessed that he did, too. Under the circumstances, how could our minds have occasionally wandered in the direction they did?

The answer, of course, as any behavioral scientist knows, is: How could they not—at least for a while? Brothers and sisters are friends, confidants, life partners, and more. But they are also, simply and fundamentally, males and females—and no matter the relationship, no matter the life history, no matter whether two people are strangers or kin, there will always be some measure of cross-gender complexity that goes with that difference.

You may have spent every day of your childhood with your big sister, but if you're a boy, that doesn't mean you can figure out a thing about why she likes the toys she likes, how she can read the books she reads, and what she sees in the giggling circle of girls she calls her friends. You may adore and treasure your little brother, but if you're a girl, that doesn't mean you don't see him for the brawling, childish, barely civilized thing he is—or that you have any understanding about how his mysterious little mind works.

From babyhood on, opposite-sex siblings approach each other with a sort of anthropological puzzlement. There is sexual curiosity, of course—a kind of my-parts-and-your-parts fascination that is mostly about learning basic anatomy but also about a kind of primal titillation. The titillation piece usually goes away quickly—snuffed out entirely by rules and taboos that are equal parts biology and social training. What remains, however, are the rich and often irreconcilable differences that always separate the sexes, but that brothers and sisters can put to use in ways that are unique among other opposite-sex groups.

Siblings growing up in all-boy broods like mine may easily fall together into a band-of-brothers clan, approaching the world in the same way and with the same temperament. But there's a gender pressure-cooking effect that goes on in those situations, too, as male traits get learned and relearned—and too often overlearned. There is little live-in experience with the different skills needed to engage with the female half of the human species. All-girl broods are similarly deprived of the chance to practice the skills they'll need to engage with the boys and men who will inevitably populate their worlds.

In some ways we all spend our entire lives turning the Rubik's Cube of the opposite sex without ever getting all of the colors to line up the right way. But the more you learn to work the puzzle when you're a child—the more you're required to consider the behavioral, sexual, and temperamental dimensions of the brother or sister who shares your childhood—the better you'll do in the big, complicated, mixed-sex life outside the home.

College women like to say that they can tell if a college boy grew up with a sister. He may be as loud and loutish as any other dorm rat, but he also knows when it's time to dial it down. You can't call it manners, exactly—that's going too far—but it's at least an awareness that his idea of fun is not the same as the girls' and that sometimes he ought to behave accordingly. College men similarly insist that they can tell if a girl grew up with a brother. There's a toughness to her, a winking lack of seriousness that feels ever so slightly male. What human beings think we observe about one another and what scientists agree we're observing are not always the same things. But in this case, our perceptions are spot on.

Early in a child's life, the gender of your siblings doesn't make a whole lot of difference, mostly because kids of both sexes, whether in the home or out, tend to mix very freely. Girls and boys in day care, pre-K, and kindergarten play together indiscriminately, surely noticing gender but not acting on the difference in any meaningful way. All that begins to change about the time kids turn six and enter first grade. At that point, an inexorable segregation by sex begins, some of which is societally imposed. Boys and girls who may have shared a common bathroom in the classroom when they were in kindergarten are now steered to separate accommodations just like adults. Organized playground games that once were co-ed will often be single-sex, with boys competing against boys and girls against girls. Brownies and Boy Scouts, girls' summer camps and boys' summer camps—all sort the sexes further. But the culture isn't the only thing at work, and a lot of the drift into two separate worlds is initiated by the kids themselves. The play and behavioral styles of the two genders are simply too different—with girls more inclined to gather into playgroups of three or four and engage in cooperative games and fantasy play, and boys more inclined to move in large, highly physical packs—for the groups to mix easily.

For a boy with a sister at home or a girl with a brother, that opposite-sex sibling now takes on a lot more meaning than he or she used to—a live-in member of a different tribe that, outside the home, is increasingly closing its ranks to you. Such a situation presents a lot of opportunities for learning. "As segregated playgroups form," says UCLA's Tom Weisner, "the sibling world may become the only world in which you have an opposite-sex peer who you can talk to and observe and learn from. Having regular, everyday contact like that has a powerful effect on you, one that's very different from the effect a same-sex sibling has."

The learning that takes place is not always conscious; indeed, it's often merely a function of necessity and habituation. The first time your older brother gives you a noogie or plays the pull-my-finger game may be shocking. By the five hundredth time, you barely notice it. The first time you see your sister lose herself in an afternoon of fantasy play with a little set of plastic ponies or princess figurines, you may try to pull her into a more rousing game. By the tenth time, you learn to let her be—or maybe even join her in her world for a while. Such learning plays out over the course of an entire childhood, and during those years, brothers and sisters may whipsaw back and forth between embracing the traits of their opposite-gender siblings and rejecting them.

Deborah Cohen, the married mother of two boys, grew up with an older brother who deeply—and openly—wished she had been a boy. "When I was born, the story goes that Joey was waiting expectantly with our grandmother for the call from the hospital," she says. "When he heard 'It's a girl!' his shoulders slumped and he stalked outside to play. I grew up idolizing him and became such a tomboy, probably to measure up. I'd round up the neighborhood kids at his behest for after-dinner curb-ball games; I still have the glove we oiled, stuffed with a baseball, and put under my mattress to break in. We were kindred spirits in our family of four kids; our two sisters were from a different planet as far as we were concerned."

Such total-immersion training in the ways of the opposite sex is generally a bad thing only if it occurs in an atmosphere in which parents and other authority figures are complicit in conveying the idea that a child's gender is somehow inferior to the other gender. That kind of message is hardly without historical or cultural precedent, but in most homes, a child grows up no worse for what Cohen experienced. Indeed, in her case, her upbringing might have left her better able to cope with the job of running her current household in which she is outnumbered three to one by the other sex. Cohen's brother, Joey, never got to see how well his handiwork turned out; he died of cancer nearly twenty years ago, yet his little sister remains grateful for the things he taught her.

"I still find myself wondering what he'd say about this or that," Cohen says. "I still want to tell him about something interesting I've seen or done."

Kimberly Updegraff of Arizona State has conducted some of the field's best studies on the ways brothers and sisters interact, focusing principally on adolescence—a crucible for all things related to gender, sex, and sexuality. Her landmark study was published in 2000, but its findings remain fresh and its insights keen today. Updegraff surveyed 197 families in central Pennsylvania, scattered among eighteen different school districts. All of the families had a firstborn child in eighth, ninth, or tenth grade, and at least one younger sibling. Updegraff also recruited

357 friends of the children in the target families—divided more or less evenly between the friends of the firstborns and the friends of the later-borns. In total, she had more than 700 subjects.

Each of the children in the sample group was interviewed one on one for up to three hours, and all of them answered a survey about their own personalities and the personalities of their friends in the study. The survey included such questions as "How much do you share your feelings and inner secrets with your best friend? How much do you go to your best friend for advice and support?" The subjects were also asked to agree or disagree on a five-point scale with such statements as "I make my friends do what I want to do." All of those questions were clearly designed to get at the traits that are traditionally associated with either masculine or feminine behavior, and all were intended to provide Up-degraff with some insight into how much the mere fact of having a sib of the opposite sex caused you to acquire some of their gender-based traits yourself.

As Updegraff anticipated, the results of the study did show that the traits rub off—but only to a degree. Girls growing up with a brother scored higher in both the surveys and the interviews on measures of assertiveness, showing a markedly greater tendency to try to exert control over their friends and playgroups. Not only that, the girls also tended to choose female friends who were unusually low in the same traits themselves, as if they were trying to boost their dominance quotient even higher by ensuring that the people around them would willingly submit.

Among boys growing up with sisters—particularly older sisters— the results were very different. Rather than emulating their big sisters, the boys tended to de-identify with them, essentially doubling down on stereotypically male dominance traits, at least outside the home. Curiously, the boys also picked friends who had the same hypermale traits themselves. Unusually assertive boys playing with other unusually assertive boys is a recipe for constant conflict and dominance struggles, but that appeared to be the way the subjects liked things. "Sisters in that group had the least masculine pals," Updegraff wrote, "while the brothers had the most masculine."

A lot of caveats have to be applied to Updegraff's findings, the first being that it is never wise to assign traits such as dominance and cooperativeness to opposite sides of the gender divide as if males and females alike don't exhibit both traits. They do, of course—even if they do so to different degrees—and sometimes a cooperative boy or a domineering girl would be that way regardless of the sex of the siblings living in the home. What's more, in any brother-sister relationship, age gap is always a factor. Generally, the bigger the difference in ages, the less involved brothers and sisters are with each other, and the less they are influenced by the other in the formation of their personalities. From one to three years is the optimal gap for sibling influence; much beyond that, and an older sister or brother becomes a little less like a sib and a little more like an aunt or uncle, which dilutes their temperament-shaping power.

Whatever influence brothers and sisters do have over one another hardly stops at adolescence, instead continuing as young teens mature and the sex-segregated playgroups of elementary and middle school reintegrate into mixed-sex social and dating circles. It's then that having an opposite-sex sibling pays particular dividends, as William Ickes, a psychologist at the University of Texas, Arlington, proved. In 2005, Ickes designed a study in which he recruited a total of forty male and female undergrads, each of whom had an opposite-sex sibling. He divided them into male-female pairs and set them chatting as if they were on a date, while video cameras rolled. He also had the subjects fill out a questionnaire afterward, describing the encounter. Since all of the people participating in the study had opposite-sex siblings, Ickes wasn't looking for how that fact alone might affect their interactions with the opposite sex—he assumed it would, as studies like Updegraff's had already shown. What he was looking for instead was whether it made a difference if that opposite-sex sib was older or younger. As it turned out, it did make a difference—a big one.

The males in the study who had older sisters scored significantly higher than those with younger sisters in terms of how much and how openly they talked during the sessions with the females. They also tended to ask more questions—a rare and highly prized trait on the dating market, at least judging by reports from frustrated women dating incurious men. Those males were rewarded in the study with more gazes from the women as well as more verbal reinforcers. Afterward, the women also gave the men higher likability scores.

"Younger brothers with older sisters were an instant hit with the women they were paired with," says Ickes. "It seemed that they had learned what a woman thinks and what her expectations are." Among younger women with older brothers, the results weren't as clear, but the differences still existed, with little sisters of big brothers more inclined than the other women to initiate conversation with men, to smile at them, and to elicit smiles in return. "Even though the effects were weaker for women," Ickes says, "both sexes proved to be better at breaking the ice with an opposite-sex stranger when they've had practice in the home. It's one more way our siblings have a long-term influence on our behavior."

There's almost no downside to the cross-gender mentoring brothers and sisters can provide each other—except one: Sometimes younger sibs can so admire cross-gender big sibs that they'll try to re-create a big sister or brother in any future girlfriend or boyfriend. It's unlikely that there's much in the way of surrogate incest going on here—an attempt to playact a sexual relationship with a well-loved but off-limits brother or sister. Rather, it's more about comfort level—feeling such an abiding sense of safety and familiarity with a particular type of partner that no other type will do. Not only can that be emotionally limiting, it can also hobble new relationships before they even get a chance to get started, since no partner modeled after a sibling ideal is ever likely to measure up to the original.

In Suzanne Finstad's Warren Beatty biography, she writes extensively of Beatty's long and starry romantic history, filled with over-the-title names such as Natalie Wood and Julie Christie, but she also observes that a disproportionate number of those women fit what she called "his pattern of dating girlfriends in the mold of [his sister] Shirley MacLaine." She cites particularly his relationship with Russian ballerina Maya Plisetskaya, whom he began dating when he was filming the 1967 movie *Bonnie and Clyde*. Beatty was thirty at the time; Plisetskaya was forty-four. "She was a dancer, she was older than Beatty, and she was gifted," Finstad writes—all traits consistent with MacLaine's. Plisetskaya, however, was also married.

It would be another twenty-five years before Beatty, at fifty-five, would finally get married himself, though even in his thirties he professed a desire to settle down and be done at last with the romantic hunt. While a whole range of variables determines why any one person comes to marriage so late—or avoids it altogether—in a culture that values the institution so highly, it can't help to have a gold-standard sibling like Shirley MacLaine, against whom most other women would likely seem to pale.

. . .

The role sisters and brothers play in schooling their siblings about the opposite sex is by no means a fixed or assured thing—in part because a child's own sexual identity can take a while to come into focus. Like adults, children have a sort of natural set point for sexuality and gender expressiveness, one that changes from person to person. Some kids are fiercely tactile—in a way that would almost be called sensual if it occurred in an adult—while others are cooler and more physically remote. Some boys are born with an all-male swagger, and some girls seem to have popped from the womb with frilliness encoded in every gene. All of these things are societally and familially influenced, but the mere fact that kids in the same culture or even the same household can be so different speaks to the way their personalities and sexual temperament come at least partly precooked. And a lot of that variety occurs just among straight-ahead, plain vanilla, heterosexual kids. Things get even more complex in families in which a brother or sister is gay or lesbian.

One of the least surprising moments in the history of my family occurred the day Steve decided to come out. Such a disclosure is difficult for any child—all the more so for Steve, who made his announcement in 1971. The Stonewall riots that launched the gay rights movement had occurred less than two years before. Homosexuality was still illegal in many parts of the country and could be prosecuted accordingly, and most people still casually tossed about homophobic epithets that have become as culturally forbidden today as racial slurs are.

Still, Steve's disclosure was not the stuff of family headlines. In a time when other boys were watching *Gunsmoke*, Steve was swanning over Lucille Ball. When the sounds of early 1960s rock were everywhere, he was hunkering down with *My Fair Lady* and *Gypsy* LPs. I grew up to the caterwauling of Ethel Merman not because I wanted to but because I shared a room with Steve and we owned a stereo. When he called my mother late one evening during his first year in college, catching her on one of the lucid moments she had in the thick of her drug addiction, and announced he was gay—a relatively new term at the time but one we had all heard—she reacted with genuine equanimity. She told him she'd always assumed as much and allowed as how she was glad he felt comfortable enough to tell her. When he pressed her about whether she understood the full implications of what he was saying—that this was real and it was for life—she assured him that she did.

"But you wish I wasn't gay," he said—spoiling for a fight, as he now admits.

"Yes, I do," she answered, "but only because I think your life would be easier than it's going to be now. But you've got to be happy."

It was an extraordinary response, particularly because it occurred in the era in which it did. Garry and Bruce and I were only marginally more surprised at the news than our mother had been. The next time Steve came to Baltimore for a visit we had no shortage of questions, but we tried to follow his lead about when it was all right to ask them and when we should stop, when it was okay to be flip and when we had crossed a line. At one point Bruce, who was fourteen, looked at Steve with an affected, anthropological inquisitiveness and said, "Teach me the ways of your people." He expected it to get a laugh and I actually thought it was funny, since it both captured and defused the strangeness he felt and did so in a way that was more sophisticated than his years. Steve did not agree, and his response was chilly—and we all calibrated accordingly.

If my family was behaviorally atypical, we were biologically very typical, at least in some ways. Studies of the roots of homosexuality have advanced a lot in the past four decades, and while the old "lifestyle choice" canard has long since been demolished, a full scientific understanding of what does determine sexual orientation has been slower in coming. One explanation is the size of the sibling brood. Biological anthropologist Paul Vasey of the University of Lethbridge in Alberta, Canada, has been conducting studies in Samoa of a phenomenon he calls the maternal fecundity theory. As the term suggests, Vasey believes that the mere fact that a woman has a lot of children might make it somewhat likelier that at least one of her sons will be gay.

On its face, such an idea is self-evident, since by dint of mere probability, the more children any woman has, the greater the odds not only that one will be gay but that one will be a concert pianist or a pro football player or a heart surgeon or a criminal. The larger any sample group, the larger the universe of possibilities. But there's more to it than arithmetic; there's also genes.

Vasey chose Samoa for his work because the comparatively isolated island culture makes it possible to run experiments in which fewer confounding variables come into play. His studies involved comparing the fecundity of mothers of heterosexual boys with that of mothers of gay boys—or *fa'afafine*, a Samoan term that means "in the manner of a woman." The *fa'afafine* are actually more than merely gay. They also assume some of the traditional female roles in the Samoan culture. Whatever their particular social position, they face less of the discrimination gays do in much of the rest of the world and instead are simply viewed as a sort of third, legitimate gender. Vasey's surveys did reveal that the average *fa'afafine* had more siblings than the average heterosexual boy, and not only did the mothers of the boys tend to produce more children, so did the sisters when they grew up.

The reason for that may lie in a neat bit of reproductive balancing.

The mothers of gay boys, Vasey suggests, carry a gene that codes for androphilia—or a particularly robust attraction to men—which would help account for the mothers' own prodigious reproduction. A boy who inherits the gene may be androphilic, too—in other words, gay—and be less likely to wind up reproducing at all (at least in the era before surrogacy and reproductive technology made it a little easier for men without female mates to become fathers). In terms of total baby count, this ought to be a wash, since the mother's overproduction is offset by the *fa'afafine*'s nonproduction. That makes the gene useless in survival terms—or at least it would ordinarily. But the sisters inherit androphilic tendencies, too, and with their own prolific breeding, push the family's reproductive output into positive territory. What's more, childless uncles can and do serve as trusted alloparents, providing the children in the extended family with a support network larger than that of other kids—and that has survival advantages of its own.

It's easy enough to prove part of Vasey's hypothesis simply by counting the babies, uncles, and *fa'afafine* in any one extended clan, but the mechanism that underlies it is not yet clear. Vasey himself conceded that if the androphilic gene does exist, he can't say exactly how it works. "The girls may begin menstruation earlier and enter menopause later, thus having longer reproductive careers," he says. "They may have physical characteristics that make them more attractive to men, or they may themselves be more interested in sex or attracted to men who have higher sex drives."

Whichever process is at work, the result is more sex, more breeding, and thus more offspring, which goes a long way toward explaining why a non-procreative trait such as homosexuality did not vanish in the early history of the human species. The female fecundity phenomenon is not unique to Samoans. Biologist Andrea Camperio Ciani has conducted related studies in Italy and found something similar there—and a human characteristic that has a toehold on the European continent is usually one that spreads readily around the world.

Intriguing as Vasey's work is, it's not the whole story. A far larger body of studies expands the role of the sibling brood further, showing that it takes more than just a lot of brothers and sisters in a family to increase the odds of producing one gay member. It takes a lot of older male siblings. As long ago as 1936, family demographers in Europe began observing that a disproportionate number of gay men had at least one older brother—and often several. Indeed, the greater the number of boys, the higher the mathematical likelihood that one of the youngest would be gay, a finding that has been replicated over the decades in many other studies. The number of older sisters does not make any difference.

For a long time, the thinking was that in these cases, homosexuality might be a learned orientation; perhaps being so low on a hypermasculine power ladder in some way feminized boys. But circumstances said otherwise. For one thing, older male sibs who died in infancy or were not carried to term seemed to count in the big-brother tally anyway, increasing the odds of homosexuality in the last son even though the survivor never had contact with the deceased. What's more, the effect also persisted when brothers were separated in babyhood and raised apart. That meant that something was likely happening in utero with each successive male sibling that in some way had its influence before the gay baby was even born.

In 2006, psychologist Anthony Bogaert of Brock University in Ontario sought to quantify more precisely how powerful the fraternal birth-order effect is, and in addition postulated a theory explaining what's behind it. In a survey of 944 men—some of whom were raised with their biological brothers, some of whom were raised apart from them, and some of whom had only stepbrothers—he found that the likelihood of homosexuality in the youngest boy increased by at least one-third for every blood brother who preceded him. Bogaert began with an estimate of roughly 3 percent for the overall share of gay males in the general population—a figure that on its face seems low and is disputed by many psychologists, some of whom put it at 10 percent or above. But even with such a conservative starting point, the findings were dramatic: A single older brother, Bogaert concluded, boosted the probability of a gay younger brother to 4 percent; two older brothers took it to 5 percent; and three or more caused it to top out at about 6 percent—double the starting point.

The likeliest explanation, Bogaert and a growing body of other scientists think, has to do with the mother's immune system. A woman's body does not recognize either a boy fetus or a girl fetus as alien—a very good thing, since it would then reject it like a transplanted organ—but it does see boys as slightly more alien than girls. Some mothers' systems may react by developing antibodies to certain sex-specific proteins a male fetus carries. Every subsequent boy baby will trigger a release of those antibodies in the womb, with the reaction getting stronger with each pregnancy. Ultimately, the antibodies may cross the placenta and have an impact on the baby's developing brain—including the area that governs sexual attraction.

The fraternal birth-order effect is not a given among male siblings, as it wasn't in my family, in which the gay brother is the oldest, not the youngest. Additionally, there are other neural-wiring variables at work that seem uninfluenced by brood size or gender and yet appear to play an equally significant role in determining orientation. One of those variables may also be involved in determining whether someone is left-handed or right-handed. All people are born with genetic coding that regulates body symmetry and asymmetry—something that goes beyond handedness to include which way the whorl in the hair at the crown of the head grows and which hemisphere of the brain will be dominant for processing language. Gender and orientation can sometimes get tangled up with this, since a closely linked suite of genes controls them as well. Gay men are 39 percent likelier to be left-handed than straight men, for example, and likelier to have a counterclockwise hair whorl as well—by a factor of nearly four, according to one study. "Characteristics like this are determined very, very early on," says psychologist Jennifer Steeves of York University in Toronto. "A baby's handedness can sometimes even be observed in utero."

Simply knowing that symmetry and sexuality interact in some way is not the same as knowing exactly how they do—much less why they do. But it does deepen science's grasp of the multiplicity of physical variables at work in shaping so fundamental a trait.

The study of homosexuality among siblings is a growing field, but as with so many other things in science, it is not a terribly egalitarian one—with far more work to date being devoted to boys than to girls. That, however, is slowly changing, too, and the studies are producing surprising results of their own. In the same way that the fraternal birth-order effect was observed culturally before it was established scientifically, nonscientists have also long noticed a curious characteristic of the hands of lesbian girls and women. In most females, the index and ring fingers are nearly the same length; in men the index finger is markedly shorter. Lesbians often follow the male pattern. In 2000, researchers at the University of California, Berkeley, helped document and legitimize the observation, showing that what began mostly as an urban legend does appear to be based in fact. As with fraternal birth order, the cause of the finger-length phenomenon may be found in utero, with higher-than-usual levels of androgens—or male hormones—during gestation, which may not only masculinize girls' hands but affect their sexual orientation.

Other, newer studies of lesbian physiology have focused on another unlikely part of the body: the inner ear. The human ear not only absorbs and processes sounds, it can actually emit them, in the form of tiny waves given off by the vibratory interaction of the eardrum and the cochlea. Known as otoacoustic emissions, these very weak vibrations generally have a lower frequency in men and a higher one in women. Studies are now revealing that among many lesbians, the waves are low-shifted in the male direction. Again, the roots appear to be gestational. "The pattern," says Vasey, "is indicative of a more male-typical prenatal hormone environment." No studies have yet shown if the siblings who preceded the girl baby into the womb played any role in establishing that environment the way older brothers do with younger, gay ones or if some other mechanism is at work.

For brothers and sisters of gays and lesbians, questions about hormones, antibodies, and brain architecture are largely academic matters, interesting when it comes to understanding the forces that shaped a loved one, perhaps, but not much beyond that. The larger issues are how all of the sibs can best absorb and embrace the news that a member of the brood is gay or lesbian, and what to do when one sib can't embrace it.

Within many families, acceptance of homosexuality splits along generational lines. Kids growing up in a world in which gay characters populate movies and TV shows, gay and lesbian couples homestead the suburbs, and civil unions if not yet same-sex marriage are widely available are a lot likelier to roll with the idea of sexual diversity in their own family than older folks who grew up in a more rigidly heterosexual world. The gay or lesbian child edging out of the closet is thus likely to have more to fear from the reaction of parents and grandparents than of brothers and sisters, and this provides an opportunity for the sibling bond to be put to work.

Ritch Savin-Williams, a Cornell University psychologist and author of the book *Mom, Dad, I'm Gay: How Families Negotiate Coming Out*, has conducted hundreds of interviews with gay and lesbian adolescents and teens, and has found that across the landscape of most families, kids prefer to play it safe by opening up to a sibling first. Not only does this allow them to gauge the mood of the family at large, it also provides a chance to war-game strategies about whom to tell next and how best to share the news. "Typically, gay kids pick their favorite sib, the one they're closest to, as their initial confidant," Savin-Williams says. "More often than not, this sibling is a sister, even if the gay child is a boy, but that is not always the case."

The advice the consigliere sib offers will vary according to the family, and while openness and honesty all around are usually the healthiest arrangement, sometimes they're not the wisest. When parents are violently homophobic, for example, their reactions can be upredictable—even dangerous. In some cases they may banish the child from the home; in others, they may withhold financial support for college or other necessities. A gay or lesbian child who is nearing adulthood may be best advised to keep some family members in the dark—at least for the short term. In fairness to older family members, Savin-Williams stresses that it is not always parents or grandparents who react badly. Sometimes it can be a member of the sibling brood itself.

"Maybe there's an older brother or sister who's fiercely homopho-bic," he says. "A confidant sibling may say to the gay child, 'You know what, I wouldn't tell Bob because he won't react too well.' I'm all for authenticity, but sometimes it can have its drawbacks."

The ideal for family candor, of course, is achieved when the parents can readily be told and everyone can sit down together and discuss the news as a group. The already scattered nature of our clan made that hard, as did the fact that while my mother accepted the news of Steve's orientation with equanimity, my father was more flip and dismissive, professing not even to believe it fully. I suspect he did know and did believe it, and, like the rest of us, had known it all along, too.

(Our maternal grandmother, remarkably, embraced Steve's sexual-ity as easily as our mother did, even greeting one of his boyfriends with a kiss on the cheek and a thank-you for making her grandson happy. Our grandfather was a bit more obstinate, and while he probably sensed that being critical or negative would have put him on the wrong side of the official family position, he did manage a bit of passive-aggressive resis-tance by handily forgetting for the rest of his life that he'd ever heard Steve was gay. "When is Stevie going to get married?" he asked Bruce and me only three years before he died, at almost ninety-two. "Grandpa," Bruce said, sighing, "Stevie doesn't like girls. Grandma knows it and she's fine with it." "Well . . . ," my grandfather spluttered, "that's before she understood what it meant.")

Even when some family members are in this kind of denial about sexual issues—sometimes *especially* when they're in denial—the more light and air that can be brought to the topic, the better. Open discussion allows questions to be asked and answered and—equally important— boundaries to be discussed and set. A heterosexual sib who once tossed about the term "That's so gay!" as a way to describe something fussy or overdone may be asked to stop—and should comply. As my brothers and I learned in the first few years after Steve came out, any boundaries that are set today may need to be modified in the future as the gay or lesbian child matures and grows and develops an identity in an often dangerous world.

A family meeting also provides the chance for kids to address any anxieties they have about what a sibling's sexuality says about their own. The short answer is usually: nothing. In the same way that having a left-handed sibling does not mean that you're unknowingly a southpaw, so, too, does having a gay or lesbian brother or sister usually bear no relevance to another sib's sexuality—though here there are no absolutes. To the extent that homosexuality has genetic roots, Savin-Williams says, there's surely not just one gene involved but several. That means that families with a homosexual member probably do carry more gay or lesbian DNA than other people. "It's possible some sibs will have some genes, but not all of them," Savin-Williams says. In those cases, the gay genes are either silent—in the same way that a blue-eyed gene may be invisibly carried by a brown-eyed person—or they affect temperament or anatomy in ways that don't influence orientation.

A final benefit of family candor is that kids who accept and embrace a brother's or sister's sexuality can support and protect that sibling, too. High school and junior high in particular are environments in which rumors and teasing can be pitiless, and a child who has come out may suffer no shortage of either. A flying wedge of brothers and sisters who can offer assistance when it's needed is an awfully handy thing to have. "If problems start," Savin-Williams says, "they need to be able to come to the gay or lesbian sibling's aid."

. . .

Family sexual issues are never easy to sort out, but the hardest of all may arise on those occasions when an erotic spark gets struck between siblings themselves. Just how often sibling incest occurs is a hard thing to determine. One study of undergraduates at six New England colleges found that 15 percent of females and 10 percent of males reported having had some kind of sexual experience with an opposite-sex sib at some point in their lives. Another study put the figure at 16 percent for females, but that study asked the girls only if they'd been subjected to forced or coerced sex. The consensual kind was not addressed.

None of those numbers are anything like ironclad—and truly definitive ones may never be forthcoming. With the secrecy and social opprobrium that surrounds incest, the act is uniquely dependent on self-reporting—and in some cases it's not even all that easy to define. When does anatomical exploration cross the line into something more? When are kids considered beyond the age of innocent curiosity and old enough to be aware of what they're up to? Actual intercourse between a sexually mature brother and sister is hard to misinterpret, but there are a lot of developmental and erotic steps before that point. Siblings in early adolescence, for example, may be engaging in some kind of familiar, naive roughhousing or other physical play, only to discover that their newly maturing bodies are reacting very differently from how they once did. Is that incest or something less? In about a third of all cases, an incestuous episode occurs only once and is never repeated, and such self-limiting behavior is particularly likely if kids simply stumble into things this way.

However much incest does take place, in some respects it's a wonder it doesn't occur more—at least when you consider what our species looks for in a mate. Your sibs are young, available, often attractive, and you have compatible—indeed, identical—backgrounds. Find a gem like that at a college mixer or on a dating website, and you could be set for life. "Imagine someone who shares similar thoughts, hobbies, ways of interpreting the world, and is physically attractive, too," says psychologist Debra Lieberman of the University of Miami. "Sounds like the perfect mate, except it's your sibling."

Such an automatic reaction is the behavior our primitive wiring sets up in us—and that's the wiring that completely runs the show in other species, in which mating between brothers and sisters takes place all the time. Yet the overwhelming majority of the time, humans are decidedly not aroused at the sight of a young, sexy sib. Often we barely notice, and to the extent that we do notice we may recoil at the thought.

There are a number of reasons for our species' nearly universal incest taboo, the most commonly cited being the avoidance of birth defects and inherited diseases. Families can carry a genetic predisposition for a disease for generations, but since the trait is a recessive one, the disease may never be expressed. If a brother and sister both carry the gene, however, pairing up can be disastrous. The risk of some kind of birth defect in cases like these is as high as 50 percent, according to some scientists, but a lot depends on the particular defect or disease and the particular family in question. Whatever the exact number, it's likely to be a whole lot lower when two unrelated people mate, a fact that our ancient ancestors recognized early on. "In primitive societies that had no incest taboo, people began noticing the incidence of offspring with abnormalities who came from brother-sister unions," says William Ickes. "To minimize those cases, they would implement a taboo."

The stay-away training starts when brothers and sisters are young, with segregated baths and bedrooms, and sometimes a severe scolding if they're caught touching or exploring each other in forbidden ways. Parents send both overt and implicit signals about what the limits are, but all of them convey the idea that sexualizing a sib is not just wrong; hitting or teasing a brother or sister is wrong, too, after all, but siblings do it all the time. Sex play, it's made clear, is bad in a deep and even unclean way. A parent doesn't have to express horror or disgust often— or even voluntarily—before a kid gets the message.

The brain—and specifically, the olfactory system—may work to keep sibs apart, too, thanks to the major histocompatibility complex (MHC), the region of the genome that produces proteins that allow humans to detect viable mates by smell. The less similar the MHC of two people is, the likelier they are to produce healthy children; the more similar it is, the likelier it is that there could be genetic complications. The metaphorical chemistry two people often speak of when they meet and are powerfully attracted to one another may in fact be a literal form of chemistry, driven in part by MHC. The same is true of the inexplicable lack of attraction people may feel toward an unrelated person who ought to be very appealing, but for some reason isn't. Brothers and sisters may love one another deeply and powerfully, but their too-similar MHC should keep things from going further.

Other cues work a keep-your-distance power of their own. Across human cultures, the mere fact of family members living in the same home can be all it takes to snuff sexuality. A mother needs no visual or olfactory evidence of relatedness to know that a child is her own, since she's the one who gave birth and has, in effect, been in possession of her child since conception. For fathers, who can never be 100 percent certain of paternity, the child's physical resemblance and the mother's general trustworthiness have to suffice. For older siblings, the first kinship cues are seeing the baby arrive in the home and then watching it be nursed by the mother. For younger sibs (or older ones who were too young to remember the birth of a baby brother or sister), the simple business of cohabiting is the first and most powerful mark of relatedness. The longer sibs live together, the more indelible that mark becomes—and that may be true even if kids are not related but simply raised as if they are.

Israelis learned this lesson early in the country's history when families of new settlers established kibbutzim, or communal farms on which they lived and worked collectively. Parents of different broods often hoped that their sons and daughters would marry across families, partly because they knew and liked the other clan and partly because that would help knit the community even closer. The children themselves may have had no real objection to the idea—at least when they were small. But when they reached sexual maturity and began seriously considering a mate, they usually found they had no attraction at all to their intended spouse. Indeed, marriage to the person was all but unthinkable. This became known as the "kibbutz effect," a contemporary label for a very old idea.

"What's in play in situations like this is a kind of learning mechanism," says psychologist Sarah Hill of Texas Christian University. "You take in information from the environment and draw conclusions about it." The conclusion that's drawn in the kibbutz case is that someone who's been part of your life for so long must be related, and a related person is simply not a viable mate. "Think of it as an if-this-then-that rule," says Hill. "In this case it's: if present, then yuck."

"Yuck" may lack a certain scientific precision, but it does nicely express the visceral nature of the aversion to incest. It takes a lot to overcome such a deeply felt distaste—yet some siblings still do. Not everyone is aware of or fears the risk of recessive diseases. Not all scientists yet agree on the role of MHC, and it's possible the scent proteins aren't as powerful as they seem. And while cultural norms forbidding incest are universal, they're not insurmountable—particularly in situations of extreme familial dysfunction. Children who experience shared trauma and who are abused or isolated from other kids may find comfort only in one another, and that can develop into shared sexuality. Sometimes alcohol or drugs can play a role, as can a simple absence of other sexual options.

"There's always been a debate among some people about whether the incest taboo exists at the personal level at all or whether it's exclusively at the cultural level," says William Ickes. "If it does exist only culturally, some people in some situations just might not have the taboo." Even if they do, it might not be strong enough to overcome the other variables.

The misfortune, abuse, and deprivation behind so many cases of incest rarely win victims much sympathy. Incest is illegal in most of the world and in some places it can be severely punished. In 1997, Allen and Patricia Muth, a brother-sister pair born in Wisconsin who met as adults, were sentenced to separate maximum-security prisons for terms of eight and five years respectively for a long-term sexual relationship that produced four children—one of them developmentally disabled. "I believe severe punishment is required in this case," the judge said at their sentencing. "I think they have to be separated." In 2010, a sibling pair in otherwise libertarian Sweden was charged with incest and faced one year in prison for the offense.

In most cases, such extreme measures are unnecessary, as the power of cultural learning—even in the absence of any innate biological aversion—overcomes everything else. Grow up in a home in which pork is forbidden, and you're likely to feel physically ill if you eat what you think is a baloney sandwich and later learn that it's ham. Drink a glass of ice water in a restaurant and you'll think nothing of it, unless someone then tells you the waiter secretly spat in it—even if no such thing happened. The same is true, in an exponentially deeper way, when you're steeped in a culture that treats the brother-sister bond as a deep and meaningful thing—but a thing that for the good of the home, the self, and the species as a whole must remain forever asexual. Learned early, it's a rule that remains imprinted for life.

My brothers and I got to know our half sister Allison—as well as our half brother Adam—slowly over the months that followed our dinner in the Chinese restaurant, and we grew more comfortable and familial in one another's company each time we met. As genes and culture usually do dictate, whatever awkward awareness I had of Allison's attractiveness at first soon vanished. But much graver worries were soon to come.

Only two years after our first meeting with Allison, we got word that she had been in a serious car accident on a dark, flat road in the middle of Iowa while on assignment for ABC. She reached down to adjust the radio or air conditioner when she was driving back from a nighttime shoot, lost control, flipped her car, and wound up in a ditch. Her forearm was shattered and her leg was badly slashed. Given the isolated spot and the nature of the crash, she might not have freed herself from the wreck. She did manage to escape, fashioned a bandage for her badly bleeding leg from her torn shirt, and was rescued by another driver, who got her to a hospital. She required multiple surgeries, a bone-setting bolt in her arm, and skin grafts on her leg, and she returned home to New York for a long period of recuperation. While she was laid up, she suffered a second blow when she learned that the man she had been seeing for many months took her convalescence as an opportunity to step out with another woman. The depth of the worry my brothers and I experienced over her injuries—and the depth of anger we shared for the man who had betrayed her, even though we'd never met him—surprised us. It was new and it was powerful and it was oddly sweet. It was, we realized, what it felt like to have a little sister.

ELEVEN

Paired and Pared

The Curious Worlds of Twins and Singletons

I f you were an only child in the early 1920s, you'd have probably wanted to avoid G. Stanley Hall. A psychologist, a professor, and the first president of the American Psychological Association, Hall knew a thing or two about how the human mind works. Often thought of as America's Sigmund Freud, he even bore a physical resemblance to the grand Austrian. When the two famously met at Hall's Clark University in 1909, it was thought of as a historic moment for modern psychology, even if the picture it produced—of two somber bearded men glaring with matching humorlessness into the camera—was equal parts earnest and comic.

Hall's severity was more than just appearances. Author of the 1883 book *The Contents of Children's Minds on Entering School*, he had some very clear ideas about the worth of boys and girls—and none of it made for very happy reading. Childhood, he taught, was a time of near savagery, during which "normal children . . . pass through stages of passionate cruelty, laziness, lying and thievery." During adolescence, "every step of the upward way is strewn with wreckage of body, mind and morals." The bloom of full teenhood was not much better, with most children becoming "emotionally unstable and pathic."

It was possible to tame and civilize such proto-people, provided you took a firm and unforgiving hand. Reasoning with children was useless, and had to be replaced with iron discipline; precociousness had to be snuffed in favor of strict pedagogy. Budding teen sexuality should be rechanneled into vigorous athletics. Failing to do so could lead to masturbation, which was a waste of sexual energy; sexuality, in turn, was a highway to debauchery.

But even such extreme measures could do little to save the luckless boy or girl born into the world without any brothers or sisters. Such solitary children were afflicted with all the shortcomings that beset other young people, but without the civilizing influence of siblings, the singleton traveled an even more perilous path. Pampered, narcissistic, socially inept, singletons would be destroyed by their childhoods before they ever reached maturity. "Being an only child," Hall wrote, "is a disease in itself."

Hall was hardly alone in his low opinion of the only child. Indeed, he was almost sunny compared to psychiatrist Abraham Arden Brill. Another of the Austrian giants, Brill studied with Jung, then emigrated to the United States, where he taught at New York University and Columbia and was the first to translate the works of Freud into English. In his 1921 book, *Basic Principles of Psychoanalysis*, Brill also addressed the sorry lot of the singleton, and wrote: "The only child is the morbid product of our present social economic system. He is usually an offspring of wealthy parents who, having been themselves brought up in luxury and anxious that their children should share their fate, refuse to have more than one or two children. By their abnormal love they not only unfit the child for life's battle but prevent him from developing into normal manhood, thus producing sexual perverts and neurotics of all descriptions. It would be best for the individual as well as the race that there should be no only children."

Over the arc of the past century, of course, Brill's and Hall's hard sentiments—like so much else of what we thought we knew about psychology—have been discredited. Generations of happy, thriving only children are proof that siblings are not the sine qua non to a happy life. But that doesn't mean that parents and psychologists don't worry over singletons all the same. The nurturing, socializing effect of siblings is a real and powerful thing, and it's reasonable—indeed only logical— to assume that kids who lack sibs might wind up *unn*urtured and *uns*ocialized. An entire childhood spent being tended by adoring parents who have no other outlet for their caretaking can produce an orchid of a child—a pampered, spoiled, hothoused thing, too temperamentally fragile to survive in the wilds of the world. Singletons will learn selfishness when they should learn sharing, inflexibility when they should learn compromise, narcissism when they should learn generosity.

Between 1925 and 1986 alone, there were more than 200 major papers published that sought to determine what type of damage is done to a child as a result of growing up alone. The findings were often mixed, with some studies unearthing no difference at all between singletons and kids with sibs and others darkly warning that there were dangers indeed. No matter which body of data was correct, the childbearing, family-raising public had already made up its mind.

A 1956 study found that one of the leading reasons couples chose to have a second child was not that they necessarily wanted a bigger family but that they wanted to spare their firstborn the burden of growing up alone. A 1974 study found that 78 percent of Americans believed that singletons are "disadvantaged." Another study published that same year described only children as "generally maladjusted, self-centered and self-willed, attention-seeking and dependent on others, temperamental and anxious, generally unhappy and unlikeable." Their only advantage? They are "somewhat more autonomous than a child with two siblings."

But singletons, at last, are getting a break. With the passage of time come better methodology and less investigative bias, and the body of work conducted since the 1970s has turned up much more reliable—and generally much happier—results. It's true that only children do not have the in-house playmates, roommates, mentors, and life mates that brothers and sisters have. And it's true that in the broadest terms, having such influences is a very good thing. But it's not equally true that not having them does any harm at all. Indeed, in one modern study after another, singletons show themselves capable of finding compensations, of filling the voids that would ordinarily be filled by siblings. As a result of that adaptability, not only do they usually perform as well as kids who have brothers and sisters on a range of social, intellectual, and cognitive scales, they often do better.

"Outcomes are more important than processes," says psychologist Toni Falbo, professor of educational psychology at the University of Texas, Austin, and an expert on the psyches of singletons. "And the outcome is that these kids wind up with the same skills other children have. The question is, How does that happen? Somehow they get adequate experience." Her work and that of others are increasingly solving that riddle.

. . .

For a demographic group that's had to put up with such heat over the decades, singletons represent a surprisingly sizable portion of the population. There are currently about 20 million one-child households in the United States. Among single mothers—itself a significant demographic group—the share raising a single child has more than doubled in the past two decades, going from 10 percent in the late 1980s and early 1990s to 23 percent today. In the UK, about 17 percent of families are home to just a single child, and in trendsetting Manhattan—where apartments are tiny, both parents typically work, and the cost of living is stratospheric—the figure is a remarkable 30 percent.

Not all parents raising singletons planned in advance to have just one child, but a significant percentage of them do, and that share is slowly creeping up. According to a 1985 U.S. Census report, 12.7 percent of eighteen- to thirty-four-year-old women reported that they intended to bear a single child and stop after that. Today, that figure is 13.9 percent.

The size of the only-child population is partly determined by historical forces as well, and those can drive the figures both up and down. During times of war there is usually a bump in the number of singletons, often because a father is killed or disabled in combat after he has begun his family but before he has completed it. Singletons are often a knock-on effect of rising divorce rates, too, as parents split up after having just one child. Hard economic times similarly drive family size down and the singleton population up, with parents deciding that a larger brood is just not something they can support. The twenty-first-century United States—with two wars, a historically severe recession, and a divorce rate that fluctuates from 25 percent to over 50 percent, depending on the demographic group—is at the mercy of all those variables.

Whatever the factors are that lead to one-child families, there's no denying that the children in those homes do live their lives as an object of parental attention in ways that multiple sibs never do. The time, money, and other forms of investment that must be so carefully husbanded when there are two, three, or more kids in the house are directed exclusively toward the one child. Sharing and turn taking—among the hardest of all skills for small children to learn and the most common causes of shoutfests and fights—is not a problem in the singleton's home.

With more disposable income to spend, there are also more treats and privileges such as movies, vacations, summer camps, private schools, and high-price colleges. Singletons are likelier to enjoy educational and extracurricular goodies such as musical instruments, newer computers, dance lessons, and after-school sports, as well as tutors and trainers to help them make the most of it all. They are less likely to be pressed into household chores—in part because a one-child home simply needs less picking up than a multi-child one does. And without a lot of kids with different preferences and temperaments to accommodate, the singleton's tastes are more often indulged.

"Think about how parents of multiple kids have to select foods for different meals to appeal to the appetites of one child and then the other," says Daniel Shaw of the University of Pittsburgh. "With only one child to cook for, the parents will cater to that child's tastes. The choice of family outings and other activities can similarly be determined by the desires of the singleton, as opposed to thinking about multiple children who vary in developmental skills and desires."

Only children may even be healthier than other kids. The mere fact that parents have just one child's schedule to juggle—and one set of pediatrician's bills to pay—means that singletons are likely to see the doctor more regularly, and to return for follow-up visits after recovering from an illness or injury. (This happy fact of the singleton's life may, paradoxically, have accounted for one of Hall's most troubling and misinterpreted findings. Over the course of his career, Hall kept a detailed archive of all of the patients brought to him for care, paying special attention to what he called "exceptional and peculiar children." There were more than 1,000 kids on that unfortunate list, and when he broke them down by family size he found that a disproportionately large number of them were singletons. That seemed to seal the deal against the only child, since Hall—this time at least—appeared to have hard numbers on his side. But a less grim—and more accurate—interpretation was simply that an only child going through a rough behavioral patch was likelier to be brought in for care than a child with brothers and sisters. Often as not, that difficult period would pass, just as it would for a child from a larger family who would never have gotten professional attention. But the singleton would have been permanently inked into Hall's book all the same.)

Pampering, of course, is only one part of the singleton's life; pressure is the other—and that's a lot less easy to take. From fish to birds to mammals to humans, the reproductive calculation is always the same: More offspring are better than fewer, since that allows you to place your genetic bets on as wide a field as possible. When human parents are raising a house full of children, simple arithmetic says that at least some of them will grow up wealthy and successful and produce a lot of kids of their own. A single child, by contrast, means you've got just one horse in the race—and that horse must be a winner. Not only do parents feel that urgency, they make sure the child does as well. "There's a pressure to achieve that constantly comes from the parents," says Shaw. "Adult singletons will often say that they wish they'd had siblings simply because there was just too much attention directed at them."

This phenomenon can occur in all one-child families anywhere in the world, but it's most evident in China, where the government has been conducting a decades-long, population-wide, longitudinal study in only-child science. In 1979, China, facing a rapidly exploding population, implemented its notorious one-child policy—or, as the ruling Communist Party called it, its "policy of birth planning." Parents were offered financial and employment incentives to stop having babies after producing just one—and threatened with penalties for failing to show such reproductive restraint.

Even in a country as regimented as China, such a sweeping social-engineering project was never going to be easy to police, and the one-child policy has indeed been inconsistently applied. Enforcement has been much stricter in cities than in rural areas, and some ethnic minorities, who make up a relatively small fraction of the population, have been exempted altogether. Parents have gamed the system on their own, sometimes in terrible ways. With the advent of in vitro screening methods such as ultrasound, for example, came the practice of selectively aborting girls and trying again to have a boy—a likelier route to family wealth and prestige. Families that do bring a daughter to term sometimes abandon her immediately after birth, a practice that fueled the overseas adoption boom as streams of baby girls left China for new families in the West.

Thirty years of such demographic manipulation have had a profound impact on China's population. To date, an estimated 250 million Chinese babies who otherwise would have been born never were. Among those children who did make it into the world and remained in China, there is currently a badly lopsided gender balance, with 32 million more boys under twenty years old than girls. That disparity will be more acutely felt over the coming years as the boys reach marrying age and find that there are just too few girls to go around, leading either to a permanent sub-population of bachelors or an unplanned-for surge of emigration as millions of young men go overseas to find wives and raise families.

That's for the future, though. For now, the lives of the Chinese singletons—particularly the boys—have more than enough challenges. The one-child policy has given rise to a generation of what are known in China as the *xiao huangdi*, or "little emperors," children from preschool age to young adulthood who think the suns and stars of Chinese culture revolve around them—in part because they do. They attend the best colleges, snag the best jobs, and in a new and exuberantly capitalist culture, grow up to make the most money. A 2004 article in *Fortune* magazine that explored the *xiao huangdi* in depth quoted a consumer-trends analyst from Ogilvy & Mather saying, "Get ready for the biggest me generation the world has ever seen."

Chinese critics themselves take a similarly dim view of the little emperors. The same *Fortune* story cited the common complaint among adults that singletons never learn to "eat bitterness," or overcome hardship and obstacles. Said one kindergarten director, who knows better than most how the *xiao huangdi* see their place in the world: "Kids these days are spoiled rotten. They have no social skills. They expect instant gratification. They're attended to hand and foot by adults so protective that if the child as much as stumbles, the whole family will curse the ground."

While that might seem like an enviable arrangement for the only children themselves, such a constant lavishing of attention does not come free. Children offered the opportunity to attend the best schools are also *expected* to do so—and to thrive there. The availability of the best jobs includes an assumption that the singletons will actually land them and get rich performing them. Billboards exhorting the only child to work hard dot the countryside, and teachers and bosses repeat the message over and over again. By some measures, the *xiao huangdi* may not be little emperors at all, but rather something more like little salarymen—China's youthful version of Japan's overworked, overpressured, badly stressed young executives of the 1980s.

"These children aren't spoiled," says Toni Falbo of the University of Texas, Austin, who traveled to China on a grant from the National Institutes of Health and studied 4,000 children in both the cities and the countryside. "They're just pressured to achieve. They're told to be obedient, to work hard, that the whole fate of the nation rests on them. That's the normal discourse."

The Chinese experience, of course, is entirely different from the American one—or, for that matter, from that of most other countries. But down at the level of the individual family, only children in any part of the world can surely sympathize with the sense of parental expectation and family responsibility experienced by singletons everywhere.

"Sometimes, I felt like I wasn't just my parents' only son, I was also their only sun," is how Tom Everett, fifty-two, an investment banker living in Denver, has often put it. Everett is in the relatively uncommon position of not only having grown up as a singleton but being the father of one himself. "Only children become the focus of what's going on in the family, good or bad. In my household I felt like if I was doing well, everybody would be doing better."

But there's a paradox at work, too. Such pressure-cooker living ought to be something that adult singletons recall with sadness and even resentment. On balance, however, Everett describes his solo upbringing as "more positive than negative"—and he's by no means alone. The majority of only children report that while they're quite aware of the fun they'd have had with a brother or sister—and quite candid that they would have liked that experience—they prefer the childhood they had. This is more than the simple human tendency to put the best possible gloss on something you can't change anyway. People who grew up in a home with only one parent, after all, rarely say they wouldn't have preferred two. Only children, by contrast, usually liked things just as they were.

You don't have to be Hall or Brill to wonder how that can be. Finding the hidden benefits that make an only child's upbringing such a positive and often fondly remembered thing has been a focus of much of the modern research. And it's Falbo who has made some of the most important contributions to this growing body of work.

The biggest and most influential of her investigations took place in 1986, and most of the research published since has validated her bedrock findings. Falbo's study was what's known as a meta-analysis—not a separate body of work in which she recruited her own sample group and conducted her own surveys, but rather a round-up and recrunching of the data from multiple existing papers. In this case, there were 115 of those studies, all revolving around singletons. Falbo strip-mined the data from those papers and then reapplied it in a new way, evaluating singletons in six critical categories of her own devising: achievement, intelligence, adjustment (including self-esteem and behavioral issues), character (including leadership skills and maturity), and sociability (including extroversion and ease of affiliation with peers). She also looked at the quality of the children's relationships with their parents.

No matter how Falbo analyzed her numbers, not only did she not see the terrible developmental deficits singletons are supposed to suffer, she actually found that they matched or exceeded the performance of children who grow up with brothers and sisters. In achievement and intelligence, singletons did better than most kids from families with three or more children, finishing behind only firstborns and children from two-child families—and then not terribly far behind. (The fact that firstborns and kids from two-child families have a slight edge probably comes from the opportunity the older child has to mentor the younger one, and the exclusive attention the younger one gets from the older.) Singletons surpassed all kids from multiple-sibling families in character and the quality of the parent-child relationship. In adjustment they finished slightly ahead of all kids with sibs, and in sociability they finished slightly behind, but in both cases the difference was so tiny that it was, for statistical purposes, a tie.

"Overall, only children were not different from the others," Falbo says. "Even though the assumption is often that they will be introverted and loners, there just didn't seem to be any association at all. In intelligence, sociability, and adjustment, they were pretty much like everyone else, and what little differences there were, actually were an advantage for only children."

Some of the qualities Falbo sought to study are admittedly hard to measure. It's not easy to find a precise metric to apply to qualities as vague as character and adjustment. But traits such as achievement and intelligence can be quantified down to the decimal points, thanks to IQ tests, SATs, grade point averages, and other academic yardsticks. And it's easy to explain why singletons score so high. Not only do they get more educational opportunities, they also grow up in a home that is simply more intellectually stimulating than one in which parents are raising multiple kids.

A single child outnumbered by grown-ups tends to strive harder to understand adult vocabulary and interests—a very different situation from the one in the multiple-child home in which the kids tend to tug the grown-ups down toward their sophistication level. Everything from the music singletons hear to the DVDs they watch to the conversations that swirl around them over the dinner table is likely to skew older. When the choice is to adapt or be left out, the singleton does what's necessary. A 1982 study that preceded Falbo's meta-analysis confirmed this fact when scientists observed mealtimes in only-child homes and multiple-sibling homes and tallied up the discrete bits of information and back-and-forth conversation that took place—separating it out from periods of silence or utilitarian exchanges such as "Pass the peas." Again and again they found that the conversations in the singleton households were more consistent and more data-rich than in multi-sib families, and it was the parents who set the tone and the topic. Everett became aware of this phenomenon early in his life—and today is happy for that experience.

"There wasn't a built-in language and sensibility of children dominating my household," he says. "As a result, I quickly got comfortable with how adults think and speak, and often did so a lot faster than my friends did. That included what we watched on TV. When I was growing up, most of my friends watched shows aimed at kids. In our house it was things like *The Dick Van Dyke Show*. It was a very sophisticated show—very subtle and smart. It taught me what was funny, and why things are funny. I watched a lot of politics, too, because my parents were watching things like that. What I didn't see much of were cartoons. That's the way things are in my house now, too. My son is only ten, but his favorite thing to watch on TV is reruns of *Friends*. He enjoys it—and he also understands it."

The vaguer measures of singleton accomplishment, such as character and adjustment, are not quite as easy to explain as intelligence and achievement, but in some respects the very mechanisms thought to do only children harm may in fact be the ones that confer extra benefits. Parental attention, for example, can indeed sometimes become doting, which is not good for any child. However, when moms and dads are very attentive to a child's needs, the child in turn learns that opening up in times of emotional distress—seeking and receiving help—is much preferable to covering up.

Similarly, the fact that singletons spend more time alone than other kids may make them not less socially successful but paradoxically more so. When you're more familiar with being alone, you're also more comfortable with it, which reduces the urgency and anxiety many kids feel in trying to find and join a social group. Singletons may make wiser choices in these situations, simply because they're content to wait until the right group comes along.

Other variables, less within the control of singletons and their parents, can determine the developmental trajectory of the only child. Being lucky enough to have a large extended family is one of them—particularly if those family members live nearby and include a lot of cousins who are close in age.

In wealthy, highly industrialized countries like the United States, easy mobility and frequent job switching mean that extended families are rarer than they once were, but they remain more common than many people think. One analysis from the Pew Research Center shows that 37 percent of Americans live their entire lives in the community in which they were born. Many of those who do move away don't go very far: As many as 80 percent of people born in New York State, for example, will never live outside of the state, a loyalty to place followed closely by natives of Louisiana, Pennsylvania, Michigan, and Ohio. The rest of the nation does not trail far behind. All that keeps extended family close at hand, and all that is a good thing for singletons, for whom cousins—and even young aunts and uncles—may become surrogate siblings. Indeed, in some ways having cousins may actually be better than having siblings, providing much of the same brother-and-sister companionship without any of the fighting, jealousy, and competition for Mom's and Dad's attention and the resources that go with it.

The near absence of such familial surrogates is one more reason China's one-child policy has been such a demographic disaster. Many young parents were themselves products of one-child families, which means that huge swaths of the newest generation of families have been entirely stripped not only of multiple sibs but of uncles, aunts, and cousins as well. That has never gone down well in a country that has long celebrated the centrality of the family and the awareness of ancestral lines, never mind the fact that it also starves only children of blood-relative playmates.

American singletons enjoy other advantages, particularly since the early 1970s, as more and more women joined the workforce and periodic recessions have increasingly made a one-income household impossible to maintain. With both parents punching a clock, day care and preschool have become not just luxuries but necessities. Big companies with generous benefit plans sometimes provide on-site day-care centers or help employees pay for outside care. Even when companies don't chip in, parents themselves have made day care a family priority, placing it high on the list of mandatory household expenses such as groceries and electricity. Some have established parenting circles or community groups that provide a form of collective care, with moms and dads in multiple families taking turns volunteering their services.

In much the way the immune systems of kids in day care are thought to boot up earlier and more vigorously because they're exposed to colds and other bugs more frequently than kids who stay at home, so, too, are the social skills of singletons brought online faster when they spend all day in the company of other kids. A similar pattern of formal socialization continues as singletons move out of day care and into grade school and beyond. Many child-care professionals rightly lament the mad over-scheduling of after-school activities that increasingly begin for all contemporary kids even before they hit first grade—the nonstop dash from soccer to gymnastics to swim class to chess club. But all the frenetic scheduling does have a particular benefit for singletons, giving them more opportunities for connecting with other kids after the school bell rings than they would get if they were simply going home to a house in which the only other people are adults.

Certainly, none of this means that even the most sanguine psychologists or the most well-adjusted singletons would be likely to argue that growing up without siblings is, as a hard rule, preferable to growing up with them. The mere fact that so many only children find so many compensations for their lack of brothers and sisters doesn't mean there wasn't something missing that had to be to compensated for in the first place. And the absence of a sibling does leave a hole that the singleton must work to fill.

But in that very act of compensation there can also be a quiet reward. Of all of the traits parents and psychologists admire in only children, it's the kids' comfort inside their own skin that is the most striking—an autonomy and self-containment that allow them to amuse themselves, to find deep, even contemplative pleasure in reading or fantasy play or whatever else is absorbing them at any moment. There's a texture and richness to that kind of total-immersion learning that might not be possible if the same kids had to cope with the distraction of a group of noisy sibs fighting or roughhousing or otherwise drawing their focus. It may be coincidence that history is full of great thinkers and artists who emerged from only-child homes—Da Vinci, FDR, Elvis, Cole Porter, Lillian Hellman, Frank Sinatra, Cary Grant—or it may be that the time and attention they were able to devote to developing their innate talents helped push them across that elusive line that separates simply being good at something from being truly extraordinary at it. The freedom to breathe and think and focus on one thing at a time is something that most people experience too rarely. For singletons, it can be a simple part of life.

"I watch my son and am always impressed by how comfortable he is with alone time," says Everett. "He may be reading, playing with Lego, practicing guitar, but whatever he's doing, he becomes completely involved with it. I'm happy he has that ability to entertain himself and deal with some of his own needs. Would that have been the case if he'd had a brother or sister? Maybe—but I don't think so."

My sister, Allison, wore a lavender jacket the night she went out to throw eggs at cars on Park Avenue. It was a new jacket, down-filled, and would have to last her the entire fall and winter season—which, on Halloween night, had barely begun. For that reason, her mother had told her to take especially good care of it. She had no idea Allison would be wearing it tonight when she went out for what was supposed to be an evening of innocent trick-or-treating with her twin brother, Adam, but was actually an evening of misdemeanor mischief with him and a group of his male friends.

It was 1997, and Allison was thirteen and not usually the type to make misdemeanor mischief, but this evening she made an exception, partly because she liked being accepted as a member of Adam's little wolf pack of friends, and partly because Adam himself would be there. As a general rule, any place on the planet one of them went was the place the other would want to be, too. So they went out egging together on Halloween night, and were neither hurt nor arrested in the process—though the lavender jacket got fairly splattered—and slipped back inside without incident.

The next morning, Adam and Allison would return to very different—and very familiar—roles. Allison would wake up for school first and go into Adam's room to make sure he was awake. She'd return to her room to get dressed, checking the clock periodically to keep them from running late. When they sat down to breakfast she'd watch him to see that he ate and would ask him if he'd done all his homework for the day. She thought of herself as a little mama and, though she never said it out loud, Adam seemed to see things that way, too. My brother and sister may have been playmates, confidants, co-equals, and best friends, but when it came to the routine business of daily living, she was the one who kept their trains running on time. That was simply the way things had always been—and it was completely typical of the complicated world of twins.

If singletons are the free radicals of the sibling world—the unpaired electrons that must bounce around in search of a bonding site and a stable state—twins may be the steadiest and most grounded of elements. Conceived in tandem, bonded in the womb, they share the world before they're even fully part of it. Fraternal twins, from the geneticist's perspective, are nothing terribly special, a random mix of their parents' genes, who may share anywhere from 10 percent to 90 percent of their own genomes, but who most of the time will shake out at about 50 percent—which makes them not a whit different from any other full siblings. Of course, other siblings don't seem to be able to read each other's minds and finish each other's thoughts and have no idea how they would proceed in a life in which their twin wasn't at their side— which is how fraternal twins themselves often experience things.

Identical twins are something even the geneticists can't wave off. They're as close as an arbitrary thing like nature can come to quality-controlled mass production—two humans stamped out from identical templates, with identical strengths and identical weaknesses, all run by an identical genetic operating system. Identical twins start life as a single cell before dividing into a pair of independent embryos, which means that not only are they similar entities, for a brief time they were the same entity. Growing up in a world with a photocopied self always at hand is something only the copies themselves can fully fathom—an experience that is at turns warm, fierce, rich, complex, and surreal.

Being a twin is by no means an unalloyed good, and both identical and fraternal pairs can start life with a lot of disadvantages. Childbirth alone can be more fraught when twins are being delivered, with a greater chance of complications and even maternal or infant death, particularly in the developing world, where labor and delivery are less likely to take place in a hospital. But even in the most high-tech setting, there can be problems. For starters, twins have a higher risk of being undersized at birth and are also likelier to be born prematurely. About 60 percent of twin pairs are premature, according to the March of Dimes, and more than half are low-birth-weight babies—five and a half pounds or less. The prematurity figure for triplets is 90 percent and close to 100 percent for all larger broods. Premature and undersized newborns are likelier to suffer from a host of problems such as respiratory disorders, heart disorders, intestinal problems, and abnormal retinal development. They are also often found to have lower IQs—though that can change over time.

This is generally so whether a mother of twins is carrying a pair of boys, a pair of girls, or a boy and a girl, but in cases of mixed-gender twins, there can be other developmental wrinkles. Premature twin boys have a 60 percent greater likelihood of developing respiratory disorders than premature twin girls do. The reasons are not entirely clear, but they are likely part of the overall edge in hardiness female humans enjoy over males throughout life—an edge that contributes to their lower incidence of disease and generally longer life spans. In terms of postpartum respiratory disorder, however, things change when a boy and girl share the womb. In those cases, the girl loses her edge, facing the same increased odds her twin brother does. This shift in risk has long been reported anecdotally, but a 2008 study from Tel Aviv University documented it, examining records from 8,858 births of very low-birth-weight infants (one to three pounds) from 1995 to 2003 and finding the mixed-twin respiratory phenomenon again and again.

The explanation for the problem may lie in hormones. Fraternal twins develop in separate amniotic sacs and have separate placentas. Identical twins may or may not have separate placentas, depending on when the two embryos divide; they will only very rarely share the same sac—from 1 in 35,000 to 1 in 60,000 pregnancies. Nonetheless, during gestation all twins do share the same womb environment, and the cross-mixing of chemistry that inevitably takes place can have an effect on development. A growing body of work is showing that this can be particularly so in terms of gender, with girls exhibiting a subtle masculinization when their twin is a boy. Behavioral studies of boy-girl twin pairs often find that the sisters tend to take more risks, exhibit more outgoing behavior, and generally behave in more dominant ways than other girls. Like my sister, they also tend to assume a parental role relative to their brothers.

Risk taking, of course, could simply be learned—a result of growing up side by side with a boy. And looking after a brother may just be caretaking and early mothering behavior. But Nancy Segal, a psychologist at California State University at Fullerton and author of two books about twins—*Entwined Lives* and *Indivisible by Two*—does not think so. She is especially struck by studies in which boy-girl twins raised apart are compared to boy-girl non-twin siblings who were raised together in a way that made them what she calls "virtual twins," adopted into the same family at the same age and same time, for example. In general, the girls in the biological boy-girl pairs showed more dominant and asser-tive personalities—even growing up without their brothers—than the girls who technically had no twin sib but grew up as if they did.

What's more, Segal says, otoacoustic emissions—the sound waves given off in sex-specific frequencies by the inner ear structures of all people—are male-shifted to a deeper frequency in girls who have a male twin. That's similar to the otoacoustic shift that has been found in some studies of lesbian physiology, which may suggest a similar hormonal influence in determining sexual orientation—though in cases of single births the reason for that change in chemistry is not clear.

"The subtle masculinization of a female twin has been shown in cattle, too," Segal says, "though they have a different placental arrange-ment, which means that it's not a perfect analogy. Still, in humans, there can be some blood sharing, and that's probably where things begin." A similar body of work has not yet been done on whether there is a cor-responding feminization of boy twins in the boy-girl pair, though there's little reason to believe that the phenomenon should run only one way.

The blending of twins' body chemistry is nothing compared to the sometimes eerie blending of their minds. Anecdotes of a sort of twin telepathy are everywhere among families raising both fraternal and identical pairs—and that includes my own. One afternoon after my sister had grown up and gotten married, she was out driving with her husband while Adam was away visiting California. She suddenly found herself overcome by a powerful unease, one she could neither account for nor control. She mentioned it to her husband, who suggested that perhaps she should call Adam when they got home to see if he was all right. She did—and he wasn't. He had broken his ankle riding an all-terrain vehicle over sand dunes with his friends, and had done so at more or less the very moment she was feeling so jumpy—nearly 3,000 miles away.

Mothers whose sons are off at war have long told similar tales of knowing when a child has been wounded or killed, and the natural impulse in both these situations is to credit moms and twins with a sort of supersensory ability, a paranormal connection to the people who mean the most to them and an innate awareness of when something has gone wrong with them. Maybe. Or maybe something less wondrous is happening. Human beings are notoriously selective observers, living in a world in which cause and effect can be hard things to measure. You set your alarm clock for 6:00 a.m. every day and not long after it sounds, the sun rises. The unmistakable implication: If you forgot to set the clock, the sun would not come up. When free-floating anxiety precedes a terrible event, the causation feels obvious and the experience becomes filled with meaning. When free-floating anxiety precedes nothing in particular, it may dissipate as inexplicably as it appeared and soon be forgotten altogether.

But even if the feeling of mother and twin intuition can't be explained magically, it can still be explained meaningfully. For many twins, the partner with whom they entered the world will always remain at its emotional center. In the best cases—most cases, actually—that does not crowd out the love they later feel for spouses and children, nor prevent them from building nuclear families of which the twin is not the central part. But nor do those later relationships ever diminish the one with their birth mate. "Allison has always been and will always be my very best friend and soul mate," is how my brother Adam—not usually given to hyperbole—puts it. "I have other best friends and soul mates, especially my wife. But there is only one Allison. I am who I am because of her." Unease when that soul mate is away or out of touch is to be expected, and the anxiety that precedes cases of seeming intuition is more likely to occur in those on-your-own periods.

Powerful as the emotional bond is between fraternal twins, it is usually even more so between identicals. Indeed, for these pairs, the closeness of the twinship does sometimes surpass all other relationships either twin will ever form. "When they're asked, more than 99 percent of identical twins will endorse the idea that 'My twin is my best friend,'" says research psychologist Tony Vernon of the University of Western Ontario. "Even if they haven't seen the twin in a while, they'll admit to being closer to that brother or sister than they are to their spouse or their children. And when a twin dies, the bereavement the survivor feels can be worse than for all other family members, too."

That grief typically comes late in life, because identical twins also tend to enjoy an edge in longevity over other people, with an average life span of 82, compared to 80.5 for fraternal twins, and slightly under 80 for Americans as a whole. The reason twins get the edge: They tend to stay in closer contact throughout their lives, even if they live in different cities. Remaining socially connected to other people is one of the greatest predictors of longevity among older people, while isolation is similarly predictive of mortality. Twins also have a substantially lower rate of suicide than the general population, according to a 2003 Danish study that tracked a whopping 21,653 pairs of same-sex twins for an equally impressive fifty-one years. That happy stat was also attributed to stronger family ties.

The fact that twin communication can be a special thing is no surprise to parents raising both identical and fraternal pairs, in part because twins often seem to have a language of their own—literally. Lisa Dreyer, mother of eight-year-old fraternal twins Sofia and Alejandra, noticed just such a thing before her daughters were even fully verbal.

"When the girls were just learning to speak, they had basic, one-word commands for my husband and me, and those were pretty clear," she says. "But I also noticed a specific pattern and inflection in their speech when they spoke with each other. They didn't do this in public or around adults, but mostly when they were in their cribs, which were side by side in their room. One of them would babble, which would make the other one laugh or react with similar babble. My husband and I would stand outside their room listening to this, absolutely stunned because it was clear they were having what sounded like a conversation. This lasted until they were almost three years old and it ended when they got to school. When I ask them about it today, they say they don't recall it."

Tempting as it is to think the girls actually were communicating in a whole new language, there's probably something subtler and, alas, less remarkable going on. "Twin language always fascinates parents," says Lisabeth DiLalla, developmental psychologist at Southern Illinois University School of Medicine. "Most twins don't exhibit this, but many do. What sounds like some magical language, however, really isn't. It's English but in a kind of shorthand that's so familiar to the twins they need no translation. This happens mostly in preschool or the early school years, before they start communicating more with teachers and other children."

Twins collaborate behaviorally in other ways. Early on, Dreyer and her husband noticed that, once their girls developed their full verbal skills, they were equally talkative—but only when they were playing together or communicating with family members. Out in the world, Sofia usually spoke for both of them. Of the two, she was inherently the one more socially at ease and simply assumed the responsibility of serving as their spokesgirl. Alejandra was perfectly happy with such an arrangement and permitted it to take place. By the time the sisters got to grade school, however, the roles changed. Both of them had learned to speak for themselves, but now it was Alejandra who was more gregarious and Sofia who was more reticent.

Here, too, the girls are not uncommon. Twins often follow a shared but staggered maturation arc, with one sib developing a particular skill while the other lags. The sib who has fallen behind then catches up. Eventually, they accumulate all of the abilities they need, but for a while it's as if they're collaborating on just one personality, dividing the labor in the service of a single whole. "You see an interesting kind of turn taking," says DiLalla. "I've had moms come in and point to one twin and say 'This year she's the outgoing one, but last year she was the introvert.' It's not that their personalities aren't developing. It's that they have each other, so things develop differently."

All of these things are true of both fraternal and identical twins, but identicals do share a greater degree of intimacy and overlap than even the closest fraternals ever could. This is largely attributable to their matching genes. It's here that their connection can often seem truly otherworldly. The Minnesota Twin Family Study (MTFS) is an ongoing research project sponsored by the University of Minnesota to investigate how twins differ; how they're similar; and in what ways genetics, environment, or both are at play. The MTFS has been under way since 1983, amassing a large registry of twin volunteers and a vast and growing library of data. Some of the most compelling results they've produced concern identical twins who were separated at birth and raised apart—perfect lab specimens for the dual influences of environment and heredity, since they share all of their genes but virtually none of their experiences. The power of those genes has proven to be extraordinary.

Among the cases MTFS researchers most like to cite is that of the Jim twins—identical brothers who never knew each other and were raised by separate parents. It is surely just coincidence that both sets of parents chose to name their babies Jim, but the parallels never seemed to stop after that: The Jims grew up to smoke the same brand of cigarettes, drink the same beer, drive the same car, and have the same opinion about baseball (they didn't like it). They married women who also had the same names, divorced them, and married other women—with matching names again. They went on vacation to the same resort at the same time, though they did not bump into each other there—and indeed never met at all until they were united by the study.

Selective observation and randomness may again be at work here; the identical names of the Jims' wives were surely no less happenstance than their own matching names. But there are other twin pairs who offer examples of similarly strange convergence. There are the identical girls separated at birth who both grew up to enjoy writing in journals—and both, when the journals were later compared, had chosen the same days to write and the same days not to write. There were the twin boys born in prewar Germany to a Jewish father and a non-Jewish mother. One left Germany, one remained, both survived—and both grew up to enjoy making funny noises in elevators. There were the two male twins who both grew up to be firemen, the two who developed the odd quirk of flushing a toilet both before and after using it.

Every bit of this may be mere chance, but at least some of it may not be. If it isn't, the explanation for what's going on does not have to lie in anything supernatural, but rather in the software that is the human brain. "Identical twins have similar—indeed identical—brain wiring," says Vernon. "They'll have matching electroencephalograms, and their brains typically operate in matching ways." That means their temperaments are likely to be similar as well, and that in turn will drive them to make similar choices.

Twins who smoke the same brand of cigarettes may do so strictly by accident, or both may share brain wiring that makes them innately outgoing and rebellious. That could push them to choose uncommon brands other people don't, smoking Dakota cigarettes, say, and drinking Shiner Bock beer. Twins who are both innately quiet and conformist may both go for Marlboro and Budweiser. The same kind of temperamental tendencies could also drive geographically separate twins to develop similar views on baseball or politics and to choose either a conservative sedan or a zippy roadster as the family car. Twins who need constant emotional stimulation and activity may both like the buzz that comes from living in cities, and thus find themselves in a lot of elevators; if they're also mischievous by nature, they may decide it's fun to make noises there, too. Twins who are prewired to be thoughtful and reflective may be identically drawn to journal writing, and the parallel hormonal and metabolic cycles that carry them through the month may prod them to write on the same days.

Matching brain wiring presents twins with matching challenges, too. Vernon's studies have found that identical twins, whether raised apart or together, correlate more than any other sibs for a behavioral trait known as negative affect—or the simple tendency to complain, overreact, and exhibit bad moods that often cloud the good ones of the people around them. Identical twins also have similar scores on a test known as the Dimensional Assessment of Personality Pathology, which measures what psychologists call "the dark triad" of behavioral traits—Machiavellianism (or deceit and manipulativeness), narcissism (which includes not just self-absorption but a sort of exploitative seductiveness), and simple psychopathy. Fraternal twins may correlate on all of these traits, too, but identicals do so at about two and a half times the rate. That means that "to the extent that identical twins do correlate, those correlations are often linked to genetics, not environment," Vernon says.

Most parents of twins do not have to reckon with such pathologies, since even among the twin population, the conditions remain comparatively uncommon. For them, the routine challenges of raising twins—fights, rivalries, learning to share, going to school—are more than enough. It's almost never easier raising two at once than one at a time, particularly in babyhood, when the work includes diaper changes and round-the-clock feedings. Just how big the workload remains as the twins get older often depends, again, on whether they are identical or fraternal. Identicals, as a very general rule, will be more cooperative and collaborative; fraternals will be less so—and that means that fraternals will fight more, too.

Nancy Segal cites a German study in which pairs of twins were given tasks to perform, such as completing an art project or solving math problems. Each twin worked independently of the other on a separate sheet at a separate table. When identical twins were being studied, they tended to coordinate their work without even seeming to plan it—moving at about the same pace and finishing at about the same time. When fraternals were involved, things became more of a race to see who would finish first and who would perform better. If the skill being tested happened to be one at which only one of the fraternals excelled—drawing a picture, say—the one who didn't have the same level of ability would sometimes not even try. For Segal's own doctoral dissertation, she ran a similar study, but this time she had the twins work together, at the same table, on a single jigsaw puzzle. The differences could not have been more stark.

"The identicals were well coordinated," Segal says. "They were happy and it was almost like they were dancing. The fraternals were more competitive and argumentative and not well matched. They were a mess." Segal has interviewed identical twins who were both artists and worked together on projects, and has seen a similar collaborative talent at play there, too. By the time the pairs were done working, they sometimes couldn't even say which twin had contributed what to the work.

(Such collaborative intimacy is more common among identical twins than among fraternals or non-twin sibling pairs, but it's not exclusive to them. Joel and Ethan Coen—two years apart and creators of such films as *Fargo*, *Raising Arizona*, and the 2007 Oscar winner for best picture, *No Country for Old Men*—are very clear in their screen credits about who does what job, with Joel listed as director and Ethan as producer. But the brothers actually collaborate much more than their screen credits let on, often sharing directing and producing chores. They even co-edit their films, though under the pseudonym Roderick Jaynes. How well is that collaborative editing working out? Consider this: "Jaynes" has twice been nominated for an Academy Award—once for *Fargo* and once for *No Country for Old Men*. If he ever wins, Oscar officials plan to accept the award on behalf of the Academy.)

With larger broods of multiple siblings—triplets, quadruplets, and beyond—things are, no surprise, exponentially more complicated than they are with twins. For one thing, not all sibs in a multiple birth of three or more will be fraternals. Sometimes there will be an identical pair thrown in. That's not quite so bad if there are at least two fraternals to go along with them. But when the brood is triplets and the breakdown is two identicals and one fraternal, that odd child may always feel a bit left out.

"When you have this arrangement, the identicals will usually be closer than the fraternal," says Segal. But, she stresses, that's not always the case. "I talked to a woman who has boy triplets with an identical pair and one fraternal, and the identicals didn't get along. Instead, they both pal around with the fraternal."

Triplets as well as larger groups may also practice the tactic of triangulation—as when two sibs form an alliance that excludes, or sometimes even punishes, the third. Triangulation can occur among all members of a family, and is especially common when marriages are in trouble and children strategically align themselves with Mom or Dad, using their loyalty as a lever to get what they want from the parent they've selected. Among triplets and other large sibling groups, these allegiances can shift with the circumstances, so that while all of the kids will get a chance to be part of the bonded group at some point, they all will also be excluded at others.

The precise dynamics of triplets and other larger sibships is, for now, only poorly understood, mostly because such extreme multiples are so rare. About 1 out of every 32 births produces twins, compared to 1 out of every 535 for triplets and above. In vitro fertilization techniques have caused this number to jump in recent years, but the boom in multiples has eased some as doctors improve their techniques and are better able to ensure that parents who want only one or two children get them.

No matter the actual head count in a multiple-birth brood, the bonds among all the kids will typically follow the pattern with twins, which means that they will all grow up closer than even the most well-matched single-birth sibs. This closeness—which is usually a very good thing—can present other challenges that parents must learn to manage. DiLalla cites studies showing that two- and three-year-old identical twins tend to be shyer than other kids; she conducted follow-up research of her own in which she recruited 100 pairs of non-twin sibs and 80 pairs of twins and evaluated their temperaments and prosocial behaviors. She found that preschool twins indeed tend to be less social, and when they move toward adolescence, they are more prone to be aggressive as well.

Much of this is due to the mere fact that twins are less motivated than other kids to seek out friends outside the home, since their best friend already lives under the same roof. When they finally do begin forming relationships with other peers, they are less skilled at it. "It sort of all fits together that there may be something going on in which twins are being less socialized rather than more," Segal says of findings like DiLalla's.

One solution, of course, is to nudge the twins apart. Parents often tie themselves into knots worrying about how similar they should allow—or force—their twins to be and how much they should try to help them establish separate identities. It's not just dressing them alike, it's taking them to the same after-school groups, providing them with the same toys or books, and introducing them into the same circles of playmates. It can even include whether or not to give them similar names—the Jane and June, Ed and Fred, Andy and Mandy phenomenon.

No matter how much or how little parents allow twins to have in common, the world outside the home will insist on seeing them as two of a kind. "Regardless of whether twins are identical or fraternal," Kramer says, "people look at that dyad a different way. There's a belief that they're more connected to one another and that they understand one another." That creates a certain pressure on the kids to live up to that stereotype.

Dreyer noticed just that public expectation early in her twins' lives and came up with a few simple countermeasures. Even in the home, she and her husband never referred to their children as "the twins," but rather as "the girls." That's something the girls themselves seemed to internalize. "If somebody asks them now if they're twins, they'll answer yes," says Dreyer. "If someone asks them if they're sisters they'll say yes to that, too, but they won't clarify further." She and her husband also never dressed the girls alike and did try to help them develop different interests. In addition, they requested that they be placed in different classes at school, mostly to encourage the quieter twin to stop relying on the more gregarious one to speak for them both—a strategy that worked.

Opinions on whether twin sibs should be in the same classroom tend to differ from family to family and school district to school district. Is separating them the only way to give them enough breathing room to develop individual identities? Does keeping them together help them adjust better, at least when they're very young? As a rule, there are no rules.

"Until recently, schools always made the decision," DiLalla says. "But lately parents have been deciding and more schools are deferring to them. That doesn't always mean the parents are right. Ultimately, it often comes down to the simple matter of whether the kids are well behaved or not. Twins who come into school showing behavior problems tend to do better when they're separated. Those who don't have these behavior problems may do better when they're kept together."

Such squishiness—maybe this, maybe that, maybe so, maybe not—

does not do much to help parents who are looking for firm guide-lines, and nor does the similar absence of fixed rules about dressing twins alike or buying them different toys or giving them separate rooms. The upside of this is that it simply may not matter. Over the course of a lifetime—a long one, given the extra years most twins get—they will make their own choices and find their own level of closeness. They will de-identify and reidentify, drift apart and drift together. The parents' role in all of this will be necessarily limited, to act as what DiLalla calls "a scaffold." What the twins build on that emotional framework will be entirely their decision. Much more often than not, they will build something lasting.

TWELVE

And On and On . . .

Siblings Through the Years

t took me until I was in early middle age to think seriously about the fact that, life and death being what they are, one day there would be fewer than four of us in my original band of brothers. When I was very young, I believed that people died in the order in which they were born and that that rule applied down to the day. A child who came into the world on April 1, 1960, would eventually leave it one day before a child born on April 2, 1960. That was pretty much the last time I gave more than passing thought to how the chronology of mortality applied to my brothers and me. It was more than four decades later that I considered the idea again, one evening when the four of us were sitting at a table at Joe Allen's restaurant in New York.

We've been having dinner at Joe Allen's for the better part of twenty-five years now. We don't get to eat there terribly often anymore, since it's not terribly often that all of us are in town at the same time. Bruce and I still live in New York City, Garry lives in Los Angeles, and Steve lives in Boston. Coordinating four schedules so that we all come together on the same evening at the same table takes some doing, and typically doesn't happen unless a special occasion like a wedding or a funeral forces the issue. Still, when such an occasion does occur, we know where we'll eat.

As with most families with a go-to restaurant, we did not choose Joe Allen's on the strength of either its food or décor—both of which are perfectly nice but also perfectly unremarkable. Human beings are seekers of the warm and the familiar—and families are exponentially more so. There's a reason the toddler insists on hearing *Goodnight Moon* night after night—sometimes multiple times on a single night—and it's not because this time the story might end differently. There's a reason extended clans return to the same lake house summer after summer. There's a reason so mundane a thing as meat loaf night becomes an inviolable part of a household's dinnertime tradition.

All such family habits are marinated in history. Each successive summer at the lake adds to the sum of all the other summers, and makes it likelier still that there will be more to come. Each meat loaf dinner or reading of *Goodnight Moon* works the same way. And the same is certainly true of every all-brothers dinner at a place like Joe Allen's.

My dark reflections on the night I contemplated our mortality began as warm thoughts. Looking around the table, I recalled how many similar evenings we'd passed together this way. It occurred to me that since I was too young when Bruce was born to remember his arrival with any clarity, I had no conscious experience of living in a world without all four of us present. Oddly—and a bit morbidly—I then thought of Ringo Starr. Shortly after John Lennon was murdered, a TV reporter asked Ringo a question about his feelings or his plans or the future of the surviving band members. "I don't know," he answered. "You'd have to ask the other two." Then he stopped himself and nodded his head. "That sounded very strange," he said. And indeed it did. Such a sentence in the past would always have ended with the words "other three."

I looked around the table again at Steve, Garry, and Bruce, none of whom was as young as he'd once been and none of whom was taking care of his health as well as I'd like—and as well as I took self-satisfied pride in doing. Bruce, after having successfully given up smoking and staying clean for years, had recently taken it up again. Garry—as always, the only athlete among us—was continuing to run in more marathons than I considered safe. Steve, while generally healthy, still has never met a steak he couldn't vacuum up in less than five minutes.

"You should all know," I suddenly announced, "that I plan to live to be one hundred, and I don't plan to bury any of my brothers. So govern yourselves accordingly."

They looked back at me, rolled their eyes, and returned to their food.

The long march of years brothers and sisters usually get to share is both a gift and an inevitable source of melancholy. You are together as your family of origin buds and grows. You are together as it matures. And you are together, too, as it decays and declines. You experience the same things, even if not always in the same ways. "Siblings," says Katherine Conger, "are like our memory banks."

For the two decades before children are old enough to leave home, they are making constant deposits into that account. The shared experiences of childhood get placed in a family's short-term vault and then, if the experiences are meaningful enough, they are transferred to long-term archiving. The day I swatted Steve with the balsa wood plank got stored quickly. The recent night I made my nine-year-old daughter laugh so hard at dinner that milk shot out of her nose—causing the seven-year-old to double over, too—has surely been filed away in their accounts already.

It's only when the sibs begin growing up and breaking away—sequentially leaving home for college and beyond—that things begin to change. No longer are they living in the same environment, exchanging only different perspectives on common experiences. All at once, and for the very first time, they're living largely separate lives. Brothers and sisters returning from college bring lessons and guidance from the adult world that are new to kids still living with Mom and Dad—and that those kids are not especially accustomed to hearing from a sibling. Conger recalls a telling experience she had during one of her interviews with sibling pairs.

"One older sibling who had gone off to school came back home, and I did a videotape with him and his little sister," she recalls. "As part of the interview he said to her, 'College is a lot tougher than I thought it would be. You'll have to knuckle down and start studying. I kind of fooled around in high school and I'm really having to work hard.' I thought it was so great for the older brother to fill his sister in on what's awaiting her out there. It's a great image."

Important as such mentoring from an emancipated sibling can be, the threshold from high school to college also marks a period in which brothers and sisters begin to disinvest from one another. Geography drives sibs apart, as do diverging academic interests, differing career pursuits, and, of course, romantic relationships. There's a centrifugal physics to all these forces, one that scatters a previously cohesive sibling band in all manner of unpredictable directions.

Conger calls this period, which can run a decade or more, the sibling moratorium, and while it can come as a jolt to the sibs themselves—especially the little brothers and sisters, who may feel abandoned—it is an essential developmental step. Once the younger sibs themselves are out in the world, they see the benefits of the separation, too.

"The moratorium tends to happen mostly when siblings are in their twenties," Conger says. "They're all trying to establish where they're going in terms of work, education, finding romance, starting a family. The sibling relationship must recede for a while, because they are working on these issues. Brothers and sisters will all become influential again in one another's lives, but not until later, when they move past that age."

Victoria Bedford of the University of Indianapolis describes this phenomenon as the "hourglass effect," a stage at which sibling closeness and interaction contracts to a narrow choke point, and only expands again when the brothers and sisters are all set and settled. At that stage, they are likelier to be living similar lives once again—even if they're living them separately—wrestling with the common challenges of raising kids, earning a living, and keeping a household solvent and afloat. Matching lives—not to mention often-matching schedules—will typically draw them closer again.

My brothers and I took longer than most to scatter—and at first we managed it only halfway. By the time we were in our twenties, we had all moved away from Baltimore. Steve and Garry migrated to Los Angeles, living in separate apartments not far from each other; Bruce and I moved to New York—or Hoboken, New Jersey, actually, for the cheaper rent, where we shared an apartment. Even as we pursued our early careers, we all remained intimately involved in one another's lives—Bruce and I especially, and unavoidably, since we lived under the same roof. Whether or not that was good for our emotional growth we did not much consider, but other people in our lives had doubts.

Not long after Bruce and I left Hoboken and moved to separate apartments in New York City, I began a several-year romance with a woman who got to know my brothers well and could not help but observe how much time we still spent on the phone together or in one another's company. She began to ask me—tactfully but tellingly—if maybe it wouldn't be good for me to be investing more of my emotional energy elsewhere. Truth be told, I'd been thinking that, too. I suspect Bruce felt the same way—and I'm certain the serial women he was dating at the time did as well. Yet the first time I shared my girlfriend's thoughts with him, he frowned and muttered, "Yoko."

He was joking—sort of—or at least he delivered the dismissal with enough of a playful tone that he seemed to be. But there was indeed a busting-up-the-Beatles quality to my girlfriend's urgings, though Bruce and I knew she was right. Ultimately, the four of us did establish more autonomous lives. No coincidence, perhaps, that only then did any of our romantic relationships begin to move toward marriage.

The very act of marrying, of course, can have its own kind of impact on sibling bonds. By definition, spouses should be each other's best friends and go-to confidants, and while plenty of people in chilly or unhappy marriages have either lost or never achieved that intimacy, few would deny that it was one of the things they hoped for at the outset. No matter how well spouses do or don't get along, however, the day-to-day collaboration that goes into making a home and raising children does crowd out a lot of the time and emotional energy they had for relationships outside the marriage. That includes siblings—and that can lead to problems. Bedford cites studies showing that romantically unattached sibs will often continue to name another sib as their primary attachment figure—scientist-speak for the most important person in their lives—but married sibs will be much less likely to return the favor. Often as not, this results in feelings of resentment, directed both at the attached brother or sister and at the romantic partner who caused the problems in the first place.

As bad as these tensions can be, they become worse if they stir up older, long-dormant ones as well. When the sib who has paired up was also the pretty one or the popular one or the one with all the dates when the kids were growing up, the feelings of inadequacy or envy that occurred back then will likely be recycled. Similarly, if the married sib was generally known to be Mom's or Dad's favorite, the renewed familial attention that comes with planning a wedding or the arrival of the first grandchild will spark problems of its own.

"The unattached sibling will feel hostile and distant and may or may not say anything about it," says Catherine Salmon. "But unless the married sibling is totally clueless, it will be obvious that something is going on." Paradoxically, it's that partnered sib who may have the tougher go. Yes, it's nice to be the one who's loved by both a sibling and a mate, but the torn loyalties that come from having to mind the feelings of both can create tensions and guilt of their own.

All of these issues can occur even when the single sibling is actually fond of the attached sibling's partner. But what happens when that's not the case—when you think your sister's new husband is a boor or a bum, or your brother's new wife is humorless or controlling? Dare the unpaired sib say anything at all? In most fraught familial situations, psychologists counsel candor and openness. But unless the undesirable partner actually seems dangerous or otherwise unstable, this is one time the honesty-in-all-things rule may not apply. "Often, it's just not going to be taken well," says Laurie Kramer. "Maybe the complaints are on target and the couple winds up getting divorced ten years later. But if you say something much earlier than that, the message just might not be heard."

This is especially so if the siblings do not have a long, shared history of mutual trust and supportiveness. "That's when you hear things like, 'You've never approved of my choices. Nothing I do is ever good enough for you,'" says Kramer.

No matter the quality of the partners the siblings choose, the passage of time does tend to smooth over a lot of conflicts. This is particularly so when an unattached sibling finds a mate as well—and most particularly when any sib becomes a parent. The primal sense of family bonding that gets stirred up when the first baby of a new generation is born can be an extraordinarily powerful thing. That's partly pure sentiment—who doesn't love babies?—and partly genetic. A family's biological legacy is a precious thing, and when the entire responsibility for passing it on is heaped on one small child, the clan draws together around that new member.

Bruce was the first of the brothers in our family to get married and the first to become a father as well, and while part of me moped enviously through his wedding and had to force a smile when he and his new wife bought an apartment and set up housekeeping, all that was swept away when his daughter Bridgette was born. For me, the new sense of family connectedness was expressed through gifts—a great, great many gifts—as well as constant visits and regular offers to babysit. For my other brothers it meant flying in from Los Angeles and spending as much time with the new baby as their schedules would allow. Not surprisingly, as Garry and I went on to have children of our own, our investment in any niece or nephew had to be dialed back, but the time we logged as Bridgette's exceedingly devoted uncles was good for us, good for the family, and, I'd like to think, good for her, too.

Not every uncle or aunt responds to a nephew or niece in quite the same way. Badly estranged siblings may extend their antipathy for one another to the next generation—though the birth of a baby may some-times warm things up at least a little. And despite the consuming at-tentiveness my brothers and I displayed toward Bridgette, studies do suggest that sisters—particularly unmarried sisters—do a better job of alloparenting nieces and nephews than brothers. "Unmarried men tend to be involved in reproductive things of their own—such as meeting women and dating," says Salmon. When uncles do get heavily involved in helping to care for a sibling's kids, some surprising studies suggest that they're likelier to do so if the sibling is a sister. "There's anthropo-logical stuff going on here," says Salmon. "You invest in your sister's children because you know they're hers. When a brother has children there can always be paternity questions."

Gay and lesbian aunts and uncles, most research continues to show, are more attentive to their nieces and nephews because they're less likely to have kids of their own—though this, again, is changing as liberalized adoption laws, new reproductive technologies, and surrogate parenting democratize parenthood more than ever. The gender of a sibling's chil-dren can draw an uncle or aunt closer as well. If you're raising daughters and have always longed for a son, you may be more motivated to spend time with a nephew than a niece—and the same holds true for a parent of boys who's always wanted a girl. In all of these cases, one overarching rule does apply: The more involved siblings are with one another's kids, the closer the sibs themselves will remain—and the closer the extended family as a whole will be as well.

While adult siblings who remain involved in one another's lives gen-erally see their continued relationship as a desirable and very re-warding thing, even those who want nothing to do with one another continue to be deeply connected all the same—whether they realize it or not. That's because the person with whom you first learned how—or how not—to manage relationships and resolve conflicts can't help but inform how you practice those same skills with all of the other people who eventually populate your world.

Parents of small children tear their hair out when their kids are fighting, and not just because of all the noise and upheaval. They also worry that siblings who can't settle their conflicts at home will be equally poor at interpersonal skills when they grow up and the stakes for getting along will be much higher. Laurie Kramer's findings that the preschoolers who have the most fights in the playroom tend to be more combative on the playground as well seems to confirm that fear, as does Lew Bank's finding that older brothers who bully their little sibs are at higher risk of carrying on that behavior outside the home.

But there are upsides to the fights, too. Bedford has conducted studies of groups of adult siblings over a twenty-year period, looking into the lingering effects of childhood battles, and has come up with some encouraging findings. In most cases, she says, as long as early-life conflicts do not cross the line from merely fractious to dangerous or abusive, most adult sibs will see the experiences as essentially positive, both in terms of what they teach them about human relationships in general and how they strengthen the sibling bond in particular. "Conflicts with siblings give you growth experience you wouldn't have outside the family," Bedford says. "You get to push limits further than you usually would with other relationships." And that can be very instructional.

Among her subjects, 75 percent said that during childhood they argued with their siblings "somewhat frequently" to "extremely frequently." But of the people who answered that way, fully 87 percent said that once they grew up, arguments with the same sibs occurred "hardly ever or not at all." About 80 percent of siblings who fought as kids also said they were consciously aware of using those experiences to their advantage when they were older, usually in one or more of four ways: personal development, social competence, parenting skills, and better managing the sibling relationship itself.

"I'm very sensitized to the fact that it's important to listen to others," said one study participant about the lessons that came from childhood conflicts. "People get over their anger and people who disagree are not terrible," said another. One subject who has always had to struggle with shyness even in adulthood said that fighting with his sibs taught him to be "more vocal" and "to argue better." Others said that they learned to have "more open and honest exchanges."

This is by no means true of all brothers and sisters. The sibling bond may be powerful and resilient, but like all human relationships, it is not indestructible—and the damage done to it by conflict can be lasting. Psychologist Deborah Gold of Duke University has closely studied adult sibling relationships and sees most of them falling into one of five categories: intimate, congenial, loyal, apathetic, and hostile.

In her 1990 study that first defined and explored these groupings, she described intimate relationships as "characterized by ardent devotion and psychological closeness. [The siblings] share a relationship based upon mutual love, concern, empathy, protection, durability, and stability." Said one adult brother in Gold's study, describing his relationship with his sister: "We're kindred souls. I can tell her anything. She's my favorite character in the whole world right now. She's part of me; she's my best friend."

Congenial sibs, Gold says, are close as well, but their relationship lacks the depth and reliability of the one the intimates share. They consider one another good friends, but not best friends, and while they remain in touch, it's not with the same frequency as intimate sibs. "We call each other every week and we take turns," said one sister. "Sometimes he does things I don't like, but I get over that quickly. He can afford to help me if I need it and I would help him if he asked me and if I could."

Loyal sibs fall a notch lower, basing their relationship more on a sense of family history and obligation than on deep warmth. They show up at events such as weddings but have little contact beyond that, even if they live nearby. "We don't bother each other . . . and we don't need each other every second," said one such sib. "But we have each other for life because we're brother and sister."

Siblings in the apathetic category are ones in a slow drift toward becoming strangers; they have no emotional involvement and make no effort to change that. "Our interests are different. It's just something I haven't given too much thought to," said one subject. "I would never in the world ask him for help and can't envision that he would come to me."

Documentary filmmakers Ken and Ric Burns are famously part of this group—though in some cases their relationship seems to be even chillier than mere indifference. In a 1999 interview with the *New York Times*, Ric compared his relationship with his brother to the "benign indifference" New Yorkers often seem to exhibit for one another. "That's the way Ken and I are now," he said. "It's kind of good to be left alone to do what you each do. Like New Yorkers say: 'Don't be my friend. Leave me alone. Do whatever it is you want to do. Other than that, get out of my face.'"

When you're famous, however—particularly when you're famous in the same field—the public keeps trying to push you back together, if only to watch the sparks fly. *New York* magazine's story on power siblings was published just three years after the *New York Times* piece on the Burns boys, and by then the brothers seemed to have grown even more hostile. "Ken likes to say I'm more intellectual than he is, which is a subtle put-down on his part," Ric told the magazine, exhibiting a family member's characteristic ability to see passive-aggression—rightly or wrongly—in what outsiders might see as a compliment. "Just when I think he's irretrievably a horrifying son of a bitch, he'll do some act of amazing generosity. He said to me a year ago, 'Why don't we just not bug each other anymore. There's room enough in the world—there's room enough in this *family*—for two documentary filmmakers.'"

When saying "Why don't we just not bug each other anymore" qualifies as an act of amazing generosity, you know a relationship is in trouble. Ken, for his part, gave as good as he got—but far more subtly. Commenting on Ric's filmmaking career—which includes 1999's spectacular *New York: A Documentary Film*—he said, "Of all the imitators of my style, no one has done it better than Ric." That had to hurt, and while Ken also took care to insist that, next to his two children, nothing means more to him than the love of his brother, he has an awfully ambiguous way of expressing that love in print.

The Burnses may never descend to the lowest of Gold's five categories of sibling attachment—the hostile category—but they don't seem to be all that far away. In some ways, hostile sibs are, paradoxically, more emotionally invested in each other than apathetic sibs are. The passion of the intimate sibs has been turned completely on its head and become a passionate enmity; contact is virtually nonexistent, and that void is filled by a powerful loathing. "I feel this contempt and this dislike and this anger very strongly," said a study subject. "I wouldn't go to his funeral and I'd rather starve than ask him for help."

Like so many other things in the field of psychology, the distribution of relationships along this spectrum follows a bell curve. In Gold's sample, 17 percent of siblings fell into the intimate category, 28 percent were congenial, 35 percent were loyal, 10 percent were apathetic, and 10 percent were hostile. Gold herself concedes that her findings need to be interpreted cautiously, in part because her sample group was relatively small, and in part because human subjects are notoriously poor at accurately describing their feelings about such intimate matters. A recent fight may have darkened a sib's mood temporarily, causing the relationship to be downgraded when the survey was taken. A surprise birthday card may have fleetingly boosted the rating. Even the most hostile siblings may sometimes merely be passing through a stage—a moratorium driven not by lives that have taken different developmental directions but by a fight or a slight that, for a time at least, seems irreconcilable.

Steve did not speak to Bruce or me for the better part of a year once after a trip we all made to Baltimore as adults for our grandfather's ninetieth birthday. Like all of our family gatherings in the hometown of origin, this one could not help but stir up childhood memories—memories that in Steve's case included leaving a Baltimore home for a boarding school banishment that left him feeling tossed aside and often unloved. He came to town that weekend, bringing with him a favorite movie that he'd hoped would be the occasion for a family night around the TV. When Bruce and I said that it was not a movie that interested us and that we'd just as soon not watch it, Steve stalked out, left town, and declared that he was through with us.

It was the tiniest of sparks, perhaps, and his reaction was surely far larger than what was warranted for the offense we'd committed, but that offense ignited an explosive drum of emotion for him all the same. He did write us off for a period of months, and while I've never asked him how he spent that time, I imagine he used a bit of it to tease apart the hurts he experienced as a child from the ones he would unavoidably feel as an adult, and in doing that was able to forgive us. I, similarly, began to appreciate better how different his upbringing had been from mine and to remember that he bore a different set of scars as a result—ones that I would do well to keep in mind.

The fact that we did back away from that abyss was by no means a guaranteed thing. In childhood, your siblings may be an obligatory part of your life—"relationships you can't get a divorce from," as Conger puts it. But in adulthood, this dynamic is reversed. Indeed, in some ways, siblings become the most optional of your close kin. Grown children who have poor relationships with their parents still tend to feel an obligation to them, especially as the parents age. Unhappy spouses may eventually divorce, but they will often spend years trying to resolve their differences first, if only to spare their children the trauma of a broken home. And it's the rarest of parents who ever cuts off all ties with a child, no matter how fraught the relationship may be. Siblings, however, are done with the most intimately entwined phase of their relationship when childhood ends, and have more freedom to stand back and reevaluate things when they're grown. If they don't like what they see, they can act on that antipathy. "Adult siblings are less likely to put up with a bad relationship over time," says Bedford simply. "They realize life is short." The sibs in Gold's apathetic and hostile categories clearly made their choices with that idea in mind.

The University of Pittsburgh's Daniel Shaw has seen this phenomenon, too. "When I've done radio shows about siblings," he says, "I'm sometimes floored by the number of people who call in and say they have miserable relationships with their brothers and sisters."

Just which sib relationships will wind up on the ash heap and which will be saved and even improved depends on a lot of variables. One of them is simply the curative presence of sisters. In most mixed-sex sibling broods, the default position is for sisters to be the kin keepers—the ones who maintain the family photo albums, remember all the birthdays, and see to it that scattered clans get called back together at holiday time. Females are also likelier to be the family biographers, knowing whose second cousin is related to whose great aunt—and, for that matter, what a second cousin and a great aunt are in the first place. This is especially so when a sister is either the oldest or the youngest, and thus more invested in the family unit than middle-borns, who may grow up feeling less central to the overall dynamic of the clan.

Sisters, similarly, may serve as sibling peacemakers. The image of males as closemouthed and averse to sharing their feelings has much more than a grain of truth to it—at least in comparison to females. This makes estranged brothers more likely to remain that way than estranged sisters, with each passing year of silence or indifference further hardening the hostility.

Sisters, by contrast, are likelier to try to work things out with a sib when they themselves are part of the estranged pair, and likelier as well to try a little shuttle diplomacy between two brothers who aren't communicating. That idea has seeped into the popular culture. It's not for nothing that one of the most poignant scenes in the epic *Godfather* films occurs when the Corleone sister, Connie, begs younger brother Michael to forgive older brother Fredo for betraying the family. "He's so helpless without you," she pleads. Michael seems to relent, taking Fredo in a fierce and fraternal embrace at their mother's funeral. The fact that Michael nonetheless has Fredo killed at the end of the movie admittedly diminishes the authenticity of the reconciliation, but it makes Connie's efforts no less worthy—and no less typical of the power of a peacemaking sister.

The common phenomenon of sibling rivalry may also play a role in shaping the relationships of adult siblings, particularly adult brothers, and here the problem can sometimes be intractable. Deborah Gold has studied the way the primal competition that defines childhood—which brother makes the soccer team or gets the better grades or merely winds up taller—can continue into adulthood, with the metrics now changing to who has the better job or the bigger income or even the sexier wife.

"Almost from day one, the fundamental developmental markers—who gets a tooth first, who crawls, walks, and speaks first—are held up on a larger-than-life scale," said Gold in an article in *Psychology Today*. The rivalry may have its earliest roots in the struggle for Mom's and Dad's approval, but it goes on well past the point that Mom and Dad are paying attention—or in some cases are even alive anymore.

What makes things especially difficult in cases of adult brother-brother competition is that while the world at large does not give a hoot about the kinds of things that were the source of competition when the sibs were children, it renders judgments in very real ways about adult achievements. Famous brothers must often tread very carefully around their unfamous ones; rich brothers may be deeply resented by their middle-class ones. "In our society, men are supposed to be achievement oriented, aggressive," Gold explained. "They're supposed to succeed." That race for that success may be one reason that, in a 1990s study of 7,700 adult sibs, the brother-brother pairs had less regular contact than brother-sister or, especially, sister-sister.

Brothers are hardly hopeless, of course, and most do have the ability to mend the cracks in their relationship and even avoid them in the first place. In the 2006 book *Men in Relationships*, Victoria Bedford and psychologist Paula Avioli of Kean University wrote about a twenty-year, longitudinal study of brothers from three wartime eras: World War II, Korea, and Vietnam. Not surprisingly, the sibling styles varied widely across those very different periods, even if just thirty-five years spanned all three. Not surprisingly, either, it was the Vietnam cohort—the baby boomers, who came of age in an era of feminism and increased emotional openness—who tended to have the most complex and candid relationships with their brothers. As a result, those relationships were also likelier to be more durable and to recover better when there'd been a breach. The brothers of that era were "more likely to be understanding of differences," wrote Bedford and Avioli, "and at ease in the realm of emotional support, whether as receiver or provider."

That did not mean that the brothers from the World War II and Korean War eras were not, in their own more circumscribed ways, deeply committed to their bonds with their brothers. Indeed, the nature of the survey proved that they were. "The fact that these men remained in the study for twenty years to document the meaning of brothers to them is testimony of the importance of the relationship," said the authors.

No matter the gender, era, or temperaments of any adult sibling group, nothing will test their relationships quite as much as the challenge of tending to aging parents. Just as no two siblings got the same level of attention, validation, and love from Mom and Dad when they were children, so do no two give back to them in precisely the same way when the caretaking roles switch.

Who should take the lead in looking after elderly parents can be a source of constant conflict, but certain patterns do emerge. Simple proximity can often be where the discussions begin and end. An adult child who lives five minutes away from the parents' home in Philadelphia is a lot likelier to be checking on them regularly than one who lives in San

Diego—or even in New Jersey, for that matter. Gender, again, is critical, too. All other things being equal, the kin-keeping tendencies of a sister will emerge at this stage of a family's life as well, and when that happens, brothers are typically content to let the women take the lead. Birth order is another big player, with firstborns the likeliest to do the heavy lifting in caring for parents, last-borns the next likeliest, and middle children doing the least work. For the middling who always felt overlooked in childhood, there can be something of a flip-off quality to this, a conscious or unconscious way of punishing parents for perceived inattentiveness. For other middle kids, it may simply be a matter of habit. When your family of origin was always less central to your emotional life than it was to that of your older and younger siblings, you're accustomed to letting those brothers and sisters take charge. In general, says Catherine Salmon, "first- and last-born children are more likely to report being very close to parents and having more contact with them."

The fact that brothers and sisters often enter their parents' declining years knowing in advance—if only in an unspoken way—which one of them will be doing most of the elder care can help keep arguments to a minimum, since there are less likely to be any surprises. It's a lot harder to avoid problems when it comes to the much more complicated matter of dividing the shared inheritance.

Parents with an even modest estate to divide among their children may well think that the best approach is the one they used when the kids were small and the bounty being apportioned was cake or Halloween candy or a bucket of crayons: Everyone gets the same amount, and that means no one complains. Those same parents, however, might also consider this: How well did that strategy actually work back then? It's not just the number of crayons you get, after all—it's who got the blue one or who got the red one. It's not just the size of the piece of cake—it's whose has the little frosting flower. If moms and dads were struck by the ability of their children to find injustice in even the most equitable arrangements, should they really be surprised when those same kids are adults and the stakes being divided are real estate, cash, or a family business? And in fairness to the sibs, there can be merit in the grievances.

Should the oldest daughter who's done the overwhelming share of the caretaking work really get no more of a bequest than the middle son who moved away twenty-five years ago and has come home just once a year for the holidays? Shouldn't the loyal son who followed the family tradition and became the third in a generational line of lawyers or doctors or carpenters be rewarded more generously than the one who defied Dad's wishes and became an artist or a real estate speculator? And what happens when one child has gotten independently wealthy and another barely scrapes by? Surely no one would argue with giving more money to the child who needs it most, right? Wrong. That child, Bedford warns, may be seen as being "rewarded for failure," while the success of the other sib is essentially being penalized. The unfortunate solution to these problems is that there often is no solution at all. Equal division of the estate will anger some sibs; unequal division will anger others.

My brothers' and my emerging relationship with our half brother and half sister nearly came to grief just a few years after we reconnected, as a result of our own inheritance issues. One summer, our father and paternal grandmother died within a month of each other. She was ninety and had lived long, if not always well. He was just sixty-seven and died frail and gaunt, his body and mind laid waste by emphysema, the result of a lifetime of heavy smoking. Both of them died with considerable wealth inherited from my paternal grandfather, and while my father did leave my brothers and me a small, almost token bequest, nearly all of his wealth flowed to his widow. Upon his death, nearly all of our grandmother's did as well.

This, of course, meant that that entire inheritance would eventually flow from my father's widow to her children. And that, in turn, meant that Steve, Garry, Bruce, and I, who were effectively divorced by our father when his marriage to our mother broke up, would be effectively disinherited by him, too. Our father's justification, which we were told he had expressed to his lawyer and his wife (though he did not state it explicitly in his will), was that our mother had inherited a comfortable trust fund of her own from her father and that that would eventually come to us. It was a fair enough argument, and the small amount of money he did leave us was better than nothing at all. But reason was not at work here—and nor was simple greed. Deeper feelings of resentment and betrayal were, and we expressed our pique by refusing to sign a stack of required estate papers, which froze any transfer of assets until we complied.

Adam and Allison, concerned about ensuring an income for their mother, were as unhappy with us as we were with the will. The stalemate stood for a few weeks, until our uncle Richard brokered a peace, carving out an additional bequest—also a comparatively modest one—from his own inheritance for the four of us. It was a generous act and it worked as he'd hoped. We relented and signed the estate documents, and all six sibs pressed on together—and actually got past the nastiness quickly. It helped, I think, that Adam and Allison were empathic enough to understand our feelings—and that Steve, Garry, Bruce, and I were self-aware enough to be a little embarrassed at having behaved so churlishly.

For us, it was the passage of even a short stretch of time, and the easing of bruised feelings that came with it, that was the most powerful palliative. For all sibs—no matter the quality of the relationship or the cause of a rift—the inexorable advance of the calendar can work a similar curative magic. This is especially so among aging and elderly brothers and sisters. If young adulthood is defined by a scattering of the siblings, late adulthood is defined by an opposite phenomenon—a gravitational gathering as dispersed broods are drawn back together. For many aging brothers and sisters, reconnecting with siblings in this way can literally be a lifesaving choice.

There are few things that enhance longevity more as we age than sharing our lives—and even our homes—with somebody else, particularly when that somebody knows us deeply and well. This is more important than ever in an era in which life expectancy continues to rise and growing numbers of seniors are living into their eighties and beyond. The United States is already home to up to 95,000 people who are at least 100 years old—and that population cohort is expected to explode to 800,000 by 2050. The older people get, the likelier they are to outlive a spouse—leaving them alone at just the point in their lives when they're least equipped to get by without companionship. That's when aged siblings can step in to help—and that's what more and more are now doing, the scientists and demographers say.

Many siblings at this stage of life choose to live together, or at least within arm's reach—either sharing a home or living as neighbors, or sometimes moving into the same retirement community or assisted-living facility. But even siblings who aren't widowed and may not live near their brothers and sisters get a similar benefit from simply reconnecting with one another or, if they're already connected, integrating more fully into one another's lives.

"The relationship is especially strong between sisters," who are more likely to be predeceased by their spouses than brothers are, says Judy Dunn of King's College. "It is a source of help, a source of support, and indeed one of the most important such sources to them."

It's also a very natural source. There's a reason older people reminisce together so much, and it's not just because fading short-term memory makes recollections from long ago the only reliable ones. Rather, it's because there's a familiarity and intimacy to shared experiences. They're the comfort food of memories, but unlike real comfort food, they're nutritious in a very real way. It's precisely that sense of having an emotional home that helps work the life-extending magic demographers so often observe, and it's precisely the lack of that groundedness that can make years shorter—or at least poorer.

Staying close to stay alive seems like a coolly pragmatic transaction, but it's one in which the benefits manifestly flow to all the parties involved. What's more, there's nothing cool or detached about it. Late-life sibling bonds have roots that may reach back a century, spanning a stretch of shared time that's longer than the lives of some nations. Every moment lived in that joint history is in some way active in the aged sibs' current lives—in a way that is very real and very deeply felt. "When asked what contributes to the importance of the sibling relationship most," says Dunn, "elderly brothers and sisters will say it's the shared early experiences, which cast a long shadow for all of us."

That shadow, like all shadows, is a thing created by light. And siblings—old or young, living nearby or far away—shine a very bright one.

Epilogue

As easy and misguided as it was for psychologists of the past to dismiss the significance of the sibling relationship, so, too, is there a risk of sometimes overstating things. Lives can be lived richly and fully, of course, without close siblings. The other relationships available to us all, both within and outside our families, offer all manner of emotional and developmental rewards that can fill the gaps left by a lack of brothers and sisters. But growing up in a house full of sibs and failing to make the most of that lucky accident of birth is like inheriting a thousand acres of fertile farmland and never planting it. You can always get your food elsewhere, but think of what you're allowing to lie fallow.

I didn't see my father often in the latter part of his life. I moved to New York when I was only twenty-five and at one point lived just a few blocks from him on the Upper East Side, and yet the best we could typically manage was a dinner date once or twice a year. On one such occasion, when his emphysema was beginning to tighten its grip on his breathing and he was starting to look like the sickly, prematurely old man that he was, we met in a restaurant near his apartment that he described as a "steak house." It was, as I discovered when I arrived, nothing of the kind. It had an Italian name, an Italian menu, red-checked tablecloths, and even a boccie court in a back room, where older Italian men would regularly come to play. But it prominently featured steak on its menu as well, and my father was of the businessmen's generation that saw any restaurant that took the trouble to do that—and had the tough and scruffy look this restaurant did—as deserving of the "steak house" honorific. It made me feel warmly toward him, and it's a detail I carry with me even fifteen years after his death.

We sat down at our table and it was only then that I noticed a thick manila envelope he was carrying with him. He had, he said, been cleaning out some drawers and had stumbled across some old photographs of my brothers and me (one of which is the photo on the dust jacket of this book). He opened the envelope and spilled the pictures out on the table and my jaw dropped. Like most families, we exhaustively chronicled our history in photographs, and like most families as well, over the course of decades, we became exceedingly familiar with every square millimeter of every one of them. None of them held any surprises. Here, however, was a huge cache of pictures I had never seen—all taken in the summer after my parents separated for the last time, all completely new to me. It was the photographic equivalent of those oft-told tales of brain surgery in which different parts of a conscious patient's gray matter are stimulated and completely forgotten scenes or smells or sounds from childhood come pouring back.

Not every picture in the pile was of all four of us together, though most of them were. In nearly every single one, however, we were in some physical contact—typically with our arms slung around one another's shoulders in a sort of protective scrum. Maybe we were just trying to squeeze together so we could all fit in the frame; maybe we were just yielding to a biomechanical impulse to find the most comfortable position for a free limb. But I don't think so. The era—just post-divorce—and the closeness of the clinch said something else.

"I can't believe these exist," I said to my father, going slowly through each one.

He seemed less moved. "I didn't know what to do with them and I didn't just want to throw them out," he said, "so I thought you'd want them."

It was a remarkably disturbing—and remarkably candid—thing to say. I would never have expected my father to cherish the pictures; I would have expected more than a better-you-than-the-trash-can shrug when he gave them to me. And yet I wasn't terribly troubled by his comment. He and I reconciled whatever there was to reconcile long before he died. I bore him little lingering malice for the sometimes angry, often indifferent parent he had been. I bore him little malice for his absence. He was very young when he got married, very unready for what fatherhood meant, and he spent too much of his life trying to outrun his own emotional ghosts to have much energy left for us. Since his death, I have missed him in small, telling moments. He hated living in Baltimore but loved the old Colts, and I'd have liked to have called him up when the Cleveland Browns moved to town and became the Baltimore Ravens. There's a joke I still wish I could tell him, too—about an Englishman, a Frenchman, and a New Yorker about to be eaten by cannibals. It would surely have elicited one of his deep, raspy laughs.

But all that is freeze-framed in history—very much like the envelope of pictures I carried home with me from the not-a-steak-house restaurant and later copied and sent to my brothers. What is not frozen in time, however—what is still alive and changing and breathing and thriving—are the relationships the four of us share with one another and with our half sibs as well. I've researched this book and reported my findings with the habits and practices of more than twenty-five years as a science journalist. But I've lived it and tried to tell the tale from my much deeper experiences as a brother.

I may have been lucky in the siblings I got, and all six of us may have been lucky in the way we were able to parlay the challenges we faced into greater closeness and loyalty, as opposed to greater distance. But if there's anything my research and my own history have taught me, it's that in the overwhelming share of cases, our relationships with our siblings—whether easy and loving or fraught and fractious—deserve all the care, tending, and watering we can give them. Nature, after all, plays for keeps. Any human life will have more than its share of pain and grief—and it will end in death no matter what. And yet the life of any-one with a sibling begins with a sidekick and traveling companion who can be with you the entire way. Wasting that relationship is folly of the first order. It's true when we're kids, it's true when we're adults, and it's surely true when we're aging and alone. To the extent that this book has a mission, it's to argue for the sibling ideal—and for better under-standing and preserving those bonds.

Mothers and fathers who don't get too exercised when their children are fighting with one another are right to maintain such an even strain, since fighting is an unavoidable—and not unhealthy—part of the sibling relationship. But parents who believe the sib bonds can't suffer long-term damage if the fights get out of hand are overlearning the lesson. The bonds are tough, but they're destructible—with scars and resentments that can linger for a lifetime. Parents should be mindful of that, as should the siblings themselves.

Kids who grow up close to one another also grow up loyal to one another—and loyalty, in turn, breeds a sense of security. There's a lot to be said for the feeling that when danger lurks, you've always got a brother or sister or a whole band of them to gather you in and keep you safe. Again, it's too much to say that kids without sibs venture into the world timid and exposed, but it's not too much to say that they're required to do the extra work of raising a posse on their own as opposed to taking advantage of the one they've got at home. Parents of singletons can gently help a child cultivate a core group of friends. Parents of multiple kids can stress to the entire brood the value of collective loyalty, not just as one of the benefits of siblinghood, but as one of the duties.

Wisdom, too, comes from having siblings. The studies showing an IQ advantage for firstborns and, to a lesser extent, for other older kids in a family have enough caveats and qualifiers connected to them that it's hard to say much definitively. What's more, even if the IQ edge is a real thing, it's easy for all kids to get enough intellectual stimulation elsewhere to make up for any lack at home. But being smart is not the same as being wise—especially when you're talking about emotional and intellectual wisdom—and here siblings do help.

The studies showing the dividends that can be paid in later life by learning to resolve the battles of the playroom or by heeding well the cross-gender mentoring that comes from an opposite-sex sib are real and robust. We do carry that early guidance with us and we do put it to use, even if in some cases the lessons are inverse ones—understanding what never worked when you were fighting with a brother or sister and resolving to do the opposite as an adult.

Sibling rivalry, the studies show, can sharpen our competitive edge, but it can also leave us feeling bitter or undeserving. This is particularly so if parents don't take care to recognize as early as possible each of their children's strengths and reward their achievements with equal enthusiasm. That may be a little harder if one child's accomplishments are high-visibility ones—star of the school play, quarterback of the football team—and another has quieter, lower-profile gifts. But working to keep the attention scales balanced is vital all the same. It's also essential to remember that not all of the burden falls on the parents. Siblings whose competition was hostile or unhappy when they were children still do have the power to fix things as adults. It may be unfortunate that documentary filmmakers Ken and Ric Burns feud like they do, but it's also true that they're adults and at this point the fault is no one's but their own.

Such accountability is a part of what it means to be a sibling even during childhood, though more, clearly, is expected of us as we grow up. All grown sibs must find their own way to move beyond the disputes of the past, assuming they want to. Sometimes it takes an explosive clearing of the air to do it—though in the case of combative relationships, there have probably been too many of those already. Sometimes it takes a sit-down and a handshake and an agreement to speak no more of what is past. Sometimes individual counseling can help one sib move on and better embrace the other. Sometimes shared vacations for the extended family or making it a point to get together for regular, communal dinners can help.

Steve, Garry, Bruce, and I never had much conflict to overcome, so things have admittedly been easier for us. But the mellowing that comes with years has still helped us move beyond those things that did cause divisions. There are arguments, certainly, and we exasperate one another in ways we always have—with my bombast, Garry's stubbornness, Steve's touchiness, and Bruce's short fuse. But those roles are so familiar by now that we can resolve differences almost by rote. We by no means speak every day. We do e-mail nearly every day—often multiple times a day, typically in a four-way chain in which we exchange something funny or childish, serious or problematic. When two of us are together, we make jokes at the expense of the other two; when three of us are together, the fourth one takes the pounding in absentia. We're all completely aware that this happens.

Our four-male generation has produced a second generation of five girls and just one boy—which somehow seems symmetrical. I have two daughters, as does Bruce; Garry has a boy and a girl. Steve, like many gay men who have not had children, is a deeply loyal uncle and alloparent. Our sister, Allison, is the mother of two boys and our brother Adam is the father of one. Our uncle Richard, who has multiple grandchildren of his own, has served as something of a patriarch to the extended brood of his lost brother and has filled that role with grace.

Like all of the siblings in our generation, all of the new generation of cousins are together in the same room or restaurant too rarely. We do try to teach the children about the perishability of family bonds and do remind them always to look after those relationships. When Bruce's fifteen-year-old daughter, Bridgette, learned that my nine-year-old daughter, Elisa, was being teased by some classmates, she became incensed and asked if she could pick her little cousin up from school one day—if only so she could come home with Elisa's tormentors' teeth in her pocket. We discouraged such vigilantism, but I was delighted with the protective sentiment.

Ultimately, it's that kind of family-first watchfulness—among cousins certainly, but among siblings especially—that may most movingly capture the brother-sister bond. And it needn't always involve protecting a sib from a bully—indeed, it needn't ever. Sometimes it's nothing more than knowing, almost preternaturally, where and when you're needed and then being there. It's a lesson I learned most powerfully from Garry.

Though athleticism was never much in evidence in our brood, we all took naturally and enthusiastically to the theater arts. We'd been raised on show tunes, taken trips to Broadway, and been encouraged to perform in plays and talent shows at school and at camp. The times being the times, this led to no end of teasing and peer-group snickering about our heterosexual bona fides. That troubled us a little, but we pressed on anyway, since we loved the stage and loved the lights and could sing and act with more than passable skill.

At least three of us could. I could deliver a line reading or monologue perfectly nicely, but get me singing, and I was at sea. My search for a key was a meandering exercise, during which I'd sample most of the notes on offer before settling on one that may or may not have had anything to do with the one the accompanist had already chosen. That, however, was only when I was singing alone. When I was singing with my brothers, which I did whenever I could, I was fine. They'd set the musical rails on either side of me, and as long as I took care not to jump the track, I could get to the end of a song and maybe even pull off a little bit of harmony.

That's what made it such a frightening prospect when I was in eighth grade and Garry was in seventh and we had auditioned together for the school talent show and gotten a slot. The idea of performing didn't bother me, but what scared the daylights out of me was the day of the dress rehearsal, when I showed up at the auditorium in the blue sport jacket, white turtleneck, and pressed gray pants I would be wearing the next night and learned that Garry, whose class had been on a field trip, was late returning—leaving me to take the stage alone. While the audience would be made up entirely of the other kids in the show and two or three teachers, my unmasking would be no less humiliating—and word of it would spread no less rapidly.

I waited out the rehearsal as the acts that came before us in the program took their turns onstage, scanning the back of the room intermittently for any sign of Garry—or even one of his classmates, which would at least be an indication that he had returned. But there was no Garry and I was at last called forward. I made my way slowly and unsteadily to the stage and explained in something of a croak that my brother had not yet gotten back and that I would be rehearsing alone. The first song was "Cabaret," I think, or perhaps it was "Mame"—both were hot Broadway properties at the time—but it really didn't matter, since I had no idea how I would get through either one. The piano struck up and I gamely began, but managed no more than a few quavering notes before my voice seized and my throat closed up, and I feigned a cough as if I had simply choked on something. Precisely the disaster I had dreaded was unfolding. I looked once more at the back of the house and, at precisely that moment, Garry—five foot nothing of prepubescent, turtleneck-and-sport-jacketed cavalry—entered. In a movie, he would have loped to the stage in slow motion. In real life, he simply trotted to it, hopped up, and sat on the stool next to mine.

"I'm sorry I'm late," he said.

"Let's start again," the teacher at the piano answered.

We did, and tore through our songs confidently and well. The next night, during the actual performance, a camera flashed while we were singing and we were later given an eight-by-ten of the shot. I look extremely happy in that picture—and I was. Garry had my back—just as I would have his, and so it would always go in our four-boy mob.

ACKNOWLEDGMENTS

My fascination with the sibling bond has been a lifetime thing, with its roots sunk deep in my own relationships with my four brothers and my little sister—Steve, Garry, Bruce, Adam, and Allison. It is to them that I owe the first and greatest thanks for making this book possible. In ways big and small, I have always learned from them—and in ways big and small, I'd like to think I've given back in kind.

I owe another debt of gratitude to Carolyn Sayre, a former colleague at *Time* magazine, who ably assisted me in researching this book, and who—both at *Time* and in this project—has never been anything but a delight and a consummate journalistic professional. I hope we have the chance to work together again.

Thanks, too, go to *Time*. This book began as a pair of cover stories I wrote for the magazine in 2006 and 2007, and I was generously permitted to repurpose those stories and the reporting behind them here. The interviews and research I conducted in preparing those pieces were more than matched by reporting files contributed by a number of *Time*'s field reporters. Those journalists are Jessica Carsen, Wendy Cole, Dan Cray, and Sonja Steptoe.

The world of sibling research is an increasingly well-populated one, and it would hardly have been possible to interview every investigator at every college, university, or lab who is now exploring the field. I did try to sample as widely as possible from the most prominent researchers doing the most revealing work and, as is often the case, the more deeply I dug, the more names I found. The psychologists, sociologists, and other scientists or experts who agreed to be interviewed or whose work was cited in this book are:

Susan Averett, Lafayette College; Paula Avioli, Kean University; Jennifer Barber, University of Michigan; Lew Bank, Oregon Social Learning Center; Victoria Bedford, University of Indianapolis; Anthony Bogaert, Brock University, Ontario; Bo Cleveland, Penn State University; Katherine Conger, University of California, Davis; Ben Dattner, New York University; Lisabeth DiLalla, Southern Illinois University; Judy Dunn, King's College, London; Patricia East, University of California, San Diego; Toni Falbo, University of Texas, Austin; Mark Feinberg, Penn State University; Catherine Hamilton-Giachritsis, University of Birmingham; Frederick Gibbons, Iowa State University; Deborah Gold, Duke University; Judith Rich Harris, author of *The Nurture Assumption*, among other works; Mavis Hetherington, University of Virginia; Sarah Hill, Texas Christian University; William Ickes, University of Texas, Arlington; Jennifer Jenkins, University of Toronto; Laurie Kramer, University of Illinois, Urbana-Champaign; Debra Lieberman, University of Miami; Eleanor Maccoby, Stanford University; Shirley McGuire, University of San Francisco; Susan McHale, Penn State University; Douglas Mock, University of Oklahoma; Virginia Noland, University of Florida; Thomas O'Connor, University of Rochester; Robert Plomin, King's College; Joe Rodgers, University of Oklahoma; Karen Rook, University of California, Irvine; Hildy Ross, University of Toronto; Catherine Salmon, University of Redlands; Ritch Savin-Williams, Cornell University; Nancy Segal, California State University at Fullerton; Daniel Shaw, University of

Pittsburgh; Clare Stocker, University of Denver; Jim Snyder, Oregon Social Learning Center; Jennifer Steeves, York University, Toronto; Elizabeth Stormshak, University of Oregon; Frank Sulloway, University of California, Berkeley; Corinna Jenkins Tucker, University of New Hampshire; Kimberly Updegraff, Arizona State University; Walter Vandereycken, University of Leuven, Belgium; Paul Vasey, University of Lethbridge, Alberta; Tony Vernon, University of Western Ontario; Brenda Volling, University of Michigan; Tom Weisner, UCLA; Shawn Whiteman, Purdue University; Alan Wichman, Ohio State University; Robert Zajonc, Stanford University; and Richard Zweigenhaft, Guilford College.

In citing the experiences of actual siblings, I have used the subjects' ages when the interviews were conducted, which in some cases was 2006; I have also altered some names, particularly in the case of children, whose relationships and life situations may have changed considerably in the intervening years.

As always, I can't say that this book—or any of my others—would have ever seen the light without the wise guidance of Joy Harris, of the Joy Harris Literary Agency. We've been on a long journey together—and it's one that I trust is not nearly over. Thanks as well to Jake Morrissey of Riverhead Books, who took a shine to the idea of a book about brothers and sisters—and provided me a much-needed six-month extension when the vagaries of life made that necessary.

Finally, my deepest love and gratitude to my wife, Alejandra (the middle sister between two brothers), and our daughters, Elisa and Paloma, who daily learn the joys and rewards—and occasional challenges—of sisterhood. Thanks to all three for tolerating the lone male in our elegant house o' chix, and, I promise, no more working on weekends (for a while, at least).

INDEX